OPEN DATA STRUCTURES

OPEN DATA STRUCTURES

by
Chitragandha Dutta | Lavanya Das

Wordpen Academics
Publishing Science That Matter

ISBN: 978-93-6084-767-8

Published by : **WORDPEN ACADEMICS**
4736/23, Ansari Road, Darya Ganj,
New Delhi – 110 002
Phone: +91-011-35004336
E-mail: info@wordpenacademics.com

Printed at **:** **Replika Press Pvt. Ltd.**

Exclusive Distributor: ***Bio-Green Books, New Delhi***

Preface

"Open Data Structures" is a culmination of collaborative efforts aimed at providing an accessible and comprehensive resource for students, educators, and practitioners in the field of computer science and data structures. This book represents an open-access initiative, fostering a culture of knowledge sharing and collaboration to empower learners around the world.

In the realm of computer science, data structures serve as the fundamental building blocks for organizing, storing, and manipulating data efficiently. From arrays and linked lists to trees, graphs, and beyond, a deep understanding of data structures is essential for solving complex problems and developing efficient algorithms in various domains, including software engineering, artificial intelligence, and bioinformatics.

As editors of this volume, we have endeavored to compile a diverse array of data structures, algorithms, and implementations, drawing upon the expertise and contributions of numerous authors and collaborators. Through a blend of theoretical explanations, practical examples, and open-source implementations in various programming languages, this book provides readers with the tools and knowledge needed to master data structures and algorithmic techniques.

Our overarching goal in presenting this book is to democratize access to high-quality educational resources in computer science, particularly in the areas of data structures and algorithms. By making this book freely available under an open-access license, we aim to remove barriers to learning and empower individuals from diverse backgrounds to pursue their interests in computer science and software engineering.

We extend our sincere gratitude to all the authors, contributors, and reviewers who have generously shared their expertise, insights, and time to make this project possible. It is our hope that this book will serve as a valuable resource for learners and educators alike, fostering a culture of collaboration, innovation, and lifelong learning in the field of computer science.

Chitragandha Dutta | Lavanya Das

Contents

Chapter 1

Introduction

Every computer science curriculum in the world includes a course on data structures and algorithms. Data structures are *that* important; they improve our quality of life and even save lives on a regular basis. Many multi-million and several multi-billion dollar companies have been built around data structures.

How can this be? If we stop to think about it, we realize that we interact with data structures constantly.

- Open a file: File system data structures are used to locate the parts of that file on disk so they can be retrieved. This isn't easy; disks contain hundreds of millions of blocks. The contents of your file could be stored on any one of them.

- Look up a contact on your phone: A data structure is used to look up a phone number in your contact list based on partial information even before you finish dialing/typing. This isn't easy; your phone may contain information about a lot of people—everyone you have ever contacted via phone or email—and your phone doesn't have a very fast processor or a lot of memory.

- Log in to your favourite social network: The network servers use your login information to look up your account information. This isn't easy; the most popular social networks have hundreds of millions of active users.

- Do a web search: The search engine uses data structures to find the web pages containing your search terms. This isn't easy; there are over 8.5 billion web pages on the Internet and each page contains a lot of potential search terms.

- Phone emergency services (9-1-1): The emergency services network looks up your phone number in a data structure that maps phone numbers to addresses so that police cars, ambulances, or fire trucks can be sent there without delay. This is important; the person making the call may not be able to provide the exact address they are calling from and a delay can mean the difference between life or death.

1.1 The Need for Efficiency

In the next section, we look at the operations supported by the most commonly used data structures. Anyone with a bit of programming experience will see that these operations are not hard to implement correctly. We can store the data in an array or a linked list and each operation can be implemented by iterating over all the elements of the array or list and possibly adding or removing an element.

This kind of implementation is easy, but not very efficient. Does this really matter? Computers are becoming faster and faster. Maybe the obvious implementation is good enough. Let's do some rough calculations to find out.

Number of operations: Imagine an application with a moderately-sized data set, say of one million (10^6), items. It is reasonable, in most applications, to assume that the application will want to look up each item at least once. This means we can expect to do at least one million (10^6) searches in this data. If each of these 10^6 searches inspects each of the 10^6 items, this gives a total of $10^6 \times 10^6 = 10^{12}$ (one thousand billion) inspections.

Processor speeds: At the time of writing, even a very fast desktop computer can not do more than one billion (10^9) operations per second.[1] This

[1]Computer speeds are at most a few gigahertz (billions of cycles per second), and each operation typically takes a few cycles.

means that this application will take at least $10^{12}/10^9 = 1000$ seconds, or roughly 16 minutes and 40 seconds. Sixteen minutes is an eon in computer time, but a person might be willing to put up with it (if he or she were headed out for a coffee break).

Bigger data sets: Now consider a company like Google, that indexes over 8.5 billion web pages. By our calculations, doing any kind of query over this data would take at least 8.5 seconds. We already know that this isn't the case; web searches complete in much less than 8.5 seconds, and they do much more complicated queries than just asking if a particular page is in their list of indexed pages. At the time of writing, Google receives approximately 4,500 queries per second, meaning that they would require at least $4,500 \times 8.5 = 38,250$ very fast servers just to keep up.

The solution: These examples tell us that the obvious implementations of data structures do not scale well when the number of items, n, in the data structure and the number of operations, m, performed on the data structure are both large. In these cases, the time (measured in, say, machine instructions) is roughly $\mathsf{n} \times m$.

The solution, of course, is to carefully organize data within the data structure so that not every operation requires every data item to be inspected. Although it sounds impossible at first, we will see data structures where a search requires looking at only two items on average, independent of the number of items stored in the data structure. In our billion instruction per second computer it takes only 0.000000002 seconds to search in a data structure containing a billion items (or a trillion, or a quadrillion, or even a quintillion items).

We will also see implementations of data structures that keep the items in sorted order, where the number of items inspected during an operation grows very slowly as a function of the number of items in the data structure. For example, we can maintain a sorted set of one billion items while inspecting at most 60 items during any operation. In our billion instruction per second computer, these operations take 0.00000006 seconds each.

The remainder of this chapter briefly reviews some of the main concepts used throughout the rest of the book. Section 1.2 describes the interfaces implemented by all of the data structures described in this book and should be considered required reading. The remaining sections discuss:

- some mathematical review including exponentials, logarithms, factorials, asymptotic (big-Oh) notation, probability, and randomization;
- the model of computation;
- correctness, running time, and space;
- an overview of the rest of the chapters; and
- the sample code and typesetting conventions.

A reader with or without a background in these areas can easily skip them now and come back to them later if necessary.

1.2 Interfaces

When discussing data structures, it is important to understand the difference between a data structure's interface and its implementation. An interface describes what a data structure does, while an implementation describes how the data structure does it.

An *interface*, sometimes also called an *abstract data type*, defines the set of operations supported by a data structure and the semantics, or meaning, of those operations. An interface tells us nothing about how the data structure implements these operations; it only provides a list of supported operations along with specifications about what types of arguments each operation accepts and the value returned by each operation.

A data structure *implementation*, on the other hand, includes the internal representation of the data structure as well as the definitions of the algorithms that implement the operations supported by the data structure. Thus, there can be many implementations of a single interface. For example, in Chapter 2, we will see implementations of the `List` interface using arrays and in Chapter 3 we will see implementations of the `List` interface using pointer-based data structures. Each implements the same interface, `List`, but in different ways.

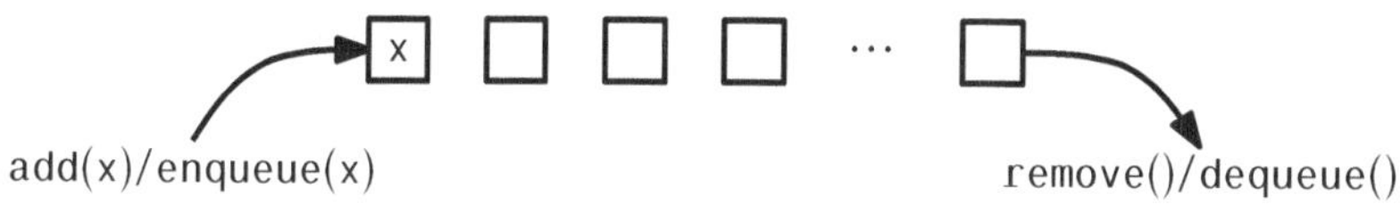

Figure 1.1: A FIFO Queue.

1.2.1 The Queue, Stack, and Deque Interfaces

The Queue interface represents a collection of elements to which we can add elements and remove the next element. More precisely, the operations supported by the Queue interface are

- add(x): add the value x to the Queue
- remove(): remove the next (previously added) value, y, from the Queue and return y

Notice that the remove() operation takes no argument. The Queue's *queueing discipline* decides which element should be removed. There are many possible queueing disciplines, the most common of which include FIFO, priority, and LIFO.

A *FIFO (first-in-first-out) Queue*, which is illustrated in Figure 1.1, removes items in the same order they were added, much in the same way a queue (or line-up) works when checking out at a cash register in a grocery store. This is the most common kind of Queue so the qualifier FIFO is often omitted. In other texts, the add(x) and remove() operations on a FIFO Queue are often called enqueue(x) and dequeue(), respectively.

A *priority Queue*, illustrated in Figure 1.2, always removes the smallest element from the Queue, breaking ties arbitrarily. This is similar to the way in which patients are triaged in a hospital emergency room. As patients arrive they are evaluated and then placed in a waiting room. When a doctor becomes available he or she first treats the patient with the most life-threatening condition. The remove(x) operation on a priority Queue is usually called deleteMin() in other texts.

A very common queueing discipline is the LIFO (last-in-first-out) discipline, illustrated in Figure 1.3. In a *LIFO Queue*, the most recently added element is the next one removed. This is best visualized in terms of a stack of plates; plates are placed on the top of the stack and also

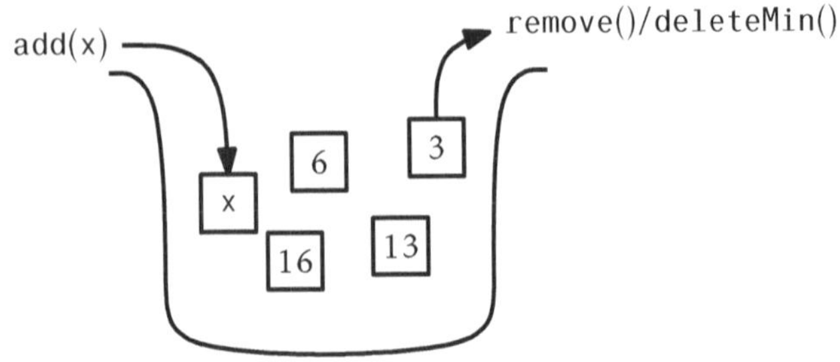

Figure 1.2: A priority Queue.

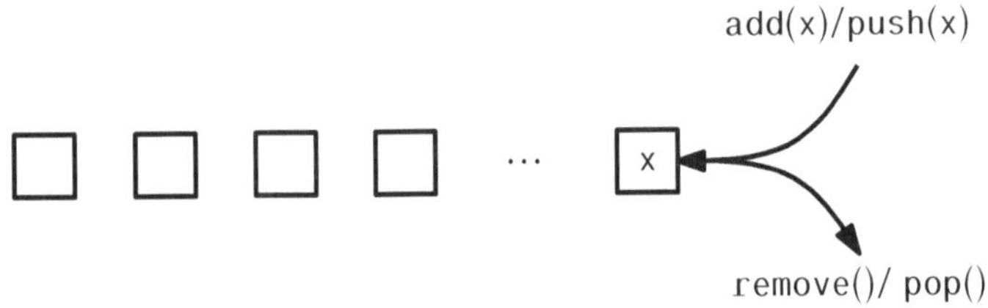

Figure 1.3: A stack.

removed from the top of the stack. This structure is so common that it gets its own name: Stack. Often, when discussing a Stack, the names of add(x) and remove() are changed to push(x) and pop(); this is to avoid confusing the LIFO and FIFO queueing disciplines.

A Deque is a generalization of both the FIFO Queue and LIFO Queue (Stack). A Deque represents a sequence of elements, with a front and a back. Elements can be added at the front of the sequence or the back of the sequence. The names of the Deque operations are self-explanatory: addFirst(x), removeFirst(), addLast(x), and removeLast(). It is worth noting that a Stack can be implemented using only addFirst(x) and removeFirst() while a FIFO Queue can be implemented using addLast(x) and removeFirst().

1.2.2 The List Interface: Linear Sequences

This book will talk very little about the FIFO Queue, Stack, or Deque interfaces. This is because these interfaces are subsumed by the List interface. A List, illustrated in Figure 1.4, represents a sequence, $x_0,\ldots,x_{n-1}$,

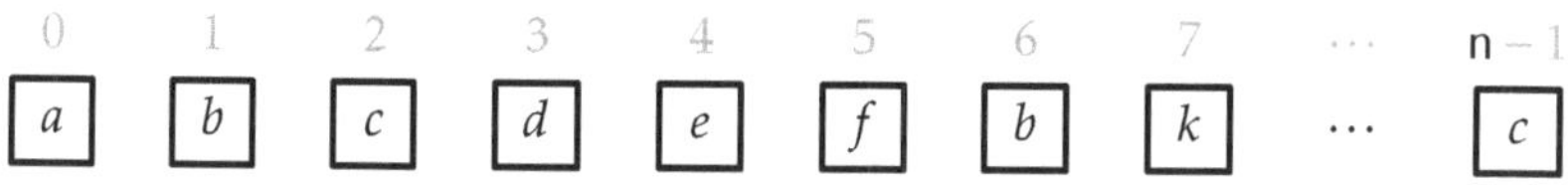

Figure 1.4: A List represents a sequence indexed by $0,1,2,\ldots,n$. In this List a call to get(2) would return the value c.

of values. The List interface includes the following operations:

1. size(): return n, the length of the list

2. get(i): return the value x_i

3. set(i, x): set the value of x_i equal to x

4. add(i, x): add x at position i, displacing $x_i,\ldots,x_{n-1}$;
   Set $x_{j+1} = x_j$, for all $j \in \{n-1,\ldots,i\}$, increment n, and set $x_i = x$

5. remove(i) remove the value x_i, displacing $x_{i+1},\ldots,x_{n-1}$;
   Set $x_j = x_{j+1}$, for all $j \in \{i,\ldots,n-2\}$ and decrement n

Notice that these operations are easily sufficient to implement the Deque interface:

$$\begin{aligned}
\text{addFirst}(x) &\Rightarrow \text{add}(0,x)\\
\text{removeFirst}() &\Rightarrow \text{remove}(0)\\
\text{addLast}(x) &\Rightarrow \text{add}(\text{size}(),x)\\
\text{removeLast}() &\Rightarrow \text{remove}(\text{size}()-1)
\end{aligned}$$

Although we will normally not discuss the Stack, Deque and FIFO Queue interfaces in subsequent chapters, the terms Stack and Deque are sometimes used in the names of data structures that implement the List interface. When this happens, it highlights the fact that these data structures can be used to implement the Stack or Deque interface very efficiently. For example, the ArrayDeque class is an implementation of the List interface that implements all the Deque operations in constant time per operation.

1.2.3 The USet Interface: Unordered Sets

The USet interface represents an unordered set of unique elements, which mimics a mathematical *set*. A USet contains n *distinct* elements; no element appears more than once; the elements are in no specific order. A USet supports the following operations:

1. size(): return the number, n, of elements in the set

2. add(x): add the element x to the set if not already present;
   Add x to the set provided that there is no element y in the set such that x equals y. Return true if x was added to the set and false otherwise.

3. remove(x): remove x from the set;
   Find an element y in the set such that x equals y and remove y. Return y, or null if no such element exists.

4. find(x): find x in the set if it exists;
   Find an element y in the set such that y equals x. Return y, or null if no such element exists.

These definitions are a bit fussy about distinguishing x, the element we are removing or finding, from y, the element we may remove or find. This is because x and y might actually be distinct objects that are nevertheless treated as equal.[2] Such a distinction is useful because it allows for the creation of *dictionaries* or *maps* that map keys onto values.

To create a dictionary/map, one forms compound objects called Pairs, each of which contains a *key* and a *value*. Two Pairs are treated as equal if their keys are equal. If we store some pair (k, v) in a USet and then later call the find(x) method using the pair x = (k, null) the result will be y = (k, v). In other words, it is possible to recover the value, v, given only the key, k.

[2]In Java, this is done by overriding the class's equals(y) and hashCode() methods.

1.2.4 The SSet Interface: Sorted Sets

The `SSet` interface represents a sorted set of elements. An `SSet` stores elements from some total order, so that any two elements `x` and `y` can be compared. In code examples, this will be done with a method called `compare(x,y)` in which

$$\texttt{compare(x,y)}\begin{cases} <0 & \text{if } \mathtt{x} < \mathtt{y} \\ >0 & \text{if } \mathtt{x} > \mathtt{y} \\ =0 & \text{if } \mathtt{x} = \mathtt{y} \end{cases}$$

An `SSet` supports the `size()`, `add(x)`, and `remove(x)` methods with exactly the same semantics as in the `USet` interface. The difference between a `USet` and an `SSet` is in the `find(x)` method:

4. `find(x)`: locate `x` in the sorted set;
   Find the smallest element `y` in the set such that $\mathtt{y} \ge \mathtt{x}$. Return `y` or `null` if no such element exists.

This version of the `find(x)` operation is sometimes referred to as a *successor search*. It differs in a fundamental way from `USet.find(x)` since it returns a meaningful result even when there is no element equal to `x` in the set.

The distinction between the `USet` and `SSet` `find(x)` operations is very important and often missed. The extra functionality provided by an `SSet` usually comes with a price that includes both a larger running time and a higher implementation complexity. For example, most of the `SSet` implementations discussed in this book all have `find(x)` operations with running times that are logarithmic in the size of the set. On the other hand, the implementation of a `USet` as a `ChainedHashTable` in Chapter 5 has a `find(x)` operation that runs in constant expected time. When choosing which of these structures to use, one should always use a `USet` unless the extra functionality offered by an `SSet` is truly needed.

1.3 Mathematical Background

In this section, we review some mathematical notations and tools used throughout this book, including logarithms, big-Oh notation, and probability theory. This review will be brief and is not intended as an introduction. Readers who feel they are missing this background are encouraged to read, and do exercises from, the appropriate sections of the very good (and free) textbook on mathematics for computer science [50].

1.3.1 Exponentials and Logarithms

The expression b^x denotes the number b raised to the power of x. If x is a positive integer, then this is just the value of b multiplied by itself $x-1$ times:

$$b^x = \underbrace{b \times b \times \cdots \times b}_{x} \ .$$

When x is a negative integer, $b^x = 1/b^{-x}$. When $x = 0$, $b^x = 1$. When b is not an integer, we can still define exponentiation in terms of the exponential function e^x (see below), which is itself defined in terms of the exponential series, but this is best left to a calculus text.

In this book, the expression $\log_b k$ denotes the *base-b logarithm* of k. That is, the unique value x that satisfies

$$b^x = k \ .$$

Most of the logarithms in this book are base 2 (*binary logarithms*). For these, we omit the base, so that $\log k$ is shorthand for $\log_2 k$.

An informal, but useful, way to think about logarithms is to think of $\log_b k$ as the number of times we have to divide k by b before the result is less than or equal to 1. For example, when one does binary search, each comparison reduces the number of possible answers by a factor of 2. This is repeated until there is at most one possible answer. Therefore, the number of comparison done by binary search when there are initially at most $n+1$ possible answers is at most $\lceil \log_2(n+1) \rceil$.

Another logarithm that comes up several times in this book is the *natural logarithm*. Here we use the notation $\ln k$ to denote $\log_e k$, where e — *Euler's constant* — is given by

$$e = \lim_{n\to\infty} \left(1 + \frac{1}{n}\right)^n \approx 2.71828 \ .$$

The natural logarithm comes up frequently because it is the value of a particularly common integral:

$$\int_1^k 1/x\,\mathrm{d}x = \ln k \ .$$

Two of the most common manipulations we do with logarithms are removing them from an exponent:

$$b^{\log_b k} = k$$

and changing the base of a logarithm:

$$\log_b k = \frac{\log_a k}{\log_a b} \ .$$

For example, we can use these two manipulations to compare the natural and binary logarithms

$$\ln k = \frac{\log k}{\log e} = \frac{\log k}{(\ln e)/(\ln 2)} = (\ln 2)(\log k) \approx 0.693147 \log k \ .$$

1.3.2 Factorials

In one or two places in this book, the *factorial* function is used. For a non-negative integer n, the notation $n!$ (pronounced "n factorial") is defined to mean

$$n! = 1 \cdot 2 \cdot 3 \cdot \cdots \cdot n \ .$$

Factorials appear because $n!$ counts the number of distinct permutations, i.e., orderings, of n distinct elements. For the special case $n = 0$, $0!$ is defined as 1.

The quantity $n!$ can be approximated using *Stirling's Approximation*:

$$n! = \sqrt{2\pi n}\left(\frac{n}{e}\right)^n e^{\alpha(n)} \ ,$$

where

$$\frac{1}{12n+1} < \alpha(n) < \frac{1}{12n} \ .$$

Stirling's Approximation also approximates $\ln(n!)$:

$$\ln(n!) = n \ln n - n + \frac{1}{2}\ln(2\pi n) + \alpha(n)$$

(In fact, Stirling's Approximation is most easily proven by approximating $\ln(n!) = \ln 1 + \ln 2 + \cdots + \ln n$ by the integral $\int_1^n \ln n \, dn = n \ln n - n + 1$.)

Related to the factorial function are the *binomial coefficients*. For a non-negative integer n and an integer $k \in \{0, \ldots, n\}$, the notation $\binom{n}{k}$ denotes:

$$\binom{n}{k} = \frac{n!}{k!(n-k)!} \quad .$$

The binomial coefficient $\binom{n}{k}$ (pronounced "n choose k") counts the number of subsets of an n element set that have size k, i.e., the number of ways of choosing k distinct integers from the set $\{1, \ldots, n\}$.

1.3.3 Asymptotic Notation

When analyzing data structures in this book, we want to talk about the running times of various operations. The exact running times will, of course, vary from computer to computer and even from run to run on an individual computer. When we talk about the running time of an operation we are referring to the number of computer instructions performed during the operation. Even for simple code, this quantity can be difficult to compute exactly. Therefore, instead of analyzing running times exactly, we will use the so-called *big-Oh notation*: For a function $f(n)$, $O(f(n))$ denotes a set of functions,

$$O(f(n)) = \left\{ \begin{array}{c} g(n) : \text{there exists } c > 0 \text{, and } n_0 \text{ such that} \\ g(n) \leq c \cdot f(n) \text{ for all } n \geq n_0 \end{array} \right\} \quad .$$

Thinking graphically, this set consists of the functions $g(n)$ where $c \cdot f(n)$ starts to dominate $g(n)$ when n is sufficiently large.

We generally use asymptotic notation to simplify functions. For example, in place of $5n\log n + 8n - 200$ we can write $O(n\log n)$. This is proven as follows:

$$\begin{aligned} 5n\log n + 8n - 200 &\leq 5n\log n + 8n \\ &\leq 5n\log n + 8n\log n \qquad \text{for } n \geq 2 \text{ (so that } \log n \geq 1) \\ &\leq 13n\log n \quad . \end{aligned}$$

This demonstrates that the function $f(n) = 5n\log n + 8n - 200$ is in the set $O(n\log n)$ using the constants $c = 13$ and $n_0 = 2$.

A number of useful shortcuts can be applied when using asymptotic notation. First:

$$O(n^{c_1}) \subset O(n^{c_2}) \ ,$$

for any $c_1 < c_2$. Second: For any constants $a, b, c > 0$,

$$O(a) \subset O(\log n) \subset O(n^b) \subset O(c^n) \ .$$

These inclusion relations can be multiplied by any positive value, and they still hold. For example, multiplying by n yields:

$$O(n) \subset O(n \log n) \subset O(n^{1+b}) \subset O(nc^n) \ .$$

Continuing in a long and distinguished tradition, we will abuse this notation by writing things like $f_1(n) = O(f(n))$ when what we really mean is $f_1(n) \in O(f(n))$. We will also make statements like "the running time of this operation is $O(f(n))$" when this statement should be "the running time of this operation is *a member of* $O(f(n))$." These shortcuts are mainly to avoid awkward language and to make it easier to use asymptotic notation within strings of equations.

A particularly strange example of this occurs when we write statements like

$$T(n) = 2\log n + O(1) \ .$$

Again, this would be more correctly written as

$$T(n) \le 2\log n + [\text{some member of } O(1)] \ .$$

The expression $O(1)$ also brings up another issue. Since there is no variable in this expression, it may not be clear which variable is getting arbitrarily large. Without context, there is no way to tell. In the example above, since the only variable in the rest of the equation is n, we can assume that this should be read as $T(n) = 2\log n + O(f(n))$, where $f(n) = 1$.

Big-Oh notation is not new or unique to computer science. It was used by the number theorist Paul Bachmann as early as 1894, and is immensely useful for describing the running times of computer algorithms. Consider the following piece of code:

Simple
```
void snippet() {
  for (int i = 0; i < n; i++)
    a[i] = i;
}
```

One execution of this method involves

- 1 assignment (`int i = 0`),
- $n+1$ comparisons ($i < n$),
- n increments ($i++$),
- n array offset calculations ($a[i]$), and
- n indirect assignments ($a[i] = i$).

So we could write this running time as

$$T(n) = a + b(n+1) + cn + dn + en \ ,$$

where a, b, c, d, and e are constants that depend on the machine running the code and represent the time to perform assignments, comparisons, increment operations, array offset calculations, and indirect assignments, respectively. However, if this expression represents the running time of two lines of code, then clearly this kind of analysis will not be tractable to complicated code or algorithms. Using big-Oh notation, the running time can be simplified to

$$T(n) = O(n) \ .$$

Not only is this more compact, but it also gives nearly as much information. The fact that the running time depends on the constants a, b, c, d, and e in the above example means that, in general, it will not be possible to compare two running times to know which is faster without knowing the values of these constants. Even if we make the effort to determine these constants (say, through timing tests), then our conclusion will only be valid for the machine we run our tests on.

Big-Oh notation allows us to reason at a much higher level, making it possible to analyze more complicated functions. If two algorithms have the same big-Oh running time, then we won't know which is faster, and there may not be a clear winner. One may be faster on one machine, and the other may be faster on a different machine. However, if the two algorithms have demonstrably different big-Oh running times, then we can be certain that the one with the smaller running time will be faster *for large enough values of* n.

An example of how big-Oh notation allows us to compare two different functions is shown in Figure 1.5, which compares the rate of grown of $f_1(n) = 15n$ versus $f_2(n) = 2n\log n$. It might be that $f_1(n)$ is the running time of a complicated linear time algorithm while $f_2(n)$ is the running time of a considerably simpler algorithm based on the divide-and-conquer paradigm. This illustrates that, although $f_1(n)$ is greater than $f_2(n)$ for small values of n, the opposite is true for large values of n. Eventually $f_1(n)$ wins out, by an increasingly wide margin. Analysis using big-Oh notation told us that this would happen, since $O(n) \subset O(n\log n)$.

In a few cases, we will use asymptotic notation on functions with more than one variable. There seems to be no standard for this, but for our purposes, the following definition is sufficient:

$$O(f(n_1,\ldots,n_k)) = \left\{\begin{array}{c} g(n_1,\ldots,n_k) : \text{there exists } c > 0, \text{ and } z \text{ such that} \\ g(n_1,\ldots,n_k) \le c \cdot f(n_1,\ldots,n_k) \\ \text{for all } n_1,\ldots,n_k \text{ such that } g(n_1,\ldots,n_k) \ge z \end{array}\right\} .$$

This definition captures the situation we really care about: when the arguments $n_1,\ldots,n_k$ make g take on large values. This definition also agrees with the univariate definition of $O(f(n))$ when $f(n)$ is an increasing function of n. The reader should be warned that, although this works for our purposes, other texts may treat multivariate functions and asymptotic notation differently.

1.3.4 Randomization and Probability

Some of the data structures presented in this book are *randomized*; they make random choices that are independent of the data being stored in them or the operations being performed on them. For this reason, performing the same set of operations more than once using these structures could result in different running times. When analyzing these data struc-

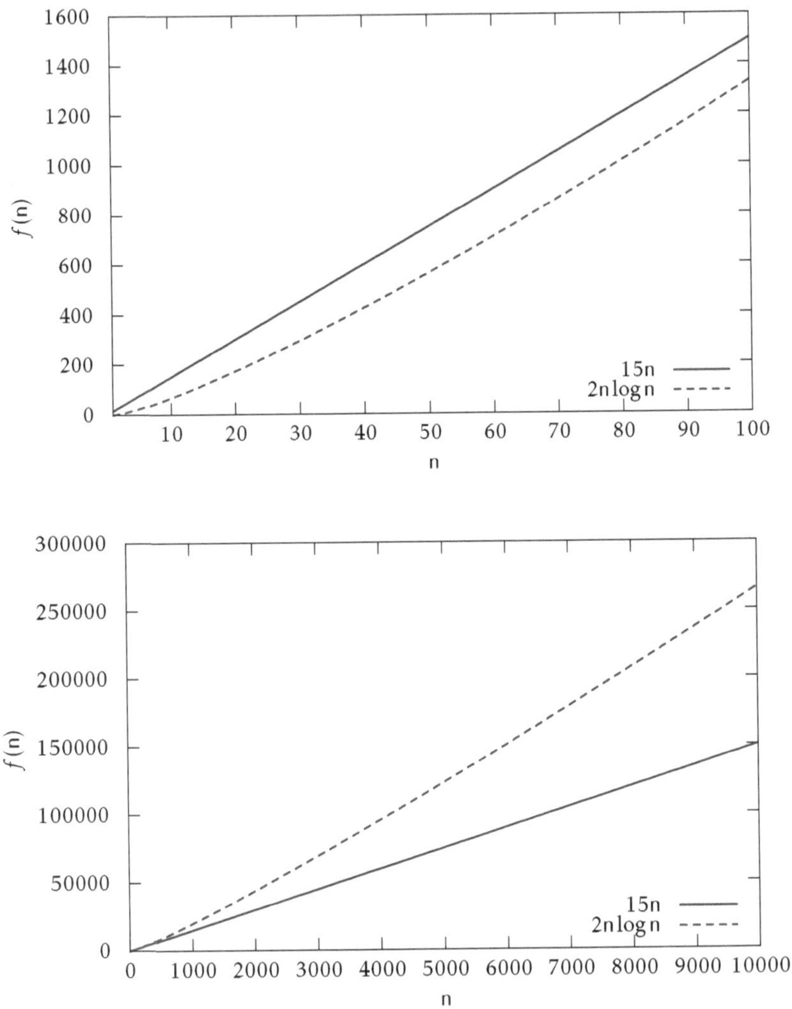

Figure 1.5: Plots of 15n versus 2n log n.

tures we are interested in their average or *expected* running times.

Formally, the running time of an operation on a randomized data structure is a random variable, and we want to study its *expected value*. For a discrete random variable X taking on values in some countable universe U, the expected value of X, denoted by $\mathrm{E}[X]$, is given by the formula

$$\mathrm{E}[X] = \sum_{x \in U} x \cdot \Pr\{X = x\} \ .$$

Here $\Pr\{\mathcal{E}\}$ denotes the probability that the event $\mathcal{E}$ occurs. In all of the examples in this book, these probabilities are only with respect to the random choices made by the randomized data structure; there is no assumption that the data stored in the structure, nor the sequence of operations performed on the data structure, is random.

One of the most important properties of expected values is *linearity of expectation*. For any two random variables X and Y,

$$\mathrm{E}[X + Y] = \mathrm{E}[X] + \mathrm{E}[Y] \ .$$

More generally, for any random variables $X_1, \ldots, X_k$,

$$\mathrm{E}\left[\sum_{i=1}^{k} X_k\right] = \sum_{i=1}^{k} \mathrm{E}[X_i] \ .$$

Linearity of expectation allows us to break down complicated random variables (like the left hand sides of the above equations) into sums of simpler random variables (the right hand sides).

A useful trick, that we will use repeatedly, is defining *indicator random variables*. These binary variables are useful when we want to count something and are best illustrated by an example. Suppose we toss a fair coin k times and we want to know the expected number of times the coin turns up as heads. Intuitively, we know the answer is $k/2$, but if we try to prove it using the definition of expected value, we get

$$\begin{aligned} \mathrm{E}[X] &= \sum_{i=0}^{k} i \cdot \Pr\{X = i\} \\ &= \sum_{i=0}^{k} i \cdot \binom{k}{i} / 2^k \end{aligned}$$

$$= k \cdot \sum_{i=0}^{k-1} \binom{k-1}{i} / 2^k$$
$$= k/2 \ .$$

This requires that we know enough to calculate that $\Pr\{X = i\} = \binom{k}{i}/2^k$, and that we know the binomial identities $i\binom{k}{i} = k\binom{k-1}{i}$ and $\sum_{i=0}^{k} \binom{k}{i} = 2^k$.

Using indicator variables and linearity of expectation makes things much easier. For each $i \in \{1,\ldots,k\}$, define the indicator random variable

$$I_i = \begin{cases} 1 & \text{if the } i\text{th coin toss is heads} \\ 0 & \text{otherwise.} \end{cases}$$

Then

$$\mathrm{E}[I_i] = (1/2)1 + (1/2)0 = 1/2 \ .$$

Now, $X = \sum_{i=1}^{k} I_i$, so

$$\begin{aligned} \mathrm{E}[X] &= \mathrm{E}\left[\sum_{i=1}^{k} I_i\right] \\ &= \sum_{i=1}^{k} \mathrm{E}[I_i] \\ &= \sum_{i=1}^{k} 1/2 \\ &= k/2 \ . \end{aligned}$$

This is a bit more long-winded, but doesn't require that we know any magical identities or compute any non-trivial probabilities. Even better, it agrees with the intuition that we expect half the coins to turn up as heads precisely because each individual coin turns up as heads with a probability of 1/2.

1.4 The Model of Computation

In this book, we will analyze the theoretical running times of operations on the data structures we study. To do this precisely, we need a mathematical model of computation. For this, we use the *w-bit word-RAM* model.

RAM stands for Random Access Machine. In this model, we have access to a random access memory consisting of *cells*, each of which stores a w-bit *word*. This implies that a memory cell can represent, for example, any integer in the set $\{0,\ldots,2^{w}-1\}$.

In the word-RAM model, basic operations on words take constant time. This includes arithmetic operations (+, −, ∗, /, %), comparisons (<, >, =, ≤, ≥), and bitwise boolean operations (bitwise-AND, OR, and exclusive-OR).

Any cell can be read or written in constant time. A computer's memory is managed by a memory management system from which we can allocate or deallocate a block of memory of any size we would like. Allocating a block of memory of size k takes $O(k)$ time and returns a reference (a pointer) to the newly-allocated memory block. This reference is small enough to be represented by a single word.

The word-size w is a very important parameter of this model. The only assumption we will make about w is the lower-bound $w \geq \log n$, where n is the number of elements stored in any of our data structures. This is a fairly modest assumption, since otherwise a word is not even big enough to count the number of elements stored in the data structure.

Space is measured in words, so that when we talk about the amount of space used by a data structure, we are referring to the number of words of memory used by the structure. All of our data structures store values of a generic type T, and we assume an element of type T occupies one word of memory. (In reality, we are storing references to objects of type T, and these references occupy only one word of memory.)

The w-bit word-RAM model is a fairly close match for the (32-bit) Java Virtual Machine (JVM) when $w = 32$. The data structures presented in this book don't use any special tricks that are not implementable on the JVM and most other architectures.

1.5 Correctness, Time Complexity, and Space Complexity

When studying the performance of a data structure, there are three things that matter most:

Correctness: The data structure should correctly implement its interface.

Time complexity: The running times of operations on the data structure should be as small as possible.

Space complexity: The data structure should use as little memory as possible.

In this introductory text, we will take correctness as a given; we won't consider data structures that give incorrect answers to queries or don't perform updates properly. We will, however, see data structures that make an extra effort to keep space usage to a minimum. This won't usually affect the (asymptotic) running times of operations, but can make the data structures a little slower in practice.

When studying running times in the context of data structures we tend to come across three different kinds of running time guarantees:

Worst-case running times: These are the strongest kind of running time guarantees. If a data structure operation has a worst-case running time of $f(\mathsf{n})$, then one of these operations *never* takes longer than $f(\mathsf{n})$ time.

Amortized running times: If we say that the amortized running time of an operation in a data structure is $f(\mathsf{n})$, then this means that the cost of a typical operation is at most $f(\mathsf{n})$. More precisely, if a data structure has an amortized running time of $f(\mathsf{n})$, then a sequence of m operations takes at most $mf(\mathsf{n})$ time. Some individual operations may take more than $f(\mathsf{n})$ time but the average, over the entire sequence of operations, is at most $f(\mathsf{n})$.

Expected running times: If we say that the expected running time of an operation on a data structure is $f(\mathsf{n})$, this means that the actual running time is a random variable (see Section 1.3.4) and the expected value of this random variable is at most $f(\mathsf{n})$. The randomization here is with respect to random choices made by the data structure.

To understand the difference between worst-case, amortized, and expected running times, it helps to consider a financial example. Consider the cost of buying a house:

Worst-case versus amortized cost: Suppose that a home costs \$120 000. In order to buy this home, we might get a 120 month (10 year) mortgage with monthly payments of \$1 200 per month. In this case, the worst-case monthly cost of paying this mortgage is \$1 200 per month.

If we have enough cash on hand, we might choose to buy the house outright, with one payment of \$120 000. In this case, over a period of 10 years, the amortized monthly cost of buying this house is

$$\$120\,000/120 \text{ months} = \$1\,000 \text{ per month} \ .$$

This is much less than the \$1 200 per month we would have to pay if we took out a mortgage.

Worst-case versus expected cost: Next, consider the issue of fire insurance on our \$120 000 home. By studying hundreds of thousands of cases, insurance companies have determined that the expected amount of fire damage caused to a home like ours is \$10 per month. This is a very small number, since most homes never have fires, a few homes may have some small fires that cause a bit of smoke damage, and a tiny number of homes burn right to their foundations. Based on this information, the insurance company charges \$15 per month for fire insurance.

Now it's decision time. Should we pay the \$15 worst-case monthly cost for fire insurance, or should we gamble and self-insure at an expected cost of \$10 per month? Clearly, the \$10 per month costs less *in expectation*, but we have to be able to accept the possibility that the *actual cost* may be much higher. In the unlikely event that the entire house burns down, the actual cost will be \$120 000.

These financial examples also offer insight into why we sometimes settle for an amortized or expected running time over a worst-case running time. It is often possible to get a lower expected or amortized running time than a worst-case running time. At the very least, it is very often possible to get a much simpler data structure if one is willing to settle for amortized or expected running times.

1.6 Code Samples

The code samples in this book are written in the Java programming language. However, to make the book accessible to readers not familiar with all of Java's constructs and keywords, the code samples have been simplified. For example, a reader won't find any of the keywords `public`, `protected`, `private`, or `static`. A reader also won't find much discussion about class hierarchies. Which interfaces a particular class implements or which class it extends, if relevant to the discussion, should be clear from the accompanying text.

These conventions should make the code samples understandable by anyone with a background in any of the languages from the ALGOL tradition, including B, C, C++, C#, Objective-C, D, Java, JavaScript, and so on. Readers who want the full details of all implementations are encouraged to look at the Java source code that accompanies this book.

This book mixes mathematical analyses of running times with Java source code for the algorithms being analyzed. This means that some equations contain variables also found in the source code. These variables are typeset consistently, both within the source code and within equations. The most common such variable is the variable n that, without exception, always refers to the number of items currently stored in the data structure.

1.7 List of Data Structures

Tables 1.1 and 1.2 summarize the performance of data structures in this book that implement each of the interfaces, `List`, `USet`, and `SSet`, described in Section 1.2. Figure 1.6 shows the dependencies between various chapters in this book. A dashed arrow indicates only a weak dependency, in which only a small part of the chapter depends on a previous chapter or only the main results of the previous chapter.

List implementations			
	get(i)/set(i,x)	add(i,x)/remove(i)	
ArrayStack	$O(1)$	$O(1+n-i)^A$	§ 2.1
ArrayDeque	$O(1)$	$O(1+\min\{i,n-i\})^A$	§ 2.4
DualArrayDeque	$O(1)$	$O(1+\min\{i,n-i\})^A$	§ 2.5
RootishArrayStack	$O(1)$	$O(1+n-i)^A$	§ 2.6
DLList	$O(1+\min\{i,n-i\})$	$O(1+\min\{i,n-i\})$	§ 3.2
SEList	$O(1+\min\{i,n-i\}/b)$	$O(b+\min\{i,n-i\}/b)^A$	§ 3.3
SkiplistList	$O(\log n)^E$	$O(\log n)^E$	§ 4.3

USet implementations			
	find(x)	add(x)/remove(x)	
ChainedHashTable	$O(1)^E$	$O(1)^{A,E}$	§ 5.1
LinearHashTable	$O(1)^E$	$O(1)^{A,E}$	§ 5.2

^{A} Denotes an *amortized* running time.
^{E} Denotes an *expected* running time.

Table 1.1: Summary of List and USet implementations.

SSet implementations			
	find(x)	add(x)/remove(x)	
SkiplistSSet	$O(\log n)^E$	$O(\log n)^E$	§ 4.2
Treap	$O(\log n)^E$	$O(\log n)^E$	§ 7.2
ScapegoatTree	$O(\log n)$	$O(\log n)^A$	§ 8.1
RedBlackTree	$O(\log n)$	$O(\log n)$	§ 9.2
BinaryTrie[I]	$O(w)$	$O(w)$	§ 13.1
XFastTrie[I]	$O(\log w)^{A,E}$	$O(w)^{A,E}$	§ 13.2
YFastTrie[I]	$O(\log w)^{A,E}$	$O(\log w)^{A,E}$	§ 13.3
BTree	$O(\log n)$	$O(B + \log n)^A$	§ 14.2
BTree[X]	$O(\log_B n)$	$O(\log_B n)$	§ 14.2

(Priority) Queue implementations			
	findMin()	add(x)/remove()	
BinaryHeap	$O(1)$	$O(\log n)^A$	§ 10.1
MeldableHeap	$O(1)$	$O(\log n)^E$	§ 10.2

[I] This structure can only store w-bit integer data.

[X] This denotes the running time in the external-memory model; see Chapter 14.

Table 1.2: Summary of SSet and priority Queue implementations.

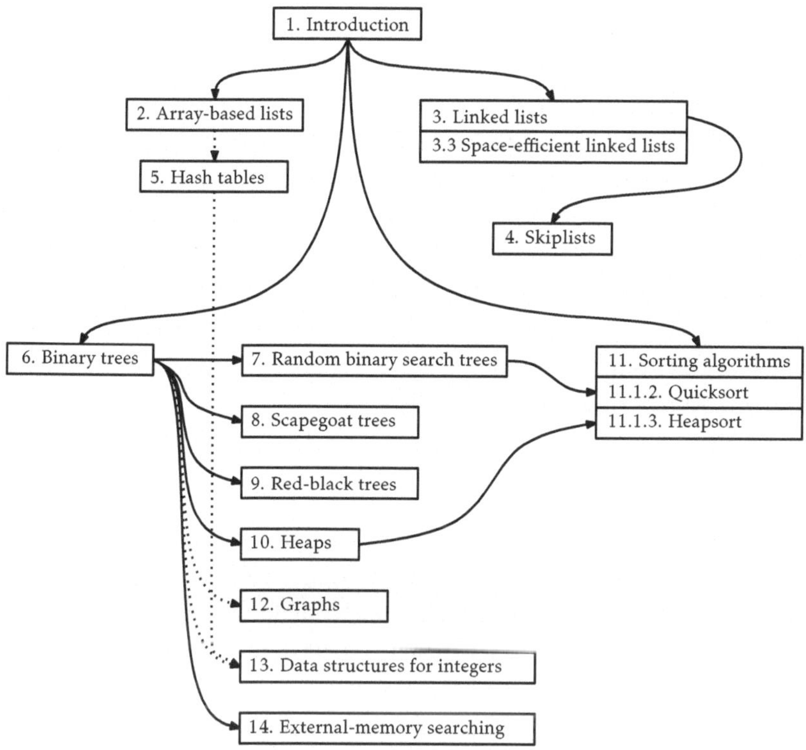

Figure 1.6: The dependencies between chapters in this book.

1.8 Discussion and Exercises

The `List`, `USet`, and `SSet` interfaces described in Section 1.2 are influenced by the Java Collections Framework [54]. These are essentially simplified versions of the `List`, `Set`, `Map`, `SortedSet`, and `SortedMap` interfaces found in the Java Collections Framework. The accompanying source code includes wrapper classes for making `USet` and `SSet` implementations into `Set`, `Map`, `SortedSet`, and `SortedMap` implementations.

For a superb (and free) treatment of the mathematics discussed in this chapter, including asymptotic notation, logarithms, factorials, Stirling's approximation, basic probability, and lots more, see the textbook by Leyman, Leighton, and Meyer [50]. For a gentle calculus text that includes formal definitions of exponentials and logarithms, see the (freely available) classic text by Thompson [73].

For more information on basic probability, especially as it relates to computer science, see the textbook by Ross [65]. Another good reference, which covers both asymptotic notation and probability, is the textbook by Graham, Knuth, and Patashnik [37].

Readers wanting to brush up on their Java programming can find many Java tutorials online [56].

Exercise 1.1. This exercise is designed to help familiarize the reader with choosing the right data structure for the right problem. If implemented, the parts of this exercise should be done by making use of an implementation of the relevant interface (`Stack`, `Queue`, `Deque`, `USet`, or `SSet`) provided by the Java Collections Framework.

Solve the following problems by reading a text file one line at a time and performing operations on each line in the appropriate data structure(s). Your implementations should be fast enough that even files containing a million lines can be processed in a few seconds.

1. Read the input one line at a time and then write the lines out in reverse order, so that the last input line is printed first, then the second last input line, and so on.

2. Read the first 50 lines of input and then write them out in reverse order. Read the next 50 lines and then write them out in reverse

order. Do this until there are no more lines left to read, at which point any remaining lines should be output in reverse order.

In other words, your output will start with the 50th line, then the 49th, then the 48th, and so on down to the first line. This will be followed by the 100th line, followed by the 99th, and so on down to the 51st line. And so on.

Your code should never have to store more than 50 lines at any given time.

3. Read the input one line at a time. At any point after reading the first 42 lines, if some line is blank (i.e., a string of length 0), then output the line that occured 42 lines prior to that one. For example, if Line 242 is blank, then your program should output line 200. This program should be implemented so that it never stores more than 43 lines of the input at any given time.

4. Read the input one line at a time and write each line to the output if it is not a duplicate of some previous input line. Take special care so that a file with a lot of duplicate lines does not use more memory than what is required for the number of unique lines.

5. Read the input one line at a time and write each line to the output only if you have already read this line before. (The end result is that you remove the first occurrence of each line.) Take special care so that a file with a lot of duplicate lines does not use more memory than what is required for the number of unique lines.

6. Read the entire input one line at a time. Then output all lines sorted by length, with the shortest lines first. In the case where two lines have the same length, resolve their order using the usual "sorted order." Duplicate lines should be printed only once.

7. Do the same as the previous question except that duplicate lines should be printed the same number of times that they appear in the input.

8. Read the entire input one line at a time and then output the even numbered lines (starting with the first line, line 0) followed by the odd-numbered lines.

9. Read the entire input one line at a time and randomly permute the lines before outputting them. To be clear: You should not modify the contents of any line. Instead, the same collection of lines should be printed, but in a random order.

Exercise 1.2. A *Dyck word* is a sequence of +1's and -1's with the property that the sum of any prefix of the sequence is never negative. For example, $+1,-1,+1,-1$ is a Dyck word, but $+1,-1,-1,+1$ is not a Dyck word since the prefix $+1-1-1<0$. Describe any relationship between Dyck words and Stack push(x) and pop() operations.

Exercise 1.3. A *matched string* is a sequence of {, }, (,), [, and] characters that are properly matched. For example, "{{()[]}}" is a matched string, but this "{{()]}" is not, since the second { is matched with a]. Show how to use a stack so that, given a string of length n, you can determine if it is a matched string in $O(n)$ time.

Exercise 1.4. Suppose you have a Stack, s, that supports only the push(x) and pop() operations. Show how, using only a FIFO Queue, q, you can reverse the order of all elements in s.

Exercise 1.5. Using a USet, implement a Bag. A Bag is like a USet—it supports the add(x), remove(x) and find(x) methods—but it allows duplicate elements to be stored. The find(x) operation in a Bag returns some element (if any) that is equal to x. In addition, a Bag supports the findAll(x) operation that returns a list of all elements in the Bag that are equal to x.

Exercise 1.6. From scratch, write and test implementations of the List, USet and SSet interfaces. These do not have to be efficient. They can be used later to test the correctness and performance of more efficient implementations. (The easiest way to do this is to store the elements in an array.)

Exercise 1.7. Work to improve the performance of your implementations from the previous question using any tricks you can think of. Experiment and think about how you could improve the performance of add(i, x) and remove(i) in your List implementation. Think about how you could improve the performance of the find(x) operation in your USet and SSet implementations. This exercise is designed to give you a feel for how difficult it can be to obtain efficient implementations of these interfaces.

Chapter 2

Array-Based Lists

In this chapter, we will study implementations of the `List` and `Queue` interfaces where the underlying data is stored in an array, called the *backing array*. The following table summarizes the running times of operations for the data structures presented in this chapter:

	get(i)/set(i,x)	add(i,x)/remove(i)
ArrayStack	$O(1)$	$O(n-i)$
ArrayDeque	$O(1)$	$O(\min\{i,n-i\})$
DualArrayDeque	$O(1)$	$O(\min\{i,n-i\})$
RootishArrayStack	$O(1)$	$O(n-i)$

Data structures that work by storing data in a single array have many advantages and limitations in common:

- Arrays offer constant time access to any value in the array. This is what allows get(i) and set(i,x) to run in constant time.
- Arrays are not very dynamic. Adding or removing an element near the middle of a list means that a large number of elements in the array need to be shifted to make room for the newly added element or to fill in the gap created by the deleted element. This is why the operations add(i,x) and remove(i) have running times that depend on n and i.
- Arrays cannot expand or shrink. When the number of elements in the data structure exceeds the size of the backing array, a new array

needs to be allocated and the data from the old array needs to be copied into the new array. This is an expensive operation.

The third point is important. The running times cited in the table above do not include the cost associated with growing and shrinking the backing array. We will see that, if carefully managed, the cost of growing and shrinking the backing array does not add much to the cost of an *average* operation. More precisely, if we start with an empty data structure, and perform any sequence of m add(i,x) or remove(i) operations, then the total cost of growing and shrinking the backing array, over the entire sequence of m operations is $O(m)$. Although some individual operations are more expensive, the amortized cost, when amortized over all m operations, is only $O(1)$ per operation.

2.1 ArrayStack: Fast Stack Operations Using an Array

An ArrayStack implements the list interface using an array a, called the *backing array*. The list element with index i is stored in a[i]. At most times, a is larger than strictly necessary, so an integer n is used to keep track of the number of elements actually stored in a. In this way, the list elements are stored in a[0],...,a[n − 1] and, at all times, a.length ≥ n.

ArrayStack

```
T[] a;
int n;
int size() {
  return n;
}
```

2.1.1 The Basics

Accessing and modifying the elements of an ArrayStack using get(i) and set(i,x) is trivial. After performing any necessary bounds-checking we simply return or set, respectively, a[i].

ArrayStack

```
T get(int i) {
```

```
    return a[i];
  }
  T set(int i, T x) {
    T y = a[i];
    a[i] = x;
    return y;
  }
```

The operations of adding and removing elements from an ArrayStack are illustrated in Figure 2.1. To implement the add(i, x) operation, we first check if a is already full. If so, we call the method resize() to increase the size of a. How resize() is implemented will be discussed later. For now, it is sufficient to know that, after a call to resize(), we can be sure that a.length > n. With this out of the way, we now shift the elements a[i],...,a[n − 1] right by one position to make room for x, set a[i] equal to x, and increment n.

ArrayStack
```
void add(int i, T x) {
  if (n + 1 > a.length) resize();
  for (int j = n; j > i; j--)
    a[j] = a[j-1];
  a[i] = x;
  n++;
}
```

If we ignore the cost of the potential call to resize(), then the cost of the add(i, x) operation is proportional to the number of elements we have to shift to make room for x. Therefore the cost of this operation (ignoring the cost of resizing a) is $O(\mathrm{n} - \mathrm{i} + 1)$.

Implementing the remove(i) operation is similar. We shift the elements a[i + 1],...,a[n − 1] left by one position (overwriting a[i]) and decrease the value of n. After doing this, we check if n is getting much smaller than a.length by checking if a.length ≥ 3n. If so, then we call resize() to reduce the size of a.

ArrayStack
```
T remove(int i) {
  T x = a[i];
```

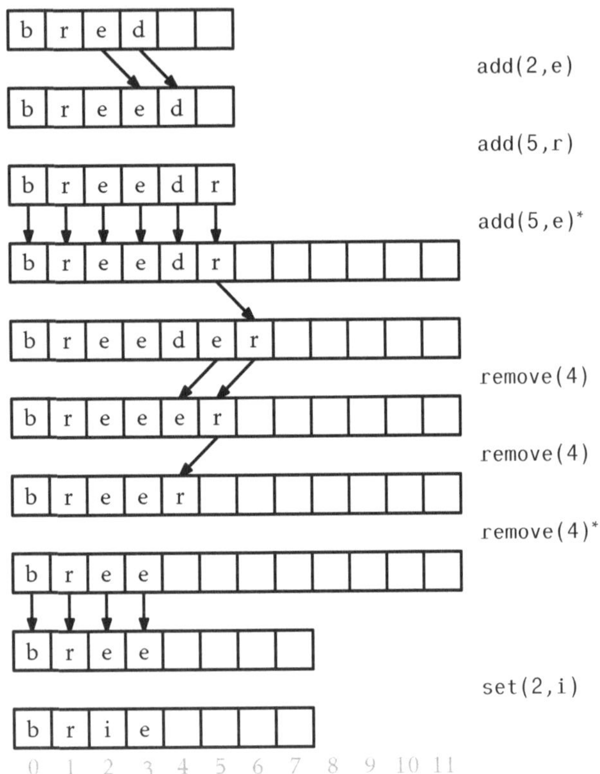

Figure 2.1: A sequence of add(i,x) and remove(i) operations on an ArrayStack. Arrows denote elements being copied. Operations that result in a call to resize() are marked with an asterisk.

```
    for (int j = i; j < n-1; j++)
      a[j] = a[j+1];
    n--;
    if (a.length >= 3*n) resize();
    return x;
}
```

If we ignore the cost of the resize() method, the cost of a remove(i) operation is proportional to the number of elements we shift, which is $O(\mathrm{n}-\mathrm{i})$.

2.1.2 Growing and Shrinking

The resize() method is fairly straightforward; it allocates a new array b whose size is 2n and copies the n elements of a into the first n positions in b, and then sets a to b. Thus, after a call to resize(), a.length = 2n.

ArrayStack

```
void resize() {
  T[] b = newArray(max(n*2,1));
  for (int i = 0; i < n; i++) {
    b[i] = a[i];
  }
  a = b;
}
```

Analyzing the actual cost of the resize() operation is easy. It allocates an array b of size 2n and copies the n elements of a into b. This takes $O(\mathrm{n})$ time.

The running time analysis from the previous section ignored the cost of calls to resize(). In this section we analyze this cost using a technique known as *amortized analysis*. This technique does not try to determine the cost of resizing during each individual add(i, x) and remove(i) operation. Instead, it considers the cost of all calls to resize() during a sequence of m calls to add(i, x) or remove(i). In particular, we will show:

Lemma 2.1. *If an empty ArrayList is created and any sequence of $m \geq 1$ calls to* add(i, x) *and* remove(i) *are performed, then the total time spent during all calls to* resize() *is $O(m)$.*

Proof. We will show that any time `resize()` is called, the number of calls to `add` or `remove` since the last call to `resize()` is at least $n/2-1$. Therefore, if n_i denotes the value of n during the ith call to `resize()` and r denotes the number of calls to `resize()`, then the total number of calls to `add(i,x)` or `remove(i)` is at least

$$\sum_{i=1}^{r}(n_i/2-1) \le m \ ,$$

which is equivalent to

$$\sum_{i=1}^{r} n_i \le 2m+2r \ .$$

On the other hand, the total time spent during all calls to `resize()` is

$$\sum_{i=1}^{r} O(n_i) \le O(m+r) = O(m) \ ,$$

since r is not more than m. All that remains is to show that the number of calls to `add(i,x)` or `remove(i)` between the $(i-1)$th and the ith call to `resize()` is at least $n_i/2$.

There are two cases to consider. In the first case, `resize()` is being called by `add(i,x)` because the backing array a is full, i.e., $\mathtt{a.length} = n = n_i$. Consider the previous call to `resize()`: after this previous call, the size of a was `a.length`, but the number of elements stored in a was at most $\mathtt{a.length}/2 = n_i/2$. But now the number of elements stored in a is $n_i = \mathtt{a.length}$, so there must have been at least $n_i/2$ calls to `add(i,x)` since the previous call to `resize()`.

The second case occurs when `resize()` is being called by `remove(i)` because $\mathtt{a.length} \ge 3n = 3n_i$. Again, after the previous call to `resize()` the number of elements stored in a was at least $\mathtt{a.length}/2-1$.[1] Now there are $n_i \le \mathtt{a.length}/3$ elements stored in a. Therefore, the number of

[1] The -1 in this formula accounts for the special case that occurs when $n=0$ and $\mathtt{a.length}=1$.

remove(i) operations since the last call to resize() is at least

$$\begin{aligned} R &\geq \text{a.length}/2 - 1 - \text{a.length}/3 \\ &= \text{a.length}/6 - 1 \\ &= (\text{a.length}/3)/2 - 1 \\ &\geq n_i/2 - 1 \ . \end{aligned}$$

In either case, the number of calls to add(i, x) or remove(i) that occur between the $(i-1)$th call to resize() and the ith call to resize() is at least $n_i/2 - 1$, as required to complete the proof. □

2.1.3 Summary

The following theorem summarizes the performance of an ArrayStack:

Theorem 2.1. *An ArrayStack implements the List interface. Ignoring the cost of calls to* resize()*, an ArrayStack supports the operations*

- get(i) *and* set(i, x) *in* $O(1)$ *time per operation; and*
- add(i, x) *and* remove(i) *in* $O(1 + n - i)$ *time per operation.*

Furthermore, beginning with an empty ArrayStack and performing any sequence of m add(i, x) *and* remove(i) *operations results in a total of $O(m)$ time spent during all calls to* resize().

The ArrayStack is an efficient way to implement a Stack. In particular, we can implement push(x) as add(n, x) and pop() as remove(n − 1), in which case these operations will run in $O(1)$ amortized time.

2.2 FastArrayStack: An Optimized ArrayStack

Much of the work done by an ArrayStack involves shifting (by add(i, x) and remove(i)) and copying (by resize()) of data. In the implementations shown above, this was done using for loops. It turns out that many programming environments have specific functions that are very efficient at copying and moving blocks of data. In the C programming language, there are the memcpy(d, s, n) and memmove(d, s, n) functions. In the C++

language there is the std :: copy(a0, a1, b) algorithm. In Java there is the System.arraycopy(s, i, d, j, n) method.

FastArrayStack
```
void resize() {
  T[] b = newArray(max(2*n,1));
  System.arraycopy(a, 0, b, 0, n);
  a = b;
}
void add(int i, T x) {
  if (n + 1 > a.length) resize();
  System.arraycopy(a, i, a, i+1, n-i);
  a[i] = x;
  n++;
}
T remove(int i) {
  T x = a[i];
  System.arraycopy(a, i+1, a, i, n-i-1);
  n--;
  if (a.length >= 3*n) resize();
  return x;
}
```

These functions are usually highly optimized and may even use special machine instructions that can do this copying much faster than we could by using a for loop. Although using these functions does not asymptotically decrease the running times, it can still be a worthwhile optimization. In the Java implementations here, the use of the native System.arraycopy(s, i, d, j, n) resulted in speedups of a factor between 2 and 3, depending on the types of operations performed. Your mileage may vary.

2.3 ArrayQueue: An Array-Based Queue

In this section, we present the ArrayQueue data structure, which implements a FIFO (first-in-first-out) queue; elements are removed (using the remove() operation) from the queue in the same order they are added (using the add(x) operation).

Notice that an ArrayStack is a poor choice for an implementation of a FIFO queue. It is not a good choice because we must choose one end of the list upon which to add elements and then remove elements from the other end. One of the two operations must work on the head of the list, which involves calling add(i, x) or remove(i) with a value of i = 0. This gives a running time proportional to n.

To obtain an efficient array-based implementation of a queue, we first notice that the problem would be easy if we had an infinite array a. We could maintain one index j that keeps track of the next element to remove and an integer n that counts the number of elements in the queue. The queue elements would always be stored in

$$a[j], a[j+1], \ldots, a[j+n-1] \ .$$

Initially, both j and n would be set to 0. To add an element, we would place it in a[j+n] and increment n. To remove an element, we would remove it from a[j], increment j, and decrement n.

Of course, the problem with this solution is that it requires an infinite array. An ArrayQueue simulates this by using a finite array a and *modular arithmetic*. This is the kind of arithmetic used when we are talking about the time of day. For example 10:00 plus five hours gives 3:00. Formally, we say that

$$10+5=15\equiv 3 \pmod{12} \ .$$

We read the latter part of this equation as "15 is congruent to 3 modulo 12." We can also treat mod as a binary operator, so that

$$15 \bmod 12 = 3 \ .$$

More generally, for an integer a and positive integer m, $a \bmod m$ is the unique integer $r \in \{0,\ldots,m-1\}$ such that $a = r + km$ for some integer k. Less formally, the value r is the remainder we get when we divide a by m. In many programming languages, including Java, the mod operator is represented using the % symbol.[2]

[2]This is sometimes referred to as the *brain-dead* mod operator, since it does not correctly implement the mathematical mod operator when the first argument is negative.

Modular arithmetic is useful for simulating an infinite array, since $i \bmod \texttt{a.length}$ always gives a value in the range $0,\ldots,\texttt{a.length}-1$. Using modular arithmetic we can store the queue elements at array locations

$$\texttt{a}[\texttt{j}\%\texttt{a.length}], \texttt{a}[(\texttt{j}+1)\%\texttt{a.length}], \ldots, \texttt{a}[(\texttt{j}+\texttt{n}-1)\%\texttt{a.length}] \ .$$

This treats the array a like a *circular array* in which array indices larger than $\texttt{a.length}-1$ "wrap around" to the beginning of the array.

The only remaining thing to worry about is taking care that the number of elements in the ArrayQueue does not exceed the size of a.

```
ArrayQueue
T[] a;
int j;
int n;
```

A sequence of add(x) and remove() operations on an ArrayQueue is illustrated in Figure 2.2. To implement add(x), we first check if a is full and, if necessary, call resize() to increase the size of a. Next, we store x in $\texttt{a}[(\texttt{j}+\texttt{n})\%\texttt{a.length}]$ and increment n.

```
ArrayQueue
boolean add(T x) {
  if (n + 1 > a.length) resize();
  a[(j+n) % a.length] = x;
  n++;
  return true;
}
```

To implement remove(), we first store a[j] so that we can return it later. Next, we decrement n and increment j (modulo a.length) by setting $\texttt{j} = (\texttt{j}+1) \bmod \texttt{a.length}$. Finally, we return the stored value of a[j]. If necessary, we may call resize() to decrease the size of a.

```
ArrayQueue
T remove() {
  if (n == 0) throw new NoSuchElementException();
  T x = a[j];
  j = (j + 1) % a.length;
```

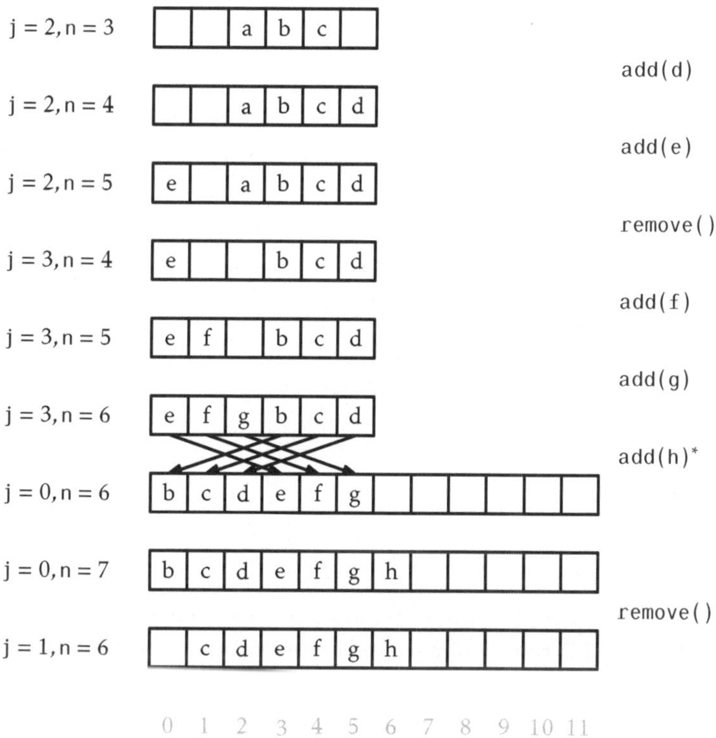

Figure 2.2: A sequence of add(x) and remove(i) operations on an ArrayQueue. Arrows denote elements being copied. Operations that result in a call to resize() are marked with an asterisk.

```
    n--;
    if (a.length >= 3*n) resize();
    return x;
}
```

Finally, the resize() operation is very similar to the resize() operation of ArrayStack. It allocates a new array b of size 2n and copies

$$a[j], a[(j+1)\%a.length], \ldots, a[(j+n-1)\%a.length]$$

onto

$$b[0], b[1], \ldots, b[n-1]$$

and sets $j = 0$.

ArrayQueue

```
void resize() {
  T[] b = newArray(max(1,n*2));
  for (int k = 0; k < n; k++)
    b[k] = a[(j+k) % a.length];
  a = b;
  j = 0;
}
```

2.3.1 Summary

The following theorem summarizes the performance of the ArrayQueue data structure:

Theorem 2.2. *An ArrayQueue implements the (FIFO) Queue interface. Ignoring the cost of calls to* resize()*, an ArrayQueue supports the operations* add(x) *and* remove() *in* $O(1)$ *time per operation. Furthermore, beginning with an empty ArrayQueue, any sequence of* m add(i,x) *and* remove(i) *operations results in a total of* $O(m)$ *time spent during all calls to* resize()*.*

2.4 ArrayDeque: Fast Deque Operations Using an Array

The ArrayQueue from the previous section is a data structure for representing a sequence that allows us to efficiently add to one end of the sequence and remove from the other end. The ArrayDeque data structure allows for efficient addition and removal at both ends. This structure implements the List interface by using the same circular array technique used to represent an ArrayQueue.

```
                         ArrayDeque
T[] a;
int j;
int n;
```

The get(i) and set(i, x) operations on an ArrayDeque are straightforward. They get or set the array element $a[(j + i) \bmod a.length]$.

```
                         ArrayDeque
T get(int i) {
  return a[(j+i)%a.length];
}
T set(int i, T x) {
  T y = a[(j+i)%a.length];
  a[(j+i)%a.length] = x;
  return y;
}
```

The implementation of add(i, x) is a little more interesting. As usual, we first check if a is full and, if necessary, call resize() to resize a. Remember that we want this operation to be fast when i is small (close to 0) or when i is large (close to n). Therefore, we check if $i < n/2$. If so, we shift the elements $a[0],\ldots,a[i-1]$ left by one position. Otherwise ($i \geq n/2$), we shift the elements $a[i],\ldots,a[n-1]$ right by one position. See Figure 2.3 for an illustration of add(i, x) and remove(x) operations on an ArrayDeque.

```
                         ArrayDeque
void add(int i, T x) {
  if (n+1 > a.length) resize();
  if (i < n/2) { // shift a[0],..,a[i-1] left one position
    j = (j == 0) ? a.length - 1 : j - 1; //(j-1)mod a.length
    for (int k = 0; k <= i-1; k++)
      a[(j+k)%a.length] = a[(j+k+1)%a.length];
```

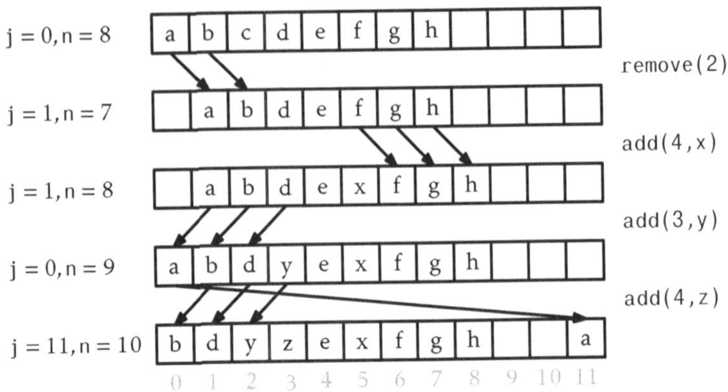

Figure 2.3: A sequence of add(i,x) and remove(i) operations on an ArrayDeque. Arrows denote elements being copied.

```
  } else { // shift a[i],..,a[n-1] right one position
    for (int k = n; k > i; k--)
      a[(j+k)%a.length] = a[(j+k-1)%a.length];
  }
  a[(j+i)%a.length] = x;
  n++;
}
```

By doing the shifting in this way, we guarantee that add(i,x) never has to shift more than $\min\{i, n-i\}$ elements. Thus, the running time of the add(i,x) operation (ignoring the cost of a resize() operation) is $O(1+\min\{i,n-i\})$.

The implementation of the remove(i) operation is similar. It either shifts elements $a[0],\ldots,a[i-1]$ right by one position or shifts the elements $a[i+1],\ldots,a[n-1]$ left by one position depending on whether $i < n/2$. Again, this means that remove(i) never spends more than $O(1+\min\{i,n-i\})$ time to shift elements.

ArrayDeque

```
T remove(int i) {
  T x = a[(j+i)%a.length];
  if (i < n/2) {  // shift a[0],..,[i-1] right one position
    for (int k = i; k > 0; k--)
```

```
            a[(j+k)%a.length] = a[(j+k-1)%a.length];
        j = (j + 1) % a.length;
    } else { // shift a[i+1],..,a[n-1] left one position
        for (int k = i; k < n-1; k++)
            a[(j+k)%a.length] = a[(j+k+1)%a.length];
    }
    n--;
    if (3*n < a.length) resize();
    return x;
}
```

2.4.1 Summary

The following theorem summarizes the performance of the ArrayDeque data structure:

Theorem 2.3. *An ArrayDeque implements the* List *interface. Ignoring the cost of calls to* resize()*, an ArrayDeque supports the operations*

- get(i) *and* set(i,x) *in $O(1)$ time per operation; and*
- add(i,x) *and* remove(i) *in $O(1+\min\{i, n-i\})$ time per operation.*

Furthermore, beginning with an empty ArrayDeque, performing any sequence of m add(i,x) *and* remove(i) *operations results in a total of $O(m)$ time spent during all calls to* resize().

2.5 DualArrayDeque: Building a Deque from Two Stacks

Next, we present a data structure, the DualArrayDeque that achieves the same performance bounds as an ArrayDeque by using two ArrayStacks. Although the asymptotic performance of the DualArrayDeque is no better than that of the ArrayDeque, it is still worth studying, since it offers a good example of how to make a sophisticated data structure by combining two simpler data structures.

A DualArrayDeque represents a list using two ArrayStacks. Recall that an ArrayStack is fast when the operations on it modify elements near the end. A DualArrayDeque places two ArrayStacks, called front and back, back-to-back so that operations are fast at either end.

```
DualArrayDeque
List<T> front;
List<T> back;
```

A DualArrayDeque does not explicitly store the number, n, of elements it contains. It doesn't need to, since it contains n = front.size() + back.size() elements. Nevertheless, when analyzing the DualArrayDeque we will still use n to denote the number of elements it contains.

```
DualArrayDeque
int size() {
  return front.size() + back.size();
}
```

The front ArrayStack stores the list elements that whose indices are 0,...,front.size() − 1, but stores them in reverse order. The back ArrayStack contains list elements with indices in front.size(),...,size() − 1 in the normal order. In this way, get(i) and set(i, x) translate into appropriate calls to get(i) or set(i, x) on either front or back, which take $O(1)$ time per operation.

```
DualArrayDeque
T get(int i) {
  if (i < front.size()) {
    return front.get(front.size()-i-1);
  } else {
    return back.get(i-front.size());
  }
}
T set(int i, T x) {
  if (i < front.size()) {
    return front.set(front.size()-i-1, x);

  } else {
    return back.set(i-front.size(), x);
  }
}
```

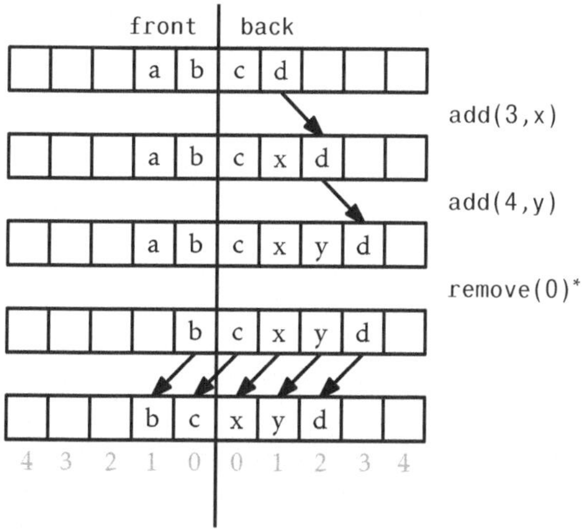

Figure 2.4: A sequence of add(i,x) and remove(i) operations on a DualArrayDeque. Arrows denote elements being copied. Operations that result in a rebalancing by balance() are marked with an asterisk.

Note that if an index i < front.size(), then it corresponds to the element of front at position front.size()−i−1, since the elements of front are stored in reverse order.

Adding and removing elements from a DualArrayDeque is illustrated in Figure 2.4. The add(i,x) operation manipulates either front or back, as appropriate:

```
DualArrayDeque
void add(int i, T x) {
  if (i < front.size()) {
    front.add(front.size()-i, x);
  } else {
    back.add(i-front.size(), x);
  }
  balance();
}
```

The add(i,x) method performs rebalancing of the two ArrayStacks front and back, by calling the balance() method. The implementation of balance() is described below, but for now it is sufficient to know that balance() ensures that, unless size() < 2, front.size() and back.size() do not differ by more than a factor of 3. In particular, $3\cdot$ front.size() $\geq$ back.size() and $3\cdot$ back.size() $\geq$ front.size().

Next we analyze the cost of add(i, x), ignoring the cost of calls to balance(). If $\mathtt{i} <$ front.size(), then add(i, x) gets implemented by the call to front.add(front.size() − i − 1, x). Since front is an ArrayStack, the cost of this is

$$O(\mathtt{front.size()} - (\mathtt{front.size()} - \mathtt{i} - 1) + 1) = O(\mathtt{i} + 1) \ . \qquad (2.1)$$

On the other hand, if $\mathtt{i} \geq$ front.size(), then add(i, x) gets implemented as back.add(i − front.size(), x). The cost of this is

$$O(\mathtt{back.size()} - (\mathtt{i} - \mathtt{front.size()}) + 1) = O(\mathtt{n} - \mathtt{i} + 1) \ . \qquad (2.2)$$

Notice that the first case (2.1) occurs when $\mathtt{i} < \mathtt{n}/4$. The second case (2.2) occurs when $\mathtt{i} \geq 3\mathtt{n}/4$. When $\mathtt{n}/4 \leq \mathtt{i} < 3\mathtt{n}/4$, we cannot be sure whether the operation affects front or back, but in either case, the operation takes $O(\mathtt{n}) = O(\mathtt{i}) = O(\mathtt{n}-\mathtt{i})$ time, since $\mathtt{i} \geq \mathtt{n}/4$ and $\mathtt{n} - \mathtt{i} > \mathtt{n}/4$. Summarizing the situation, we have

$$\text{Running time of } \mathtt{add(i,x)} \leq \begin{cases} O(1+\mathtt{i}) & \text{if } \mathtt{i} < \mathtt{n}/4 \\ O(\mathtt{n}) & \text{if } \mathtt{n}/4 \leq \mathtt{i} < 3\mathtt{n}/4 \\ O(1+\mathtt{n}-\mathtt{i}) & \text{if } \mathtt{i} \geq 3\mathtt{n}/4 \end{cases}$$

Thus, the running time of add(i, x), if we ignore the cost of the call to balance(), is $O(1 + \min\{\mathtt{i}, \mathtt{n} - \mathtt{i}\})$.

The remove(i) operation and its analysis resemble the add(i, x) operation and analysis.

DualArrayDeque

```
T remove(int i) {
  T x;
  if (i < front.size()) {
    x = front.remove(front.size()-i-1);
  } else {
    x = back.remove(i-front.size());
  }
  balance();
```

```
  return x;
}
```

2.5.1 Balancing

Finally, we turn to the balance() operation performed by add(i,x) and remove(i). This operation ensures that neither front nor back becomes too big (or too small). It ensures that, unless there are fewer than two elements, each of front and back contain at least n/4 elements. If this is not the case, then it moves elements between them so that front and back contain exactly $\lfloor n/2 \rfloor$ elements and $\lceil n/2 \rceil$ elements, respectively.

```
                         DualArrayDeque
void balance() {
  int n = size();
  if (3*front.size() < back.size()) {
    int s = n/2 - front.size();
    List<T> l1 = newStack();
    List<T> l2 = newStack();
    l1.addAll(back.subList(0,s));
    Collections.reverse(l1);
    l1.addAll(front);
    l2.addAll(back.subList(s, back.size()));
    front = l1;
    back = l2;
  } else if (3*back.size() < front.size()) {
    int s = front.size() - n/2;
    List<T> l1 = newStack();
    List<T> l2 = newStack();
    l1.addAll(front.subList(s, front.size()));
    l2.addAll(front.subList(0, s));
    Collections.reverse(l2);
    l2.addAll(back);
    front = l1;
    back = l2;
  }
}
```

Here there is little to analyze. If the balance() operation does rebalancing, then it moves $O(n)$ elements and this takes $O(n)$ time. This is bad, since balance() is called with each call to add(i, x) and remove(i). However, the following lemma shows that, on average, balance() only spends a constant amount of time per operation.

Lemma 2.2. *If an empty DualArrayDeque is created and any sequence of $m \geq 1$ calls to* add(i, x) *and* remove(i) *are performed, then the total time spent during all calls to* balance() *is $O(m)$.*

Proof. We will show that, if balance() is forced to shift elements, then the number of add(i, x) and remove(i) operations since the last time any elements were shifted by balance() is at least $n/2 - 1$. As in the proof of Lemma 2.1, this is sufficient to prove that the total time spent by balance() is $O(m)$.

We will perform our analysis using a technique knows as the *potential method*. Define the *potential*, Φ, of the DualArrayDeque as the difference in size between front and back:

$$\Phi = |\mathtt{front.size()} - \mathtt{back.size()}| \ .$$

The interesting thing about this potential is that a call to add(i, x) or remove(i) that does not do any balancing can increase the potential by at most 1.

Observe that, immediately after a call to balance() that shifts elements, the potential, Φ_0, is at most 1, since

$$\Phi_0 = |\lfloor n/2 \rfloor - \lceil n/2 \rceil| \leq 1 \ .$$

Consider the situation immediately before a call to balance() that shifts elements and suppose, without loss of generality, that balance() is shifting elements because $3\mathtt{front.size()} < \mathtt{back.size()}$. Notice that, in this case,

$$\begin{aligned} n &= \mathtt{front.size()} + \mathtt{back.size()} \\ &< \mathtt{back.size()}/3 + \mathtt{back.size()} \\ &= \frac{4}{3}\mathtt{back.size()} \end{aligned}$$

Furthermore, the potential at this point in time is

$$\begin{aligned}
\Phi_1 &= \texttt{back.size()} - \texttt{front.size()} \\
&> \texttt{back.size()} - \texttt{back.size()}/3 \\
&= \frac{2}{3}\texttt{back.size()} \\
&> \frac{2}{3} \times \frac{3}{4}\texttt{n} \\
&= \texttt{n}/2
\end{aligned}$$

Therefore, the number of calls to add(i,x) or remove(i) since the last time balance() shifted elements is at least $\Phi_1 - \Phi_0 > \texttt{n}/2 - 1$. This completes the proof. □

2.5.2 Summary

The following theorem summarizes the properties of a DualArrayDeque:

Theorem 2.4. *A DualArrayDeque implements the List interface. Ignoring the cost of calls to* resize() *and* balance()*, a DualArrayDeque supports the operations*

- get(i) *and* set(i,x) *in* $O(1)$ *time per operation; and*
- add(i,x) *and* remove(i) *in* $O(1+\min\{\texttt{i},\texttt{n}-\texttt{i}\})$ *time per operation.*

Furthermore, beginning with an empty DualArrayDeque, any sequence of m add(i,x) *and* remove(i) *operations results in a total of* $O(m)$ *time spent during all calls to* resize() *and* balance().

2.6 RootishArrayStack: A Space-Efficient Array Stack

One of the drawbacks of all previous data structures in this chapter is that, because they store their data in one or two arrays and they avoid resizing these arrays too often, the arrays frequently are not very full. For example, immediately after a resize() operation on an ArrayStack, the backing array a is only half full. Even worse, there are times when only 1/3 of a contains data.

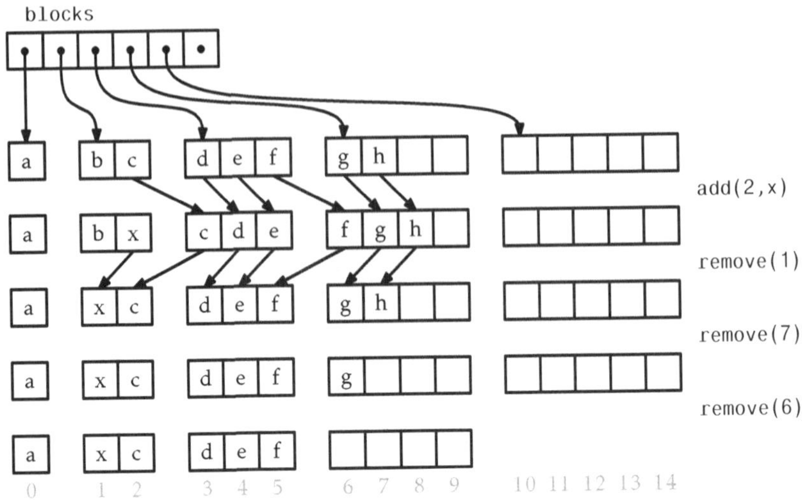

Figure 2.5: A sequence of add(i,x) and remove(i) operations on a RootishArrayStack. Arrows denote elements being copied.

In this section, we discuss the RootishArrayStack data structure, that addresses the problem of wasted space. The RootishArrayStack stores n elements using $O(\sqrt{n})$ arrays. In these arrays, at most $O(\sqrt{n})$ array locations are unused at any time. All remaining array locations are used to store data. Therefore, these data structures waste at most $O(\sqrt{n})$ space when storing n elements.

A RootishArrayStack stores its elements in a list of r arrays called *blocks* that are numbered $0,1,\ldots,r-1$. See Figure 2.5. Block b contains $b+1$ elements. Therefore, all r blocks contain a total of

$$1+2+3+\cdots+r = r(r+1)/2$$

elements. The above formula can be obtained as shown in Figure 2.6.

RootishArrayStack
```
List<T[]> blocks;
int n;
```

As we might expect, the elements of the list are laid out in order within the blocks. The list element with index 0 is stored in block 0,

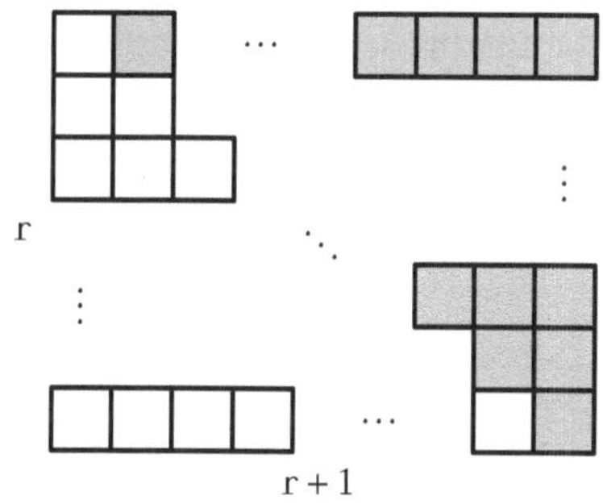

Figure 2.6: The number of white squares is $1+2+3+\cdots+r$. The number of shaded squares is the same. Together the white and shaded squares make a rectangle consisting of $r(r+1)$ squares.

elements with list indices 1 and 2 are stored in block 1, elements with list indices 3, 4, and 5 are stored in block 2, and so on. The main problem we have to address is that of determining, given an index i, which block contains i as well as the index corresponding to i within that block.

Determining the index of i within its block turns out to be easy. If index i is in block b, then the number of elements in blocks $0,\ldots,b-1$ is $b(b+1)/2$. Therefore, i is stored at location

$$j = i - b(b+1)/2$$

within block b. Somewhat more challenging is the problem of determining the value of b. The number of elements that have indices less than or equal to i is $i+1$. On the other hand, the number of elements in blocks $0,\ldots,b$ is $(b+1)(b+2)/2$. Therefore, b is the smallest integer such that

$$(b+1)(b+2)/2 \geq i+1 \ .$$

We can rewrite this equation as

$$b^2 + 3b - 2i \geq 0 \ .$$

The corresponding quadratic equation $b^2 + 3b - 2i = 0$ has two solutions: $b = (-3+\sqrt{9+8i})/2$ and $b = (-3-\sqrt{9+8i})/2$. The second solution makes no sense in our application since it always gives a negative value. Therefore, we obtain the solution $b = (-3+\sqrt{9+8i})/2$. In general, this solution is not an integer, but going back to our inequality, we want the smallest integer b such that $b \geq (-3+\sqrt{9+8i})/2$. This is simply

$$b = \left\lceil (-3+\sqrt{9+8i})/2 \right\rceil .$$

RootishArrayStack
```
int i2b(int i) {
  double db = (-3.0 + Math.sqrt(9 + 8*i)) / 2.0;
  int b = (int)Math.ceil(db);
  return b;
}
```

With this out of the way, the get(i) and set(i,x) methods are straightforward. We first compute the appropriate block b and the appropriate index j within the block and then perform the appropriate operation:

RootishArrayStack
```
T get(int i) {
  int b = i2b(i);
  int j = i - b*(b+1)/2;
  return blocks.get(b)[j];
}
T set(int i, T x) {
  int b = i2b(i);
  int j = i - b*(b+1)/2;
  T y = blocks.get(b)[j];
  blocks.get(b)[j] = x;
  return y;
}
```

If we use any of the data structures in this chapter for representing the blocks list, then get(i) and set(i,x) will each run in constant time.

The add(i,x) method will, by now, look familiar. We first check to see if our data structure is full, by checking if the number of blocks r is such that $r(r+1)/2 = n$. If so, we call grow() to add another block. With this done, we shift elements with indices $i,\ldots,n-1$ to the right by one position to make room for the new element with index i:

RootishArrayStack
```
void add(int i, T x) {
  int r = blocks.size();
  if (r*(r+1)/2 < n + 1) grow();
  n++;
  for (int j = n-1; j > i; j--)
    set(j, get(j-1));
  set(i, x);
}
```

The grow() method does what we expect. It adds a new block:

RootishArrayStack
```
void grow() {
  blocks.add(newArray(blocks.size()+1));
}
```

Ignoring the cost of the grow() operation, the cost of an add(i, x) operation is dominated by the cost of shifting and is therefore $O(1+\mathtt{n}-\mathtt{i})$, just like an ArrayStack.

The remove(i) operation is similar to add(i, x). It shifts the elements with indices $\mathtt{i}+1,\ldots,\mathtt{n}$ left by one position and then, if there is more than one empty block, it calls the shrink() method to remove all but one of the unused blocks:

RootishArrayStack
```
T remove(int i) {
  T x = get(i);
  for (int j = i; j < n-1; j++)
    set(j, get(j+1));
  n--;
  int r = blocks.size();
  if ((r-2)*(r-1)/2 >= n)  shrink();
  return x;
}
```

RootishArrayStack
```
void shrink() {
  int r = blocks.size();
```

```
    while (r > 0 && (r-2)*(r-1)/2 >= n) {
      blocks.remove(blocks.size()-1);
      r--;
    }
}
```

Once again, ignoring the cost of the shrink() operation, the cost of a remove(i) operation is dominated by the cost of shifting and is therefore $O(n-i)$.

2.6.1 Analysis of Growing and Shrinking

The above analysis of add(i,x) and remove(i) does not account for the cost of grow() and shrink(). Note that, unlike the ArrayStack.resize() operation, grow() and shrink() do not copy any data. They only allocate or free an array of size r. In some environments, this takes only constant time, while in others, it may require time proportional to r.

We note that, immediately after a call to grow() or shrink(), the situation is clear. The final block is completely empty, and all other blocks are completely full. Another call to grow() or shrink() will not happen until at least $r-1$ elements have been added or removed. Therefore, even if grow() and shrink() take $O(r)$ time, this cost can be amortized over at least $r-1$ add(i,x) or remove(i) operations, so that the amortized cost of grow() and shrink() is $O(1)$ per operation.

2.6.2 Space Usage

Next, we analyze the amount of extra space used by a RootishArrayStack. In particular, we want to count any space used by a RootishArrayStack that is not an array element currently used to hold a list element. We call all such space *wasted space*.

The remove(i) operation ensures that a RootishArrayStack never has more than two blocks that are not completely full. The number of blocks, r, used by a RootishArrayStack that stores n elements therefore satisfies

$$(r-2)(r-1) \leq n .$$

Again, using the quadratic equation on this gives

$$r \le (3+\sqrt{1+4n})/2 = O(\sqrt{n}) \ .$$

The last two blocks have sizes r and $r-1$, so the space wasted by these two blocks is at most $2r-1 = O(\sqrt{n})$. If we store the blocks in (for example) an ArrayList, then the amount of space wasted by the List that stores those r blocks is also $O(r) = O(\sqrt{n})$. The other space needed for storing n and other accounting information is $O(1)$. Therefore, the total amount of wasted space in a RootishArrayStack is $O(\sqrt{n})$.

Next, we argue that this space usage is optimal for any data structure that starts out empty and can support the addition of one item at a time. More precisely, we will show that, at some point during the addition of n items, the data structure is wasting an amount of space at least in $\sqrt{n}$ (though it may be only wasted for a moment).

Suppose we start with an empty data structure and we add n items one at a time. At the end of this process, all n items are stored in the structure and distributed among a collection of r memory blocks. If $r \ge \sqrt{n}$, then the data structure must be using r pointers (or references) to keep track of these r blocks, and these pointers are wasted space. On the other hand, if $r < \sqrt{n}$ then, by the pigeonhole principle, some block must have a size of at least $n/r > \sqrt{n}$. Consider the moment at which this block was first allocated. Immediately after it was allocated, this block was empty, and was therefore wasting $\sqrt{n}$ space. Therefore, at some point in time during the insertion of n elements, the data structure was wasting $\sqrt{n}$ space.

2.6.3 Summary

The following theorem summarizes our discussion of the RootishArray-Stack data structure:

Theorem 2.5. *A RootishArrayStack implements the List interface. Ignoring the cost of calls to* grow() *and* shrink()*, a RootishArrayStack supports the operations*

- get(i) *and* set(i, x) *in* $O(1)$ *time per operation; and*
- add(i, x) *and* remove(i) *in* $O(1+n-i)$ *time per operation.*

Furthermore, beginning with an empty RootishArrayStack, *any sequence of* m add(i, x) *and* remove(i) *operations results in a total of* $O(m)$ *time spent during all calls to* grow() *and* shrink().

The space (measured in words)[3] *used by a* RootishArrayStack *that stores* n *elements is* $n + O(\sqrt{n})$.

2.6.4 Computing Square Roots

A reader who has had some exposure to models of computation may notice that the RootishArrayStack, as described above, does not fit into the usual word-RAM model of computation (Section 1.4) because it requires taking square roots. The square root operation is generally not considered a basic operation and is therefore not usually part of the word-RAM model.

In this section, we show that the square root operation can be implemented efficiently. In particular, we show that for any integer $x \in \{0,\ldots,n\}$, $\lfloor\sqrt{x}\rfloor$ can be computed in constant-time, after $O(\sqrt{n})$ preprocessing that creates two arrays of length $O(\sqrt{n})$. The following lemma shows that we can reduce the problem of computing the square root of x to the square root of a related value x′.

Lemma 2.3. *Let* $x \geq 1$ *and let* $x' = x - a$, *where* $0 \leq a \leq \sqrt{x}$. *Then* $\sqrt{x'} \geq \sqrt{x} - 1$.

Proof. It suffices to show that

$$\sqrt{x - \sqrt{x}} \geq \sqrt{x} - 1 \ .$$

Square both sides of this inequality to get

$$x - \sqrt{x} \geq x - 2\sqrt{x} + 1$$

and gather terms to get

$$\sqrt{x} \geq 1$$

which is clearly true for any $x \geq 1$. □

[3]Recall Section 1.4 for a discussion of how memory is measured.

Start by restricting the problem a little, and assume that $2^{r} \le x < 2^{r+1}$, so that $\lfloor \log x \rfloor = r$, i.e., x is an integer having r + 1 bits in its binary representation. We can take $x' = x - (x \bmod 2^{\lfloor r/2 \rfloor})$. Now, x′ satisfies the conditions of Lemma 2.3, so $\sqrt{x} - \sqrt{x'} \le 1$. Furthermore, x′ has all of its lower-order $\lfloor r/2 \rfloor$ bits equal to 0, so there are only

$$2^{r+1-\lfloor r/2 \rfloor} \le 4 \cdot 2^{r/2} \le 4\sqrt{x}$$

possible values of x′. This means that we can use an array, sqrttab, that stores the value of $\lfloor \sqrt{x'} \rfloor$ for each possible value of x′. A little more precisely, we have

$$\mathtt{sqrttab}[i] = \left\lfloor \sqrt{i2^{\lfloor r/2 \rfloor}} \right\rfloor .$$

In this way, sqrttab[i] is within 2 of $\sqrt{x}$ for all $x \in \{i2^{\lfloor r/2 \rfloor}, \ldots, (i+1)2^{\lfloor r/2 \rfloor} - 1\}$. Stated another way, the array entry s = sqrttab[x>>$\lfloor r/2 \rfloor$] is either equal to $\lfloor \sqrt{x} \rfloor$, $\lfloor \sqrt{x} \rfloor - 1$, or $\lfloor \sqrt{x} \rfloor - 2$. From s we can determine the value of $\lfloor \sqrt{x} \rfloor$ by incrementing s until $(s+1)^2 > x$.

FastSqrt

```
int sqrt(int x, int r) {
  int s = sqrtab[x>>r/2];
  while ((s+1)*(s+1) <= x) s++; // executes at most twice
  return s;
}
```

Now, this only works for $x \in \{2^{r}, \ldots, 2^{r+1} - 1\}$ and sqrttab is a special table that only works for a particular value of $r = \lfloor \log x \rfloor$. To overcome this, we could compute $\lfloor \log n \rfloor$ different sqrttab arrays, one for each possible value of $\lfloor \log x \rfloor$. The sizes of these tables form an exponential sequence whose largest value is at most $4\sqrt{n}$, so the total size of all tables is $O(\sqrt{n})$.

However, it turns out that more than one sqrttab array is unnecessary; we only need one sqrttab array for the value $r = \lfloor \log n \rfloor$. Any value x with $\log x = r' < r$ can be *upgraded* by multiplying x by $2^{r-r'}$ and using the equation

$$\sqrt{2^{r-r'}x} = 2^{(r-r')/2}\sqrt{x} .$$

The quantity $2^{r-r'}x$ is in the range $\{2^{r}, \ldots, 2^{r+1} - 1\}$ so we can look up its square root in sqrttab. The following code implements this idea to compute $\lfloor\sqrt{\mathtt{x}}\rfloor$ for all non-negative integers x in the range $\{0,\ldots,2^{30}-1\}$ using an array, sqrttab, of size 2^{16}.

FastSqrt
```
int sqrt(int x) {
  int rp = log(x);
  int upgrade = ((r-rp)/2) * 2;
  int xp = x << upgrade;  // xp has r or r-1 bits
  int s = sqrtab[xp>>(r/2)] >> (upgrade/2);
  while ((s+1)*(s+1) <= x) s++;  // executes at most twice
  return s;
}
```

Something we have taken for granted thus far is the question of how to compute $\mathtt{r}' = \lfloor\log \mathtt{x}\rfloor$. Again, this is a problem that can be solved with an array, logtab, of size $2^{\mathtt{r}/2}$. In this case, the code is particularly simple, since $\lfloor\log \mathtt{x}\rfloor$ is just the index of the most significant 1 bit in the binary representation of x. This means that, for $\mathtt{x} > 2^{\mathtt{r}/2}$, we can right-shift the bits of x by r/2 positions before using it as an index into logtab. The following code does this using an array logtab of size 2^{16} to compute $\lfloor\log \mathtt{x}\rfloor$ for all x in the range $\{1,\ldots,2^{32}-1\}$.

FastSqrt
```
int log(int x) {
  if (x >= halfint)
    return 16 + logtab[x>>>16];
  return logtab[x];
}
```

Finally, for completeness, we include the following code that initializes logtab and sqrttab:

FastSqrt
```
void inittabs() {
  sqrtab = new int[1<<(r/2)];
  logtab = new int[1<<(r/2)];
  for (int d = 0; d < r/2; d++)
    Arrays.fill(logtab, 1<<d, 2<<d, d);
  int s = 1<<(r/4);                    // sqrt(2^(r/2))
```

```
    for (int i = 0; i < 1<<(r/2); i++) {
      if ((s+1)*(s+1) <= i << (r/2)) s++; // sqrt increases
      sqrtab[i] = s;
    }
}
```

To summarize, the computations done by the i2b(i) method can be implemented in constant time on the word-RAM using $O(\sqrt{n})$ extra memory to store the sqrttab and logtab arrays. These arrays can be rebuilt when n increases or decreases by a factor of two, and the cost of this rebuilding can be amortized over the number of add(i,x) and remove(i) operations that caused the change in n in the same way that the cost of resize() is analyzed in the ArrayStack implementation.

2.7 Discussion and Exercises

Most of the data structures described in this chapter are folklore. They can be found in implementations dating back over 30 years. For example, implementations of stacks, queues, and deques, which generalize easily to the ArrayStack, ArrayQueue and ArrayDeque structures described here, are discussed by Knuth [46, Section 2.2.2].

Brodnik *et al.* [13] seem to have been the first to describe the RootishArrayStack and prove a $\sqrt{n}$ lower-bound like that in Section 2.6.2. They also present a different structure that uses a more sophisticated choice of block sizes in order to avoid computing square roots in the i2b(i) method. Within their scheme, the block containing i is block $\lfloor \log(i+1) \rfloor$, which is simply the index of the leading 1 bit in the binary representation of $i+1$. Some computer architectures provide an instruction for computing the index of the leading 1-bit in an integer.

A structure related to the RootishArrayStack is the two-level *tiered-vector* of Goodrich and Kloss [35]. This structure supports the get(i,x) and set(i,x) operations in constant time and add(i,x) and remove(i) in $O(\sqrt{n})$ time. These running times are similar to what can be achieved with the more careful implementation of a RootishArrayStack discussed in Exercise 2.11.

Exercise 2.1. In the ArrayStack implementation, after the first call to remove(i), the backing array, a, contains $n+1$ non-null values despite the fact that the ArrayStack only contains n elements. Where is the extra non-null value? Discuss any consequences this non-null value might have on the Java Runtime Environment's memory manager.

Exercise 2.2. The List method addAll(i,c) inserts all elements of the Collection c into the list at position i. (The add(i,x) method is a special case where $c = \{x\}$.) Explain why, for the data structures in this chapter, it is not efficient to implement addAll(i,c) by repeated calls to add(i,x). Design and implement a more efficient implementation.

Exercise 2.3. Design and implement a *RandomQueue*. This is an implementation of the Queue interface in which the remove() operation removes an element that is chosen uniformly at random among all the elements currently in the queue. (Think of a RandomQueue as a bag in which we can add elements or reach in and blindly remove some random element.) The add(x) and remove() operations in a RandomQueue should run in constant time per operation.

Exercise 2.4. Design and implement a Treque (triple-ended queue). This is a List implementation in which get(i) and set(i,x) run in constant time and add(i,x) and remove(i) run in time

$$O(1+\min\{i, n-i, |n/2-i|\}) \ .$$

In other words, modifications are fast if they are near either end or near the middle of the list.

Exercise 2.5. Implement a method rotate(a,r) that "rotates" the array a so that a[i] moves to a[(i+r) mod a.length], for all $i \in \{0,\dots,\text{a.length}\}$.

Exercise 2.6. Implement a method rotate(r) that "rotates" a List so that list item i becomes list item $(i+r) \bmod n$. When run on an ArrayDeque, or a DualArrayDeque, rotate(r) should run in $O(1+\min\{r, n-r\})$ time.

Exercise 2.7. Modify the ArrayDeque implementation so that the shifting done by add(i,x), remove(i), and resize() is done using the faster System.arraycopy(s,i,d,j,n) method.

Exercise 2.8. Modify the ArrayDeque implementation so that it does not use the % operator (which is expensive on some systems). Instead, it should make use of the fact that, if a.length is a power of 2, then

$$\texttt{k\%a.length} = \texttt{k\&(a.length} - 1) \; .$$

(Here, & is the bitwise-and operator.)

Exercise 2.9. Design and implement a variant of ArrayDeque that does not do any modular arithmetic at all. Instead, all the data sits in a consecutive block, in order, inside an array. When the data overruns the beginning or the end of this array, a modified rebuild() operation is performed. The amortized cost of all operations should be the same as in an ArrayDeque.
Hint: Getting this to work is really all about how you implement the rebuild() operation. You would like rebuild() to put the data structure into a state where the data cannot run off either end until at least n/2 operations have been performed.

Test the performance of your implementation against the ArrayDeque. Optimize your implementation (by using System.arraycopy(a, i, b, i, n)) and see if you can get it to outperform the ArrayDeque implementation.

Exercise 2.10. Design and implement a version of a RootishArrayStack that has only $O(\sqrt{n})$ wasted space, but that can perform add(i, x) and remove(i, x) operations in $O(1 + \min\{i, n - i\})$ time.

Exercise 2.11. Design and implement a version of a RootishArrayStack that has only $O(\sqrt{n})$ wasted space, but that can perform add(i, x) and remove(i, x) operations in $O(1 + \min\{\sqrt{n}, n - i\})$ time. (For an idea on how to do this, see Section 3.3.)

Exercise 2.12. Design and implement a version of a RootishArrayStack that has only $O(\sqrt{n})$ wasted space, but that can perform add(i, x) and remove(i, x) operations in $O(1 + \min\{i, \sqrt{n}, n - i\})$ time. (See Section 3.3 for ideas on how to achieve this.)

Exercise 2.13. Design and implement a CubishArrayStack. This three level structure implements the List interface using $O(n^{2/3})$ wasted space. In this structure, get(i) and set(i, x) take constant time; while add(i, x) and remove(i) take $O(n^{1/3})$ amortized time.

Chapter 3

Linked Lists

In this chapter, we continue to study implementations of the `List` interface, this time using pointer-based data structures rather than arrays. The structures in this chapter are made up of nodes that contain the list items. Using references (pointers), the nodes are linked together into a sequence. We first study singly-linked lists, which can implement `Stack` and (FIFO) `Queue` operations in constant time per operation and then move on to doubly-linked lists, which can implement `Deque` operations in constant time.

Linked lists have advantages and disadvantages when compared to array-based implementations of the `List` interface. The primary disadvantage is that we lose the ability to access any element using `get(i)` or `set(i,x)` in constant time. Instead, we have to walk through the list, one element at a time, until we reach the `i`th element. The primary advantage is that they are more dynamic: Given a reference to any list node `u`, we can delete `u` or insert a node adjacent to `u` in constant time. This is true no matter where `u` is in the list.

3.1 `SLList`: A Singly-Linked List

An `SLList` (singly-linked list) is a sequence of `Node`s. Each node `u` stores a data value `u.x` and a reference `u.next` to the next node in the sequence. For the last node `w` in the sequence, `w.next` = `null`

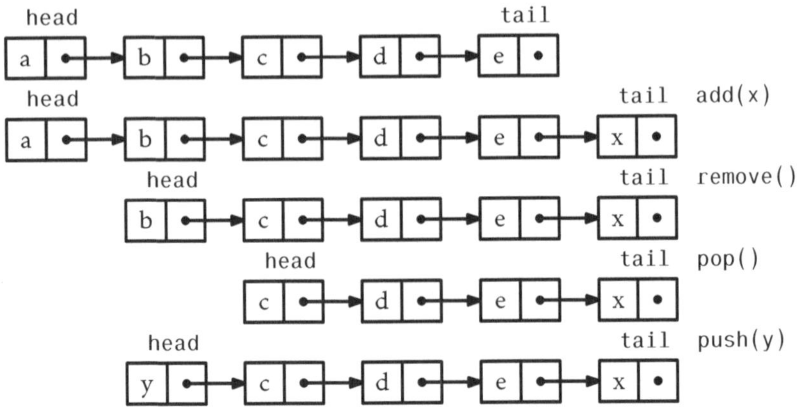

Figure 3.1: A sequence of Queue (add(x) and remove()) and Stack (push(x) and pop()) operations on an SLList.

SLList
```
class Node {
  T x;
  Node next;
}
```

For efficiency, an SLList uses variables head and tail to keep track of the first and last node in the sequence, as well as an integer n to keep track of the length of the sequence:

SLList
```
Node head;
Node tail;
int n;
```

A sequence of Stack and Queue operations on an SLList is illustrated in Figure 3.1.

An SLList can efficiently implement the Stack operations push() and pop() by adding and removing elements at the head of the sequence. The push() operation simply creates a new node u with data value x, sets u.next to the old head of the list and makes u the new head of the list. Finally, it increments n since the size of the SLList has increased by one:

```
SLList
T push(T x) {
  Node u = new Node();
  u.x = x;
  u.next = head;
  head = u;
  if (n == 0)
    tail = u;
  n++;
  return x;
}
```

The pop() operation, after checking that the SLList is not empty, removes the head by setting head = head.next and decrementing n. A special case occurs when the last element is being removed, in which case tail is set to null:

```
SLList
T pop() {
  if (n == 0)  return null;
  T x = head.x;
  head = head.next;
  if (--n == 0) tail = null;
  return x;
}
```

Clearly, both the push(x) and pop() operations run in $O(1)$ time.

3.1.1 Queue Operations

An SLList can also implement the FIFO queue operations add(x) and remove() in constant time. Removals are done from the head of the list, and are identical to the pop() operation:

```
SLList
T remove() {
  if (n == 0)  return null;
  T x = head.x;
  head = head.next;
```

```
  if (--n == 0) tail = null;
  return x;
}
```

Additions, on the other hand, are done at the tail of the list. In most cases, this is done by setting tail.next = u, where u is the newly created node that contains x. However, a special case occurs when n = 0, in which case tail = head = null. In this case, both tail and head are set to u.

SLList
```
boolean add(T x) {
  Node u = new Node();
  u.x = x;
  if (n == 0) {
    head = u;
  } else {
    tail.next = u;
  }
  tail = u;
  n++;
  return true;
}
```

Clearly, both add(x) and remove() take constant time.

3.1.2 Summary

The following theorem summarizes the performance of an SLList:

Theorem 3.1. *An SLList implements the Stack and (FIFO) Queue interfaces. The* push(x), pop(), add(x) *and* remove() *operations run in* $O(1)$ *time per operation.*

An SLList nearly implements the full set of Deque operations. The only missing operation is removing from the tail of an SLList. Removing from the tail of an SLList is difficult because it requires updating the value of tail so that it points to the node w that precedes tail in the SLList; this is the node w such that w.next = tail. Unfortunately, the only way to get to w is by traversing the SLList starting at head and taking n − 2 steps.

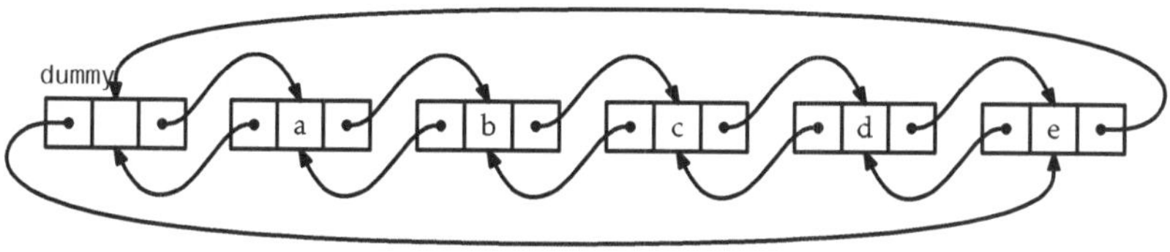

Figure 3.2: A DLList containing a,b,c,d,e.

3.2 DLList: A Doubly-Linked List

A DLList (doubly-linked list) is very similar to an SLList except that each node u in a DLList has references to both the node u.next that follows it and the node u.prev that precedes it.

```
DLList
class Node {
  T x;
  Node prev, next;
}
```

When implementing an SLList, we saw that there were always several special cases to worry about. For example, removing the last element from an SLList or adding an element to an empty SLList requires care to ensure that head and tail are correctly updated. In a DLList, the number of these special cases increases considerably. Perhaps the cleanest way to take care of all these special cases in a DLList is to introduce a dummy node. This is a node that does not contain any data, but acts as a placeholder so that there are no special nodes; every node has both a next and a prev, with dummy acting as the node that follows the last node in the list and that precedes the first node in the list. In this way, the nodes of the list are (doubly-)linked into a cycle, as illustrated in Figure 3.2.

```
DLList
int n;
Node dummy;
DLList() {
  dummy = new Node();
```

```
  dummy.next = dummy;
  dummy.prev = dummy;
  n = 0;
}
```

Finding the node with a particular index in a DLList is easy; we can either start at the head of the list (dummy.next) and work forward, or start at the tail of the list (dummy.prev) and work backward. This allows us to reach the i th node in $O(1+\min\{i, n-i\})$ time:

```
DLList
Node getNode(int i) {
  Node p = null;
  if (i < n / 2) {
    p = dummy.next;
    for (int j = 0; j < i; j++)
      p = p.next;
  } else {
    p = dummy;
    for (int j = n; j > i; j--)
      p = p.prev;
  }
  return (p);
}
```

The get(i) and set(i, x) operations are now also easy. We first find the i th node and then get or set its x value:

```
DLList
T get(int i) {
  return getNode(i).x;
}
T set(int i, T x) {
  Node u = getNode(i);
  T y = u.x;
  u.x = x;
  return y;
}
```

The running time of these operations is dominated by the time it takes to find the i th node, and is therefore $O(1+\min\{i, n-i\})$.

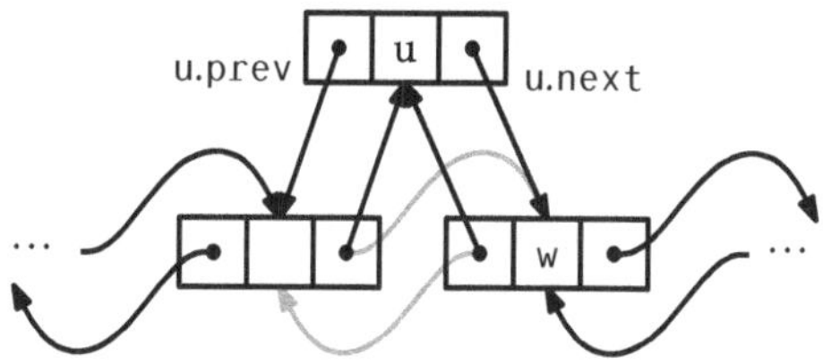

Figure 3.3: Adding the node u before the node w in a DLList.

3.2.1 Adding and Removing

If we have a reference to a node w in a DLList and we want to insert a node u before w, then this is just a matter of setting u.next = w, u.prev = w.prev, and then adjusting u.prev.next and u.next.prev. (See Figure 3.3.) Thanks to the dummy node, there is no need to worry about w.prev or w.next not existing.

DLList
```
Node addBefore(Node w, T x) {
  Node u = new Node();
  u.x = x;
  u.prev = w.prev;
  u.next = w;
  u.next.prev = u;
  u.prev.next = u;
  n++;
  return u;
}
```

Now, the list operation add(i,x) is trivial to implement. We find the ith node in the DLList and insert a new node u that contains x just before it.

DLList
```
void add(int i, T x) {
  addBefore(getNode(i), x);
}
```

The only non-constant part of the running time of add(i,x) is the time it takes to find the ith node (using getNode(i)). Thus, add(i,x) runs in $O(1+\min\{i,n-i\})$ time.

Removing a node w from a DLList is easy. We only need to adjust pointers at w.next and w.prev so that they skip over w. Again, the use of the dummy node eliminates the need to consider any special cases:

DLList
```
void remove(Node w) {
  w.prev.next = w.next;
  w.next.prev = w.prev;
  n--;
}
```

Now the remove(i) operation is trivial. We find the node with index i and remove it:

DLList
```
T remove(int i) {
  Node w = getNode(i);
  remove(w);
  return w.x;
}
```

Again, the only expensive part of this operation is finding the ith node using getNode(i), so remove(i) runs in $O(1+\min\{i,n-i\})$ time.

3.2.2 Summary

The following theorem summarizes the performance of a DLList:

Theorem 3.2. *A DLList implements the List interface. In this implementation, the* get(i), set(i,x), add(i,x) *and* remove(i) *operations run in* $O(1+\min\{i,n-i\})$ *time per operation.*

It is worth noting that, if we ignore the cost of the getNode(i) operation, then all operations on a DLList take constant time. Thus, the only expensive part of operations on a DLList is finding the relevant node.

Once we have the relevant node, adding, removing, or accessing the data at that node takes only constant time.

This is in sharp contrast to the array-based List implementations of Chapter 2; in those implementations, the relevant array item can be found in constant time. However, addition or removal requires shifting elements in the array and, in general, takes non-constant time.

For this reason, linked list structures are well-suited to applications where references to list nodes can be obtained through external means. An example of this is the LinkedHashSet data structure found in the Java Collections Framework, in which a set of items is stored in a doubly-linked list and the nodes of the doubly-linked list are stored in a hash table (discussed in Chapter 5). When elements are removed from a LinkedHashSet, the hash table is used to find the relevant list node in constant time and then the list node is deleted (also in constant time).

3.3 SEList: A Space-Efficient Linked List

One of the drawbacks of linked lists (besides the time it takes to access elements that are deep within the list) is their space usage. Each node in a DLList requires an additional two references to the next and previous nodes in the list. Two of the fields in a Node are dedicated to maintaining the list, and only one of the fields is for storing data!

An SEList (space-efficient list) reduces this wasted space using a simple idea: Rather than store individual elements in a DLList, we store a block (array) containing several items. More precisely, an SEList is parameterized by a *block size* b. Each individual node in an SEList stores a block that can hold up to b + 1 elements.

For reasons that will become clear later, it will be helpful if we can do Deque operations on each block. The data structure that we choose for this is a BDeque (bounded deque), derived from the ArrayDeque structure described in Section 2.4. The BDeque differs from the ArrayDeque in one small way: When a new BDeque is created, the size of the backing array a is fixed at b + 1 and never grows or shrinks. The important property of a BDeque is that it allows for the addition or removal of elements at either the front or back in constant time. This will be useful as elements are shifted from one block to another.

SEList
```
class BDeque extends ArrayDeque<T> {
  BDeque() {
    super(SEList.this.type());
    a = newArray(b+1);
  }
  void resize() { }
}
```

An SEList is then a doubly-linked list of blocks:

SEList
```
class Node {
  BDeque d;
  Node prev, next;
}
```

SEList
```
int n;
Node dummy;
```

3.3.1 Space Requirements

An SEList places very tight restrictions on the number of elements in a block: Unless a block is the last block, then that block contains at least $b-1$ and at most $b+1$ elements. This means that, if an SEList contains n elements, then it has at most

$$n/(b-1)+1 = O(n/b)$$

blocks. The BDeque for each block contains an array of length $b+1$ but, for every block except the last, at most a constant amount of space is wasted in this array. The remaining memory used by a block is also constant. This means that the wasted space in an SEList is only $O(b+n/b)$. By choosing a value of b within a constant factor of $\sqrt{n}$, we can make the space-overhead of an SEList approach the $\sqrt{n}$ lower bound given in Section 2.6.2.

3.3.2 Finding Elements

The first challenge we face with an SEList is finding the list item with a given index i. Note that the location of an element consists of two parts:

1. The node u that contains the block that contains the element with index i; and

2. the index j of the element within its block.

SEList
```
class Location {
  Node u;
  int j;
  Location(Node u, int j) {
    this.u = u;
    this.j = j;
  }
}
```

To find the block that contains a particular element, we proceed the same way as we do in a DLList. We either start at the front of the list and traverse in the forward direction, or at the back of the list and traverse backwards until we reach the node we want. The only difference is that, each time we move from one node to the next, we skip over a whole block of elements.

SEList
```
Location getLocation(int i) {
  if (i < n/2) {
    Node u = dummy.next;
    while (i >= u.d.size()) {
      i -= u.d.size();
      u = u.next;
    }
    return new Location(u, i);
  } else {
    Node u = dummy;
    int idx = n;
```

```
      while (i < idx) {
        u = u.prev;
        idx -= u.d.size();
      }
      return new Location(u, i-idx);
    }
}
```

Remember that, with the exception of at most one block, each block contains at least $b-1$ elements, so each step in our search gets us $b-1$ elements closer to the element we are looking for. If we are searching forward, this means that we reach the node we want after $O(1 + i/b)$ steps. If we search backwards, then we reach the node we want after $O(1+(n-i)/b)$ steps. The algorithm takes the smaller of these two quantities depending on the value of i, so the time to locate the item with index i is $O(1+\min\{i,n-i\}/b)$.

Once we know how to locate the item with index i, the get(i) and set(i, x) operations translate into getting or setting a particular index in the correct block:

```
SEList
T get(int i) {
  Location l = getLocation(i);
  return l.u.d.get(l.j);
}
T set(int i, T x) {
  Location l = getLocation(i);
  T y = l.u.d.get(l.j);
  l.u.d.set(l.j,x);
  return y;
}
```

The running times of these operations are dominated by the time it takes to locate the item, so they also run in $O(1+\min\{i,n-i\}/b)$ time.

3.3.3 Adding an Element

Adding elements to an SEList is a little more complicated. Before considering the general case, we consider the easier operation, add(x), in which x is added to the end of the list. If the last block is full (or does not exist because there are no blocks yet), then we first allocate a new block and append it to the list of blocks. Now that we are sure that the last block exists and is not full, we append x to the last block.

SEList
```
boolean add(T x) {
  Node last = dummy.prev;
  if (last == dummy || last.d.size() == b+1) {
    last = addBefore(dummy);
  }
  last.d.add(x);
  n++;
  return true;
}
```

Things get more complicated when we add to the interior of the list using add(i,x). We first locate i to get the node u whose block contains the ith list item. The problem is that we want to insert x into u's block, but we have to be prepared for the case where u's block already contains $b+1$ elements, so that it is full and there is no room for x.

Let $u_0, u_1, u_2, \ldots$ denote u, u.next, u.next.next, and so on. We explore $u_0, u_1, u_2, \ldots$ looking for a node that can provide space for x. Three cases can occur during our space exploration (see Figure 3.4):

1. We quickly (in $r+1 \leq b$ steps) find a node u_r whose block is not full. In this case, we perform r shifts of an element from one block into the next, so that the free space in u_r becomes a free space in u_0. We can then insert x into u_0's block.

2. We quickly (in $r+1 \leq b$ steps) run off the end of the list of blocks. In this case, we add a new empty block to the end of the list of blocks and proceed as in the first case.

3. After b steps we do not find any block that is not full. In this case, $u_0, \ldots, u_{b-1}$ is a sequence of b blocks that each contain $b+1$ elements. We insert a new block u_b at the end of this sequence and *spread* the original $b(b+1)$ elements so that each block of $u_0, \ldots, u_b$ contains

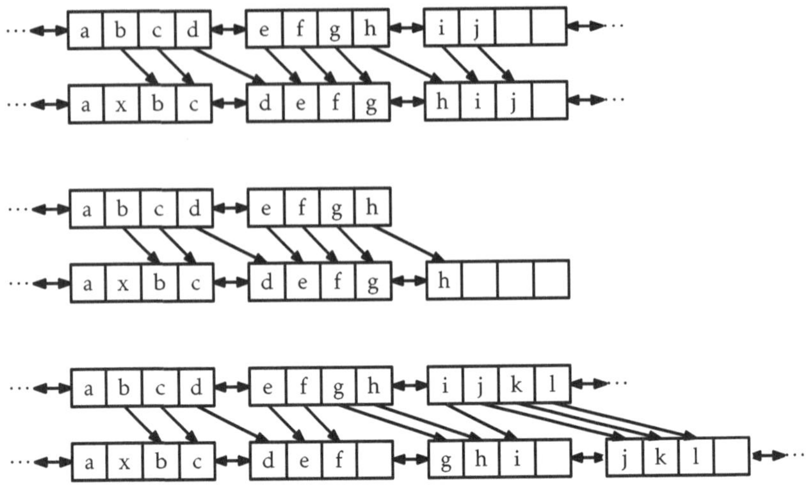

Figure 3.4: The three cases that occur during the addition of an item x in the interior of an SEList. (This SEList has block size b = 3.)

exactly b elements. Now u_0's block contains only b elements so it has room for us to insert x.

SEList
```
void add(int i, T x) {
  if (i == n) {
    add(x);
    return;
  }
  Location l = getLocation(i);
  Node u = l.u;
  int r = 0;
  while (r < b && u != dummy && u.d.size() == b+1) {
    u = u.next;
    r++;
  }
  if (r == b) {      // b blocks each with b+1 elements
    spread(l.u);
    u = l.u;
  }
```

```
    if (u == dummy) {  // ran off the end - add new node
      u = addBefore(u);
    }
    while (u != l.u) { // work backwards, shifting elements
      u.d.add(0, u.prev.d.remove(u.prev.d.size()-1));
      u = u.prev;
    }
    u.d.add(l.j, x);
    n++;
}
```

The running time of the add(i,x) operation depends on which of the three cases above occurs. Cases 1 and 2 involve examining and shifting elements through at most b blocks and take $O(\mathtt{b})$ time. Case 3 involves calling the spread(u) method, which moves $\mathtt{b}(\mathtt{b}+1)$ elements and takes $O(\mathtt{b}^2)$ time. If we ignore the cost of Case 3 (which we will account for later with amortization) this means that the total running time to locate i and perform the insertion of x is $O(\mathtt{b}+\min\{\mathtt{i},\mathtt{n}-\mathtt{i}\}/\mathtt{b})$.

3.3.4 Removing an Element

Removing an element from an SEList is similar to adding an element. We first locate the node u that contains the element with index i. Now, we have to be prepared for the case where we cannot remove an element from u without causing u's block to become smaller than $\mathtt{b}-1$.

Again, let $\mathtt{u}_0,\mathtt{u}_1,\mathtt{u}_2,\ldots$ denote u, u.next, u.next.next, and so on. We examine $\mathtt{u}_0,\mathtt{u}_1,\mathtt{u}_2,\ldots$ in order to look for a node from which we can borrow an element to make the size of $\mathtt{u}_0$'s block at least $\mathtt{b}-1$. There are three cases to consider (see Figure 3.5):

1. We quickly (in $r+1 \le \mathtt{b}$ steps) find a node whose block contains more than $\mathtt{b}-1$ elements. In this case, we perform r shifts of an element from one block into the previous one, so that the extra element in $\mathtt{u}_r$ becomes an extra element in $\mathtt{u}_0$. We can then remove the appropriate element from $\mathtt{u}_0$'s block.

2. We quickly (in $r+1 \le \mathtt{b}$ steps) run off the end of the list of blocks. In this case, $\mathtt{u}_r$ is the last block, and there is no need for $\mathtt{u}_r$'s block

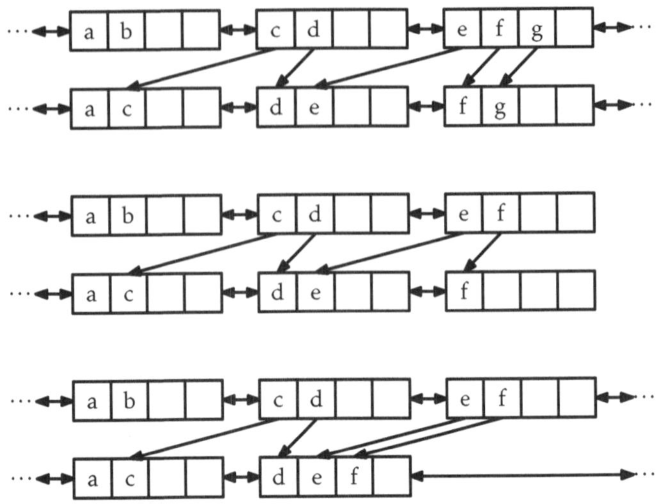

Figure 3.5: The three cases that occur during the removal of an item x in the interior of an SEList. (This SEList has block size $b = 3$.)

to contain at least $b-1$ elements. Therefore, we proceed as above, borrowing an element from u_r to make an extra element in u_0. If this causes u_r's block to become empty, then we remove it.

3. After b steps, we do not find any block containing more than $b-1$ elements. In this case, $u_0,\ldots,u_{b-1}$ is a sequence of b blocks that each contain $b-1$ elements. We *gather* these $b(b-1)$ elements into $u_0,\ldots,u_{b-2}$ so that each of these $b-1$ blocks contains exactly b elements and we remove u_{b-1}, which is now empty. Now u_0's block contains b elements and we can then remove the appropriate element from it.

SEList

```
T remove(int i) {
  Location l = getLocation(i);
  T y = l.u.d.get(l.j);
  Node u = l.u;
  int r = 0;
```

```
    while (r < b && u != dummy && u.d.size() == b-1) {
      u = u.next;
      r++;
    }
    if (r == b) {   // b blocks each with b-1 elements
      gather(l.u);
    }
    u = l.u;
    u.d.remove(l.j);
    while (u.d.size() < b-1 && u.next != dummy) {
      u.d.add(u.next.d.remove(0));
      u = u.next;
    }
    if (u.d.isEmpty()) remove(u);
    n--;
    return y;
}
```

Like the add(i,x) operation, the running time of the remove(i) operation is $O(b + \min\{i, n-i\}/b)$ if we ignore the cost of the gather(u) method that occurs in Case 3.

3.3.5 Amortized Analysis of Spreading and Gathering

Next, we consider the cost of the gather(u) and spread(u) methods that may be executed by the add(i,x) and remove(i) methods. For the sake of completeness, here they are:

```
SEList
void spread(Node u) {
  Node w = u;
  for (int j = 0; j < b; j++) {
    w = w.next;
  }
  w = addBefore(w);
  while (w != u) {
    while (w.d.size() < b)
      w.d.add(0,w.prev.d.remove(w.prev.d.size()-1));
    w = w.prev;
  }
```

```
}
```

SEList

```
void gather(Node u) {
  Node w = u;
  for (int j = 0; j < b-1; j++) {
    while (w.d.size() < b)
      w.d.add(w.next.d.remove(0));
    w = w.next;
  }
  remove(w);
}
```

The running time of each of these methods is dominated by the two nested loops. Both the inner and outer loops execute at most $b+1$ times, so the total running time of each of these methods is $O((b+1)^2) = O(b^2)$. However, the following lemma shows that these methods execute on at most one out of every b calls to add(i, x) or remove(i).

Lemma 3.1. *If an empty* SEList *is created and any sequence of $m \geq 1$ calls to* add(i, x) *and* remove(i) *is performed, then the total time spent during all calls to* spread() *and* gather() *is $O(bm)$.*

Proof. We will use the potential method of amortized analysis. We say that a node u is *fragile* if u's block does not contain b elements (so that u is either the last node, or contains $b-1$ or $b+1$ elements). Any node whose block contains b elements is *rugged*. Define the *potential* of an SEList as the number of fragile nodes it contains. We will consider only the add(i, x) operation and its relation to the number of calls to spread(u). The analysis of remove(i) and gather(u) is identical.

Notice that, if Case 1 occurs during the add(i, x) method, then only one node, u_r has the size of its block changed. Therefore, at most one node, namely u_r, goes from being rugged to being fragile. If Case 2 occurs, then a new node is created, and this node is fragile, but no other node changes size, so the number of fragile nodes increases by one. Thus, in either Case 1 or Case 2 the potential of the SEList increases by at most one.

Finally, if Case 3 occurs, it is because $u_0,\ldots,u_{b-1}$ are all fragile nodes. Then spread(u_0) is called and these b fragile nodes are replaced with b+1 rugged nodes. Finally, x is added to u_0's block, making u_0 fragile. In total the potential decreases by b − 1.

In summary, the potential starts at 0 (there are no nodes in the list). Each time Case 1 or Case 2 occurs, the potential increases by at most 1. Each time Case 3 occurs, the potential decreases by b − 1. The potential (which counts the number of fragile nodes) is never less than 0. We conclude that, for every occurrence of Case 3, there are at least b − 1 occurrences of Case 1 or Case 2. Thus, for every call to spread(u) there are at least b calls to add(i, x). This completes the proof. □

3.3.6 Summary

The following theorem summarizes the performance of the SEList data structure:

Theorem 3.3. *An SEList implements the List interface. Ignoring the cost of calls to* spread(u) *and* gather(u)*, an SEList with block size* b *supports the operations*

- get(i) *and* set(i, x) *in* $O(1+\min\{i, n-i\}/b)$ *time per operation; and*
- add(i, x) *and* remove(i) *in* $O(b+\min\{i, n-i\}/b)$ *time per operation.*

Furthermore, beginning with an empty SEList, any sequence of m add(i, x) *and* remove(i) *operations results in a total of* $O(bm)$ *time spent during all calls to* spread(u) *and* gather(u)*.*

The space (measured in words)[1] *used by an SEList that stores* n *elements is* $n+O(b+n/b)$.

The SEList is a trade-off between an ArrayList and a DLList where the relative mix of these two structures depends on the block size b. At the extreme b = 2, each SEList node stores at most three values, which is not much different than a DLList. At the other extreme, b > n, all the elements are stored in a single array, just like in an ArrayList. In between these two extremes lies a trade-off between the time it takes to

[1]Recall Section 1.4 for a discussion of how memory is measured.

add or remove a list item and the time it takes to locate a particular list item.

3.4 Discussion and Exercises

Both singly-linked and doubly-linked lists are established techniques, having been used in programs for over 40 years. They are discussed, for example, by Knuth [46, Sections 2.2.3–2.2.5]. Even the SEList data structure seems to be a well-known data structures exercise. The SEList is sometimes referred to as an *unrolled linked list* [69].

Another way to save space in a doubly-linked list is to use so-called XOR-lists. In an XOR-list, each node, u, contains only one pointer, called u.nextprev, that holds the bitwise exclusive-or of u.prev and u.next. The list itself needs to store two pointers, one to the dummy node and one to dummy.next (the first node, or dummy if the list is empty). This technique uses the fact that, if we have pointers to u and u.prev, then we can extract u.next using the formula

$$\text{u.next} = \text{u.prev}\hat{\ }\text{u.nextprev} \ .$$

(Here ^ computes the bitwise exclusive-or of its two arguments.) This technique complicates the code a little and is not possible in some languages that have garbage collection—including Java—but gives a doubly-linked list implementation that requires only one pointer per node. See Sinha's magazine article [70] for a detailed discussion of XOR-lists.

Exercise 3.1. Why is it not possible to use a dummy node in an SLList to avoid all the special cases that occur in the operations push(x), pop(), add(x), and remove()?

Exercise 3.2. Design and implement an SLList method, secondLast(), that returns the second-last element of an SLList. Do this without using the member variable, n, that keeps track of the size of the list.

Exercise 3.3. Implement the List operations get(i), set(i, x), add(i, x) and remove(i) on an SLList. Each of these operations should run in $O(1 + \text{i})$ time.

Exercise 3.4. Design and implement an SLList method, reverse() that reverses the order of elements in an SLList. This method should run in $O(n)$ time, should not use recursion, should not use any secondary data structures, and should not create any new nodes.

Exercise 3.5. Design and implement SLList and DLList methods called checkSize(). These methods walk through the list and count the number of nodes to see if this matches the value, n, stored in the list. These methods return nothing, but throw an exception if the size they compute does not match the value of n.

Exercise 3.6. Try to recreate the code for the addBefore(w) operation that creates a node, u, and adds it in a DLList just before the node w. Do not refer to this chapter. Even if your code does not exactly match the code given in this book it may still be correct. Test it and see if it works.

The next few exercises involve performing manipulations on DLLists. You should complete them without allocating any new nodes or temporary arrays. They can all be done only by changing the prev and next values of existing nodes.

Exercise 3.7. Write a DLList method isPalindrome() that returns true if the list is a *palindrome*, i.e., the element at position i is equal to the element at position $n - i - 1$ for all $i \in \{0,\ldots,n-1\}$. Your code should run in $O(n)$ time.

Exercise 3.8. Implement a method rotate(r) that "rotates" a DLList so that list item i becomes list item $(i + r) \bmod n$. This method should run in $O(1 + \min\{r, n - r\})$ time and should not modify any nodes in the list.

Exercise 3.9. Write a method, truncate(i), that truncates a DLList at position i. After executing this method, the size of the list will be i and it should contain only the elements at indices $0,\ldots,i-1$. The return value is another DLList that contains the elements at indices $i,\ldots,n-1$. This method should run in $O(\min\{i, n - i\})$ time.

Exercise 3.10. Write a DLList method, absorb(l2), that takes as an argument a DLList, l2, empties it and appends its contents, in order, to the receiver. For example, if l1 contains a,b,c and l2 contains d,e,f, then after calling l1.absorb(l2), l1 will contain a,b,c,d,e,f and l2 will be empty.

Exercise 3.11. Write a method deal() that removes all the elements with odd-numbered indices from a DLList and return a DLList containing these elements. For example, if l1, contains the elements a,b,c,d,e,f, then after calling l1.deal(), l1 should contain a,c,e and a list containing b,d,f should be returned.

Exercise 3.12. Write a method, reverse(), that reverses the order of elements in a DLList.

Exercise 3.13. This exercise walks you through an implementation of the merge-sort algorithm for sorting a DLList, as discussed in Section 11.1.1. In your implementation, perform comparisons between elements using the compareTo(x) method so that the resulting implementation can sort any DLList containing elements that implement the Comparable interface.

1. Write a DLList method called takeFirst(l2). This method takes the first node from l2 and appends it to the the receiving list. This is equivalent to add(size(),l2.remove(0)), except that it should not create a new node.

2. Write a DLList static method, merge(l1,l2), that takes two sorted lists l1 and l2, merges them, and returns a new sorted list containing the result. This causes l1 and l2 to be emptied in the proces. For example, if l1 contains a,c,d and l2 contains b,e,f, then this method returns a new list containing a,b,c,d,e,f.

3. Write a DLList method sort() that sorts the elements contained in the list using the merge sort algorithm. This recursive algorithm works in the following way:

    (a) If the list contains 0 or 1 elements then there is nothing to do. Otherwise,

    (b) Using the truncate(size()/2) method, split the list into two lists of approximately equal length, l1 and l2;

    (c) Recursively sort l1;

(d) Recursively sort l2; and, finally,

(e) Merge l1 and l2 into a single sorted list.

The next few exercises are more advanced and require a clear understanding of what happens to the minimum value stored in a Stack or Queue as items are added and removed.

Exercise 3.14. Design and implement a MinStack data structure that can store comparable elements and supports the stack operations push(x), pop(), and size(), as well as the min() operation, which returns the minimum value currently stored in the data structure. All operations should run in constant time.

Exercise 3.15. Design and implement a MinQueue data structure that can store comparable elements and supports the queue operations add(x), remove(), and size(), as well as the min() operation, which returns the minimum value currently stored in the data structure. All operations should run in constant amortized time.

Exercise 3.16. Design and implement a MinDeque data structure that can store comparable elements and supports all the deque operations addFirst(x), addLast(x) removeFirst(), removeLast() and size(), and the min() operation, which returns the minimum value currently stored in the data structure. All operations should run in constant amortized time.

The next exercises are designed to test the reader's understanding of the implementation and analysis of the space-efficient SEList:

Exercise 3.17. Prove that, if an SEList is used like a Stack (so that the only modifications to the SEList are done using push(x) ≡ add(size(), x) and pop() ≡ remove(size() − 1)), then these operations run in constant amortized time, independent of the value of b.

Exercise 3.18. Design and implement of a version of an SEList that supports all the Deque operations in constant amortized time per operation, independent of the value of b.

Exercise 3.19. Explain how to use the bitwise exclusive-or operator, ^, to swap the values of two int variables without using a third variable.

Chapter 4

Skiplists

In this chapter, we discuss a beautiful data structure: the skiplist, which has a variety of applications. Using a skiplist we can implement a `List` that has $O(\log n)$ time implementations of `get(i)`, `set(i,x)`, `add(i,x)`, and `remove(i)`. We can also implement an `SSet` in which all operations run in $O(\log n)$ expected time.

The efficiency of skiplists relies on their use of randomization. When a new element is added to a skiplist, the skiplist uses random coin tosses to determine the height of the new element. The performance of skiplists is expressed in terms of expected running times and path lengths. This expectation is taken over the random coin tosses used by the skiplist. In the implementation, the random coin tosses used by a skiplist are simulated using a pseudo-random number (or bit) generator.

4.1 The Basic Structure

Conceptually, a skiplist is a sequence of singly-linked lists $L_0, \ldots, L_h$. Each list L_r contains a subset of the items in L_{r-1}. We start with the input list L_0 that contains n items and construct L_1 from L_0, L_2 from L_1, and so on. The items in L_r are obtained by tossing a coin for each element, x, in L_{r-1} and including x in L_r if the coin turns up as heads. This process ends when we create a list L_r that is empty. An example of a skiplist is shown in Figure 4.1.

For an element, x, in a skiplist, we call the *height* of x the largest value

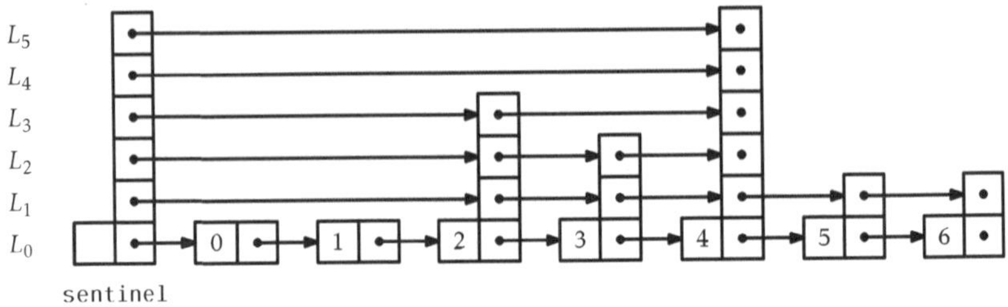

Figure 4.1: A skiplist containing seven elements.

r such that x appears in L_r. Thus, for example, elements that only appear in L_0 have height 0. If we spend a few moments thinking about it, we notice that the height of x corresponds to the following experiment: Toss a coin repeatedly until it comes up as tails. How many times did it come up as heads? The answer, not surprisingly, is that the expected height of a node is 1. (We expect to toss the coin twice before getting tails, but we don't count the last toss.) The *height* of a skiplist is the height of its tallest node.

At the head of every list is a special node, called the *sentinel*, that acts as a dummy node for the list. The key property of skiplists is that there is a short path, called the *search path*, from the sentinel in L_h to every node in L_0. Remembering how to construct a search path for a node, u, is easy (see Figure 4.2) : Start at the top left corner of your skiplist (the sentinel in L_h) and always go right unless that would overshoot u, in which case you should take a step down into the list below.

More precisely, to construct the search path for the node u in L_0, we start at the sentinel, w, in L_h. Next, we examine w.next. If w.next contains an item that appears before u in L_0, then we set w = w.next. Otherwise, we move down and continue the search at the occurrence of w in the list L_{h-1}. We continue this way until we reach the predecessor of u in L_0.

The following result, which we will prove in Section 4.4, shows that the search path is quite short:

Lemma 4.1. *The expected length of the search path for any node,* u, *in* L_0 *is at most* $2\log n + O(1) = O(\log n)$.

A space-efficient way to implement a skiplist is to define a Node, u,

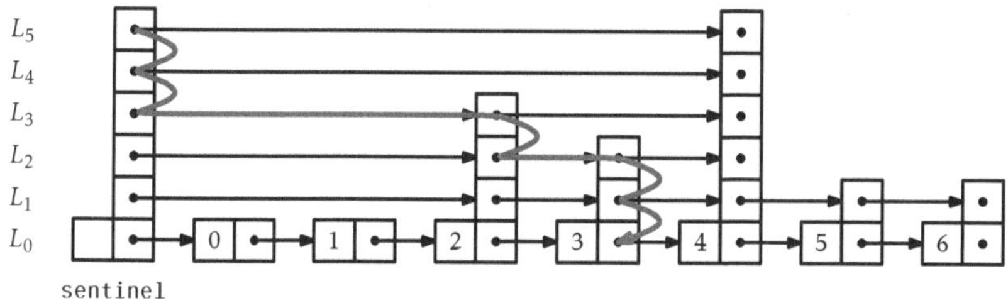

Figure 4.2: The search path for the node containing 4 in a skiplist.

as consisting of a data value, x, and an array, next, of pointers, where u.next[i] points to u's successor in the list L_i. In this way, the data, x, in a node is referenced only once, even though x may appear in several lists.

SkiplistSSet
```
class Node<T> {
  T x;
  Node<T>[] next;
  Node(T ix, int h) {
    x = ix;
    next = Array.newInstance(Node.class, h+1);
  }
  int height() {
    return next.length - 1;
  }
}
```

The next two sections of this chapter discuss two different applications of skiplists. In each of these applications, L_0 stores the main structure (a list of elements or a sorted set of elements). The primary difference between these structures is in how a search path is navigated; in particular, they differ in how they decide if a search path should go down into L_{r-1} or go right within L_r.

4.2 SkiplistSSet: An Efficient SSet

A SkiplistSSet uses a skiplist structure to implement the SSet interface. When used in this way, the list L_0 stores the elements of the SSet in sorted order. The find(x) method works by following the search path for the smallest value y such that $y \geq x$:

SkiplistSSet
```
Node<T> findPredNode(T x) {
  Node<T> u = sentinel;
  int r = h;
  while (r >= 0) {
    while (u.next[r] != null && compare(u.next[r].x,x) < 0)
      u = u.next[r];    // go right in list r
    r--;                // go down into list r-1
  }
  return u;
}
T find(T x) {
  Node<T> u = findPredNode(x);
  return u.next[0] == null ? null : u.next[0].x;
}
```

Following the search path for y is easy: when situated at some node, u, in L_r, we look right to u.next[r].x. If x > u.next[r].x, then we take a step to the right in L_r; otherwise, we move down into L_{r-1}. Each step (right or down) in this search takes only constant time; thus, by Lemma 4.1, the expected running time of find(x) is $O(\log n)$.

Before we can add an element to a SkipListSSet, we need a method to simulate tossing coins to determine the height, k, of a new node. We do so by picking a random integer, z, and counting the number of trailing 1s in the binary representation of z:[1]

SkiplistSSet
```
int pickHeight() {
  int z = rand.nextInt();
```

[1]This method does not exactly replicate the coin-tossing experiment since the value of k will always be less than the number of bits in an int. However, this will have negligible impact unless the number of elements in the structure is much greater than $2^{32} = 4294967296$.

```
  int k = 0;
  int m = 1;
  while ((z & m) != 0) {
    k++;
    m <<= 1;
  }
  return k;
}
```

To implement the add(x) method in a SkiplistSSet we search for x and then splice x into a few lists $L_0,\ldots,L_k$, where k is selected using the pickHeight() method. The easiest way to do this is to use an array, stack, that keeps track of the nodes at which the search path goes down from some list L_r into L_{r-1}. More precisely, stack[r] is the node in L_r where the search path proceeded down into L_{r-1}. The nodes that we modify to insert x are precisely the nodes stack[0],...,stack[k]. The following code implements this algorithm for add(x):

SkiplistSSet

```
boolean add(T x) {
  Node<T> u = sentinel;
  int r = h;
  int comp = 0;
  while (r >= 0) {
    while (u.next[r] != null
           && (comp = compare(u.next[r].x,x)) < 0)
      u = u.next[r];
    if (u.next[r] != null && comp == 0) return false;
    stack[r--] = u;          // going down, store u
  }
  Node<T> w = new Node<T>(x, pickHeight());
  while (h < w.height())
    stack[++h] = sentinel;   // height increased
  for (int i = 0; i < w.next.length; i++) {
    w.next[i] = stack[i].next[i];
    stack[i].next[i] = w;
  }
  n++;
  return true;
}
```

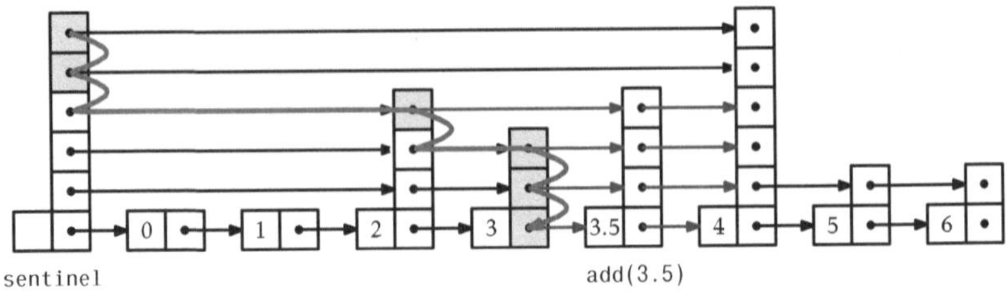

Figure 4.3: Adding the node containing 3.5 to a skiplist. The nodes stored in stack are highlighted.

Removing an element, x, is done in a similar way, except that there is no need for stack to keep track of the search path. The removal can be done as we are following the search path. We search for x and each time the search moves downward from a node u, we check if u.next.x = x and if so, we splice u out of the list:

```
SkiplistSSet
boolean remove(T x) {
  boolean removed = false;
  Node<T> u = sentinel;
  int r = h;
  int comp = 0;
  while (r >= 0) {
    while (u.next[r] != null
           && (comp = compare(u.next[r].x, x)) < 0) {
      u = u.next[r];
    }
    if (u.next[r] != null && comp == 0) {
      removed = true;
      u.next[r] = u.next[r].next[r];
      if (u == sentinel && u.next[r] == null)
        h--;  // height has gone down
    }
    r--;
  }
  if (removed) n--;
  return removed;
}
```

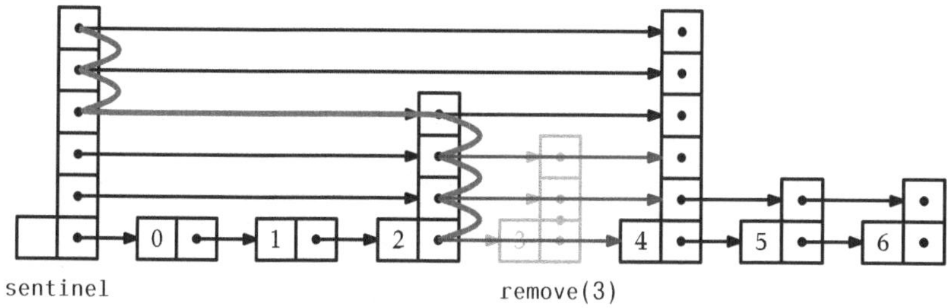

Figure 4.4: Removing the node containing 3 from a skiplist.

4.2.1 Summary

The following theorem summarizes the performance of skiplists when used to implement sorted sets:

Theorem 4.1. *SkiplistSSet implements the SSet interface. A SkiplistSSet supports the operations* add(x), remove(x), *and* find(x) *in* $O(\log n)$ *expected time per operation.*

4.3 SkiplistList: An Efficient Random-Access List

A SkiplistList implements the List interface using a skiplist structure. In a SkiplistList, L_0 contains the elements of the list in the order in which they appear in the list. As in a SkiplistSSet, elements can be added, removed, and accessed in $O(\log n)$ time.

For this to be possible, we need a way to follow the search path for the ith element in L_0. The easiest way to do this is to define the notion of the *length* of an edge in some list, L_r. We define the length of every edge in L_0 as 1. The length of an edge, e, in L_r, $r > 0$, is defined as the sum of the lengths of the edges below e in L_{r-1}. Equivalently, the length of e is the number of edges in L_0 below e. See Figure 4.5 for an example of a skiplist with the lengths of its edges shown. Since the edges of skiplists are stored in arrays, the lengths can be stored the same way:

SkiplistList
```
class Node {
```

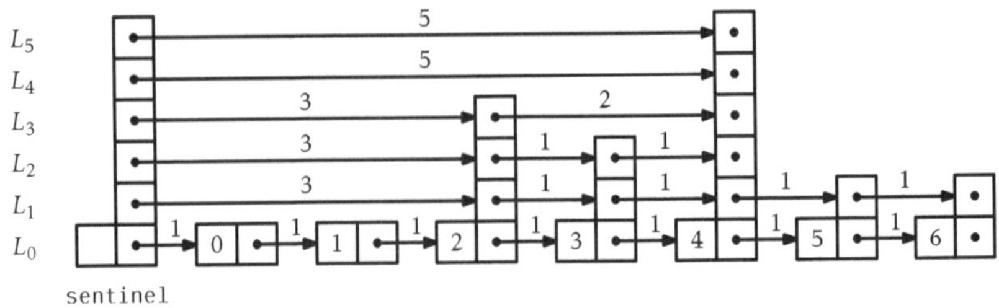

Figure 4.5: The lengths of the edges in a skiplist.

```
    T x;
    Node[] next;
    int[] length;
    Node(T ix, int h) {
      x = ix;
      next = Array.newInstance(Node.class, h+1);
      length = new int[h+1];
    }
    int height() {
      return next.length - 1;
    }
}
```

The useful property of this definition of length is that, if we are currently at a node that is at position j in L_0 and we follow an edge of length ℓ, then we move to a node whose position, in L_0, is $j+\ell$. In this way, while following a search path, we can keep track of the position, j, of the current node in L_0. When at a node, u, in L_r, we go right if j plus the length of the edge u.next[r] is less than i. Otherwise, we go down into L_{r-1}.

```
SkiplistList
Node findPred(int i) {
  Node u = sentinel;
  int r = h;
  int j = -1;    // index of the current node in list 0
  while (r >= 0) {
    while (u.next[r] != null && j + u.length[r] < i) {
      j += u.length[r];
```

```
        u = u.next[r];
      }
      r--;
    }
    return u;
  }
```

SkiplistList

```
T get(int i) {
  return findPred(i).next[0].x;
}
T set(int i, T x) {
  Node u = findPred(i).next[0];
  T y = u.x;
  u.x = x;
  return y;
}
```

Since the hardest part of the operations get(i) and set(i, x) is finding the ith node in L_0, these operations run in $O(\log n)$ time.

Adding an element to a SkiplistList at a position, i, is fairly simple. Unlike in a SkiplistSSet, we are sure that a new node will actually be added, so we can do the addition at the same time as we search for the new node's location. We first pick the height, k, of the newly inserted node, w, and then follow the search path for i. Any time the search path moves down from L_r with $r \leq k$, we splice w into L_r. The only extra care needed is to ensure that the lengths of edges are updated properly. See Figure 4.6.

Note that, each time the search path goes down at a node, u, in L_r, the length of the edge u.next[r] increases by one, since we are adding an element below that edge at position i. Splicing the node w between two nodes, u and z, works as shown in Figure 4.7. While following the search path we are already keeping track of the position, j, of u in L_0. Therefore, we know that the length of the edge from u to w is $i - j$. We can also deduce the length of the edge from w to z from the length, ℓ, of the edge from u to z. Therefore, we can splice in w and update the lengths of the edges in constant time.

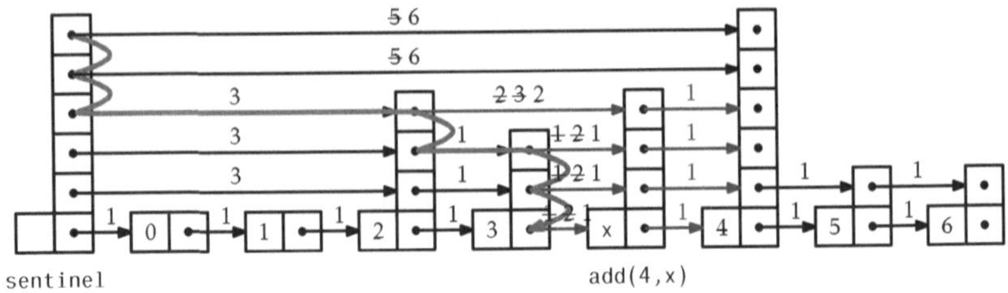

Figure 4.6: Adding an element to a SkiplistList.

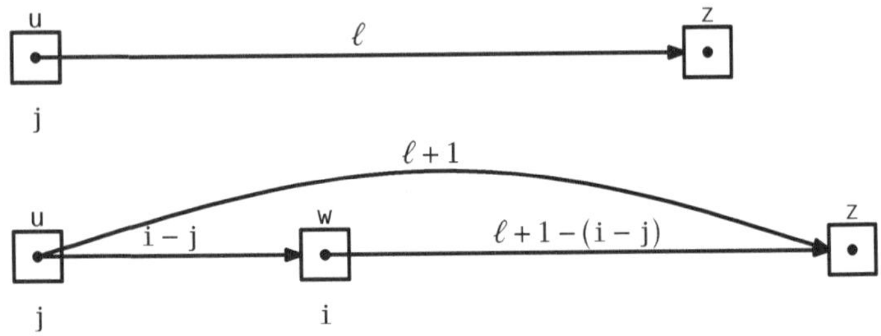

Figure 4.7: Updating the lengths of edges while splicing a node w into a skiplist.

This sounds more complicated than it is, for the code is actually quite simple:

SkiplistList
```
void add(int i, T x) {
  Node w = new Node(x, pickHeight());
  if (w.height() > h)
    h = w.height();
  add(i, w);
}
```

SkiplistList
```
Node add(int i, Node w) {
  Node u = sentinel;
  int k = w.height();
  int r = h;
  int j = -1; // index of u
  while (r >= 0) {
```

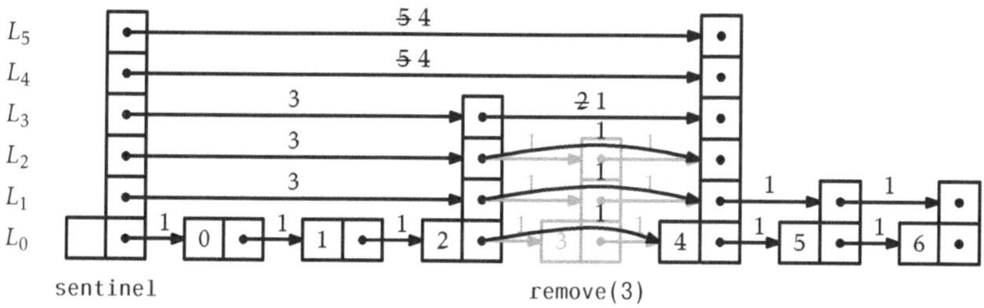

Figure 4.8: Removing an element from a SkiplistList.

```
    while (u.next[r] != null && j+u.length[r] < i) {
      j += u.length[r];
      u = u.next[r];
    }
    u.length[r]++; // accounts for new node in list 0
    if (r <= k) {
      w.next[r] = u.next[r];
      u.next[r] = w;
      w.length[r] = u.length[r] - (i - j);
      u.length[r] = i - j;
    }
    r--;
  }
  n++;
  return u;
}
```

By now, the implementation of the remove(i) operation in a SkiplistList should be obvious. We follow the search path for the node at position i. Each time the search path takes a step down from a node, u, at level r we decrement the length of the edge leaving u at that level. We also check if u.next[r] is the element of rank i and, if so, splice it out of the list at that level. An example is shown in Figure 4.8.

```
                              SkiplistList
T remove(int i) {
  T x = null;
  Node u = sentinel;
  int r = h;
```

```
  int j = -1; // index of node u
  while (r >= 0) {
    while (u.next[r] != null && j+u.length[r] < i) {
      j += u.length[r];
      u = u.next[r];
    }
    u.length[r]--;  // for the node we are removing
    if (j + u.length[r] + 1 == i && u.next[r] != null) {
      x = u.next[r].x;
      u.length[r] += u.next[r].length[r];
      u.next[r] = u.next[r].next[r];
      if (u == sentinel && u.next[r] == null)
        h--;
    }
    r--;
  }
  n--;
  return x;
}
```

4.3.1 Summary

The following theorem summarizes the performance of the SkiplistList data structure:

Theorem 4.2. *A* SkiplistList *implements the* List *interface. A* SkiplistList *supports the operations* get(i), set(i,x), add(i,x), *and* remove(i) *in* $O(\log n)$ *expected time per operation.*

4.4 Analysis of Skiplists

In this section, we analyze the expected height, size, and length of the search path in a skiplist. This section requires a background in basic probability. Several proofs are based on the following basic observation about coin tosses.

Lemma 4.2. *Let* T *be the number of times a fair coin is tossed up to and including the first time the coin comes up heads. Then* $\mathrm{E}[T] = 2$.

Proof. Suppose we stop tossing the coin the first time it comes up heads. Define the indicator variable

$$I_i = \begin{cases} 0 & \text{if the coin is tossed less than } i \text{ times} \\ 1 & \text{if the coin is tossed } i \text{ or more times} \end{cases}$$

Note that $I_i = 1$ if and only if the first $i-1$ coin tosses are tails, so $\mathrm{E}[I_i] = \Pr\{I_i = 1\} = 1/2^{i-1}$. Observe that T, the total number of coin tosses, can be written as $T = \sum_{i=1}^{\infty} I_i$. Therefore,

$$\begin{aligned} \mathrm{E}[T] &= \mathrm{E}\left[\sum_{i=1}^{\infty} I_i\right] \\ &= \sum_{i=1}^{\infty} \mathrm{E}[I_i] \\ &= \sum_{i=1}^{\infty} 1/2^{i-1} \\ &= 1 + 1/2 + 1/4 + 1/8 + \cdots \\ &= 2 \ . \end{aligned}$$

□

The next two lemmata tell us that skiplists have linear size:

Lemma 4.3. *The expected number of nodes in a skiplist containing* $\mathtt{n}$ *elements, not including occurrences of the sentinel, is* $2\mathtt{n}$.

Proof. The probability that any particular element, $\mathtt{x}$, is included in list $L_{\mathtt{r}}$ is $1/2^{\mathtt{r}}$, so the expected number of nodes in $L_{\mathtt{r}}$ is $\mathtt{n}/2^{\mathtt{r}}$.[2] Therefore, the total expected number of nodes in all lists is

$$\sum_{\mathtt{r}=0}^{\infty} \mathtt{n}/2^{\mathtt{r}} = \mathtt{n}(1 + 1/2 + 1/4 + 1/8 + \cdots) = 2\mathtt{n} \ .$$

□

Lemma 4.4. *The expected height of a skiplist containing* $\mathtt{n}$ *elements is at most* $\log \mathtt{n} + 2$.

Proof. For each $\mathtt{r} \in \{1, 2, 3, \ldots, \infty\}$, define the indicator random variable

$$I_{\mathtt{r}} = \begin{cases} 0 & \text{if } L_{\mathtt{r}} \text{ is empty} \\ 1 & \text{if } L_{\mathtt{r}} \text{ is non-empty} \end{cases}$$

[2]See Section 1.3.4 to see how this is derived using indicator variables and linearity of expectation.

The height, h, of the skiplist is then given by

$$\mathsf{h} = \sum_{i=1}^{\infty} I_{\mathsf{r}} \enspace .$$

Note that I_{r} is never more than the length, $|L_{\mathsf{r}}|$, of L_{r}, so

$$\mathrm{E}[I_{\mathsf{r}}] \le \mathrm{E}[|L_{\mathsf{r}}|] = \mathsf{n}/2^{\mathsf{r}} \enspace .$$

Therefore, we have

$$\begin{aligned}
\mathrm{E}[\mathsf{h}] &= \mathrm{E}\left[\sum_{r=1}^{\infty} I_{\mathsf{r}}\right] \\
&= \sum_{\mathsf{r}=1}^{\infty} E[I_{\mathsf{r}}] \\
&= \sum_{\mathsf{r}=1}^{\lfloor \log \mathsf{n} \rfloor} E[I_{\mathsf{r}}] + \sum_{r=\lfloor \log \mathsf{n} \rfloor + 1}^{\infty} E[I_{\mathsf{r}}] \\
&\le \sum_{\mathsf{r}=1}^{\lfloor \log \mathsf{n} \rfloor} 1 + \sum_{r=\lfloor \log \mathsf{n} \rfloor + 1}^{\infty} \mathsf{n}/2^{\mathsf{r}} \\
&\le \log \mathsf{n} + \sum_{\mathsf{r}=0}^{\infty} 1/2^{\mathsf{r}} \\
&= \log \mathsf{n} + 2 \enspace .
\end{aligned}$$

□

Lemma 4.5. *The expected number of nodes in a skiplist containing* n *elements, including all occurrences of the sentinel, is* $2\mathsf{n} + O(\log \mathsf{n})$.

Proof. By Lemma 4.3, the expected number of nodes, not including the sentinel, is $2\mathsf{n}$. The number of occurrences of the sentinel is equal to the height, h, of the skiplist so, by Lemma 4.4 the expected number of occurrences of the sentinel is at most $\log \mathsf{n} + 2 = O(\log \mathsf{n})$. □

Lemma 4.6. *The expected length of a search path in a skiplist is at most* $2\log \mathsf{n} + O(1)$.

Proof. The easiest way to see this is to consider the *reverse search path* for a node, x. This path starts at the predecessor of x in L_0. At any point in time, if the path can go up a level, then it does. If it cannot go up a level then it goes left. Thinking about this for a few moments will convince us that the reverse search path for x is identical to the search path for x, except that it is reversed.

The number of nodes that the reverse search path visits at a particular level, r, is related to the following experiment: Toss a coin. If the coin comes up as heads, then move up and stop. Otherwise, move left and repeat the experiment. The number of coin tosses before the heads represents the number of steps to the left that a reverse search path takes at a particular level.[3] Lemma 4.2 tells us that the expected number of coin tosses before the first heads is 1.

Let S_r denote the number of steps the forward search path takes at level r that go to the right. We have just argued that $E[S_r] \le 1$. Furthermore, $S_r \le |L_r|$, since we can't take more steps in L_r than the length of L_r, so

$$E[S_r] \le E[|L_r|] = n/2^r \ .$$

We can now finish as in the proof of Lemma 4.4. Let S be the length of the search path for some node, u, in a skiplist, and let h be the height of the skiplist. Then

$$\begin{aligned}
E[S] &= E\left[h + \sum_{r=0}^{\infty} S_r\right] \\
&= E[h] + \sum_{r=0}^{\infty} E[S_r] \\
&= E[h] + \sum_{r=0}^{\lfloor \log n \rfloor} E[S_r] + \sum_{r=\lfloor \log n \rfloor+1}^{\infty} E[S_r] \\
&\le E[h] + \sum_{r=0}^{\lfloor \log n \rfloor} 1 + \sum_{r=\lfloor \log n \rfloor+1}^{\infty} n/2^r \\
&\le E[h] + \sum_{r=0}^{\lfloor \log n \rfloor} 1 + \sum_{r=0}^{\infty} 1/2^r
\end{aligned}$$

[3]Note that this might overcount the number of steps to the left, since the experiment should end either at the first heads or when the search path reaches the sentinel, whichever comes first. This is not a problem since the lemma is only stating an upper bound.

$$\leq \mathrm{E}[\mathrm{h}] + \sum_{r=0}^{\lfloor \log n \rfloor} 1 + \sum_{r=0}^{\infty} 1/2^r$$
$$\leq \mathrm{E}[\mathrm{h}] + \log n + 3$$
$$\leq 2\log n + 5 \ .$$ □

The following theorem summarizes the results in this section:

Theorem 4.3. *A skiplist containing* n *elements has expected size* O(n) *and the expected length of the search path for any particular element is at most* $2\log n + O(1)$.

4.5 Discussion and Exercises

Skiplists were introduced by Pugh [62] who also presented a number of applications and extensions of skiplists [61]. Since then they have been studied extensively. Several researchers have done very precise analyses of the expected length and variance of the length of the search path for the ith element in a skiplist [45, 44, 58]. Deterministic versions [53], biased versions [8, 26], and self-adjusting versions [12] of skiplists have all been developed. Skiplist implementations have been written for various languages and frameworks and have been used in open-source database systems [71, 63]. A variant of skiplists is used in the HP-UX operating system kernel's process management structures [42]. Skiplists are even part of the Java 1.6 API [55].

Exercise 4.1. Illustrate the search paths for 2.5 and 5.5 on the skiplist in Figure 4.1.

Exercise 4.2. Illustrate the addition of the values 0.5 (with a height of 1) and then 3.5 (with a height of 2) to the skiplist in Figure 4.1.

Exercise 4.3. Illustrate the removal of the values 1 and then 3 from the skiplist in Figure 4.1.

Exercise 4.4. Illustrate the execution of remove(2) on the SkiplistList in Figure 4.5.

Exercise 4.5. Illustrate the execution of add(3, x) on the SkiplistList in Figure 4.5. Assume that pickHeight() selects a height of 4 for the newly created node.

Exercise 4.6. Show that, during an add(x) or a remove(x) operation, the expected number of pointers in a SkiplistSet that get changed is constant.

Exercise 4.7. Suppose that, instead of promoting an element from L_{i-1} into L_i based on a coin toss, we promote it with some probability p, $0 < p < 1$.

1. Show that, with this modification, the expected length of a search path is at most $(1/p)\log_{1/p} \mathtt{n} + O(1)$.
2. What is the value of p that minimizes the preceding expression?
3. What is the expected height of the skiplist?
4. What is the expected number of nodes in the skiplist?

Exercise 4.8. The find(x) method in a SkiplistSet sometimes performs *redundant comparisons*; these occur when x is compared to the same value more than once. They can occur when, for some node, u, u.next[r] = u.next[r − 1]. Show how these redundant comparisons happen and modify find(x) so that they are avoided. Analyze the expected number of comparisons done by your modified find(x) method.

Exercise 4.9. Design and implement a version of a skiplist that implements the SSet interface, but also allows fast access to elements by rank. That is, it also supports the function get(i), which returns the element whose rank is i in $O(\log \mathtt{n})$ expected time. (The rank of an element x in an SSet is the number of elements in the SSet that are less than x.)

Exercise 4.10. A *finger* in a skiplist is an array that stores the sequence of nodes on a search path at which the search path goes down. (The variable stack in the add(x) code on page 91 is a finger; the shaded nodes in Figure 4.3 show the contents of the finger.) One can think of a finger as pointing out the path to a node in the lowest list, L_0.

A *finger search* implements the find(x) operation using a finger, by walking up the list using the finger until reaching a node u such that u.x < x and u.next = null or u.next.x > x and then performing a normal search for x starting from u. It is possible to prove that the expected number of steps required for a finger search is $O(1 + \log r)$, where r is the number values in L_0 between x and the value pointed to by the finger.

Implement a subclass of Skiplist called SkiplistWithFinger that implements find(x) operations using an internal finger. This subclass stores a finger, which is then used so that every find(x) operation is implemented as a finger search. During each find(x) operation the finger is updated so that each find(x) operation uses, as a starting point, a finger that points to the result of the previous find(x) operation.

Exercise 4.11. Write a method, truncate(i), that truncates a SkiplistList at position i. After the execution of this method, the size of the list is i and it contains only the elements at indices 0,...,i − 1. The return value is another SkiplistList that contains the elements at indices i,...,n − 1. This method should run in O(log n) time.

Exercise 4.12. Write a SkiplistList method, absorb(l2), that takes as an argument a SkiplistList, l2, empties it and appends its contents, in order, to the receiver. For example, if l1 contains a, b, c and l2 contains d, e, f, then after calling l1.absorb(l2), l1 will contain a, b, c, d, e, f and l2 will be empty. This method should run in O(log n) time.

Exercise 4.13. Using the ideas from the space-efficient list, SEList, design and implement a space-efficient SSet, SESSet. To do this, store the data, in order, in an SEList, and store the blocks of this SEList in an SSet. If the original SSet implementation uses O(n) space to store n elements, then the SESSet will use enough space for n elements plus O(n/b + b) wasted space.

Exercise 4.14. Using an SSet as your underlying structure, design and implement an application that reads a (large) text file and allows you to search, interactively, for any substring contained in the text. As the user types their query, a matching part of the text (if any) should appear as a result.

Hint 1: Every substring is a prefix of some suffix, so it suffices to store all suffixes of the text file.
Hint 2: Any suffix can be represented compactly as a single integer indicating where the suffix begins in the text.
Test your application on some large texts, such as some of the books available at Project Gutenberg [1]. If done correctly, your applications will be very responsive; there should be no noticeable lag between typing keystrokes and seeing the results.

Exercise 4.15. (This excercise should be done after reading about binary search trees, in Section 6.2.) Compare skiplists with binary search trees in the following ways:

1. Explain how removing some edges of a skiplist leads to a structure that looks like a binary tree and is similar to a binary search tree.

2. Skiplists and binary search trees each use about the same number of pointers (2 per node). Skiplists make better use of those pointers, though. Explain why.

Chapter 5

Hash Tables

Hash tables are an efficient method of storing a small number, n, of integers from a large range $U = \{0, \ldots, 2^w - 1\}$. The term *hash table* includes a broad range of data structures. This chapter focuses on one of the most common implementations of hash tables, namely hashing with chaining.

Very often hash tables store types of data that are not integers. In this case, an integer *hash code* is associated with each data item and is used in the hash table. The second part of this chapter discusses how such hash codes are generated.

Some of the methods used in this chapter require random choices of integers in some specific range. In the code samples, some of these "random" integers are hard-coded constants. These constants were obtained using random bits generated from atmospheric noise.

5.1 ChainedHashTable: Hashing with Chaining

A ChainedHashTable data structure uses *hashing with chaining* to store data as an array, t, of lists. An integer, n, keeps track of the total number of items in all lists (see Figure 5.1):

ChainedHashTable

```
List<T>[] t;
int n;
```

The *hash value* of a data item x, denoted hash(x) is a value in the range

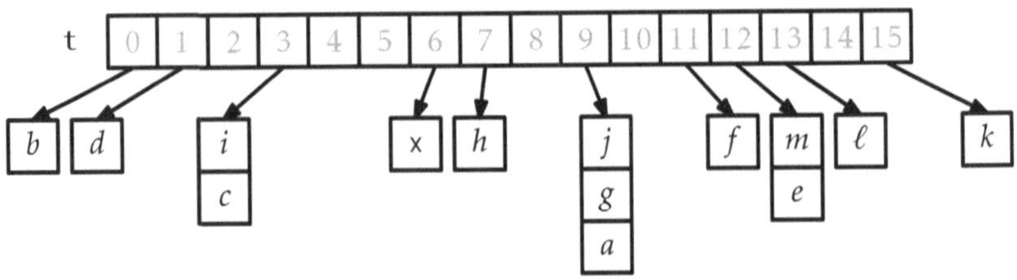

Figure 5.1: An example of a ChainedHashTable with n = 14 and t.length = 16. In this example hash(x) = 6

{0,...,t.length − 1}. All items with hash value i are stored in the list at t[i]. To ensure that lists don't get too long, we maintain the invariant

$$\mathtt{n} \leq \mathtt{t.length}$$

so that the average number of elements stored in one of these lists is n/t.length ≤ 1.

To add an element, x, to the hash table, we first check if the length of t needs to be increased and, if so, we grow t. With this out of the way we hash x to get an integer, i, in the range {0,...,t.length − 1}, and we append x to the list t[i]:

```
ChainedHashTable
boolean add(T x) {
  if (find(x) != null) return false;
  if (n+1 > t.length) resize();
  t[hash(x)].add(x);
  n++;
  return true;
}
```

Growing the table, if necessary, involves doubling the length of t and reinserting all elements into the new table. This strategy is exactly the same as the one used in the implementation of ArrayStack and the same result applies: The cost of growing is only constant when amortized over a sequence of insertions (see Lemma 2.1 on page 33).

Besides growing, the only other work done when adding a new value x to a ChainedHashTable involves appending x to the list t[hash(x)]. For any of the list implementations described in Chapters 2 or 3, this takes only constant time.

To remove an element, x, from the hash table, we iterate over the list t[hash(x)] until we find x so that we can remove it:

```
ChainedHashTable
T remove(T x) {
  Iterator<T> it = t[hash(x)].iterator();
  while (it.hasNext()) {
    T y = it.next();
    if (y.equals(x)) {
      it.remove();
      n--;
      return y;
    }
  }
  return null;
}
```

This takes $O(n_{hash(x)})$ time, where n_i denotes the length of the list stored at t[i].

Searching for the element x in a hash table is similar. We perform a linear search on the list t[hash(x)]:

```
ChainedHashTable
T find(Object x) {
  for (T y : t[hash(x)])
    if (y.equals(x))
      return y;
  return null;
}
```

Again, this takes time proportional to the length of the list t[hash(x)].

The performance of a hash table depends critically on the choice of the hash function. A good hash function will spread the elements evenly among the t.length lists, so that the expected size of the list t[hash(x)] is $O(n/t.length) = O(1)$. On the other hand, a bad hash function will hash all values (including x) to the same table location, in which case the size of the list t[hash(x)] will be n. In the next section we describe a good hash function.

5.1.1 Multiplicative Hashing

Multiplicative hashing is an efficient method of generating hash values based on modular arithmetic (discussed in Section 2.3) and integer division. It uses the div operator, which calculates the integral part of a quotient, while discarding the remainder. Formally, for any integers $a \geq 0$ and $b \geq 1$, $a \operatorname{div} b = \lfloor a/b \rfloor$.

In multiplicative hashing, we use a hash table of size 2^{d} for some integer d (called the *dimension*). The formula for hashing an integer $\mathsf{x} \in \{0,\ldots,2^{\mathsf{w}}-1\}$ is

$$\mathsf{hash}(\mathsf{x}) = ((\mathsf{z} \cdot \mathsf{x}) \bmod 2^{\mathsf{w}}) \operatorname{div} 2^{\mathsf{w}-\mathsf{d}} \enspace .$$

Here, z is a randomly chosen *odd* integer in $\{1,\ldots,2^{\mathsf{w}}-1\}$. This hash function can be realized very efficiently by observing that, by default, operations on integers are already done modulo 2^{w} where w is the number of bits in an integer. (See Figure 5.2.) Furthermore, integer division by $2^{\mathsf{w}-\mathsf{d}}$ is equivalent to dropping the rightmost $\mathsf{w}-\mathsf{d}$ bits in a binary representation (which is implemented by shifting the bits right by $\mathsf{w}-\mathsf{d}$). In this way, the code that implements the above formula is simpler than the formula itself:

ChainedHashTable
```
int hash(Object x) {
  return (z * x.hashCode()) >>> (w-d);
}
```

The following lemma, whose proof is deferred until later in this section, shows that multiplicative hashing does a good job of avoiding collisions:

Lemma 5.1. *Let* x *and* y *be any two values in* $\{0,\ldots,2^{\mathsf{w}}-1\}$ *with* $\mathsf{x} \neq \mathsf{y}$. *Then* $\Pr\{\mathsf{hash}(\mathsf{x}) = \mathsf{hash}(\mathsf{y})\} \leq 2/2^{\mathsf{d}}$.

With Lemma 5.1, the performance of remove(x), and find(x) are easy to analyze:

2^w (4294967296)	100000000000000000000000000000000
z (4102541685)	111101001000011111101000101110101
x (42)	00000000000000000000000000101010
z · x	1010000000111100100100001011101001100 10
(z · x) mod 2^w	00011110010010000101110100110010
((z · x) mod 2^w) div 2^{w-d}	00011110

Figure 5.2: The operation of the multiplicative hash function with $w = 32$ and $d = 8$.

Lemma 5.2. *For any data value* x*, the expected length of the list* t[hash(x)] *is at most* $n_x + 2$*, where* n_x *is the number of occurrences of* x *in the hash table.*

Proof. Let S be the (multi-)set of elements stored in the hash table that are not equal to x. For an element $y \in S$, define the indicator variable

$$I_y = \begin{cases} 1 & \text{if } \mathrm{hash}(x) = \mathrm{hash}(y) \\ 0 & \text{otherwise} \end{cases}$$

and notice that, by Lemma 5.1, $E[I_y] \leq 2/2^d = 2/\mathtt{t.length}$. The expected length of the list t[hash(x)] is given by

$$\begin{aligned} E[\mathtt{t[hash(x)].size()}] &= E\left[n_x + \sum_{y \in S} I_y\right] \\ &= n_x + \sum_{y \in S} E[I_y] \\ &\leq n_x + \sum_{y \in S} 2/\mathtt{t.length} \\ &\leq n_x + \sum_{y \in S} 2/n \\ &\leq n_x + (n - n_x)2/n \\ &\leq n_x + 2 \ , \end{aligned}$$

as required. □

Now, we want to prove Lemma 5.1, but first we need a result from number theory. In the following proof, we use the notation $(b_r, \ldots, b_0)_2$ to denote $\sum_{i=0}^{r} b_i 2^i$, where each b_i is a bit, either 0 or 1. In other words,

$(b_r, \ldots, b_0)_2$ is the integer whose binary representation is given by $b_r, \ldots, b_0$. We use $\star$ to denote a bit of unknown value.

Lemma 5.3. *Let S be the set of odd integers in $\{1, \ldots, 2^{\mathtt{w}} - 1\}$; let q and i be any two elements in S. Then there is exactly one value $\mathtt{z} \in S$ such that $\mathtt{z}q \bmod 2^{\mathtt{w}} = i$.*

Proof. Since the number of choices for $\mathtt{z}$ and i is the same, it is sufficient to prove that there is *at most* one value $\mathtt{z} \in S$ that satisfies $\mathtt{z}q \bmod 2^{\mathtt{w}} = i$.

Suppose, for the sake of contradiction, that there are two such values $\mathtt{z}$ and $\mathtt{z}'$, with $\mathtt{z} > \mathtt{z}'$. Then

$$\mathtt{z}q \bmod 2^{\mathtt{w}} = \mathtt{z}'q \bmod 2^{\mathtt{w}} = i$$

So

$$(\mathtt{z} - \mathtt{z}')q \bmod 2^{\mathtt{w}} = 0$$

But this means that

$$(\mathtt{z} - \mathtt{z}')q = k2^{\mathtt{w}} \tag{5.1}$$

for some integer k. Thinking in terms of binary numbers, we have

$$(\mathtt{z} - \mathtt{z}')q = k \cdot (1, \underbrace{0, \ldots, 0}_{\mathtt{w}})_2 \ ,$$

so that the $\mathtt{w}$ trailing bits in the binary representation of $(\mathtt{z} - \mathtt{z}')q$ are all 0's.

Furthermore $k \neq 0$, since $q \neq 0$ and $\mathtt{z} - \mathtt{z}' \neq 0$. Since q is odd, it has no trailing 0's in its binary representation:

$$q = (\star, \ldots, \star, 1)_2 \ .$$

Since $|\mathtt{z} - \mathtt{z}'| < 2^{\mathtt{w}}$, $\mathtt{z} - \mathtt{z}'$ has fewer than $\mathtt{w}$ trailing 0's in its binary representation:

$$\mathtt{z} - \mathtt{z}' = (\star, \ldots, \star, 1, \underbrace{0, \ldots, 0}_{<\mathtt{w}})_2 \ .$$

Therefore, the product $(\mathtt{z} - \mathtt{z}')q$ has fewer than $\mathtt{w}$ trailing 0's in its binary representation:

$$(\mathtt{z} - \mathtt{z}')q = (\star, \cdots, \star, 1, \underbrace{0, \ldots, 0}_{<\mathtt{w}})_2 \ .$$

Therefore $(z - z')q$ cannot satisfy (5.1), yielding a contradiction and completing the proof. □

The utility of Lemma 5.3 comes from the following observation: If z is chosen uniformly at random from S, then zt is uniformly distributed over S. In the following proof, it helps to think of the binary representation of z, which consists of $w - 1$ random bits followed by a 1.

Proof of Lemma 5.1. First we note that the condition $\mathrm{hash}(x) = \mathrm{hash}(y)$ is equivalent to the statement "the highest-order d bits of $zx \bmod 2^w$ and the highest-order d bits of $zy \bmod 2^w$ are the same." A necessary condition of that statement is that the highest-order d bits in the binary representation of $z(x - y) \bmod 2^w$ are either all 0's or all 1's. That is,

$$z(x-y) \bmod 2^w = (\underbrace{0,\ldots,0}_{d},\underbrace{\star,\ldots,\star}_{w-d})_2 \tag{5.2}$$

when $zx \bmod 2^w > zy \bmod 2^w$ or

$$z(x-y) \bmod 2^w = (\underbrace{1,\ldots,1}_{d},\underbrace{\star,\ldots,\star}_{w-d})_2 \ . \tag{5.3}$$

when $zx \bmod 2^w < zy \bmod 2^w$. Therefore, we only have to bound the probability that $z(x - y) \bmod 2^w$ looks like (5.2) or (5.3).

Let q be the unique odd integer such that $(x-y) \bmod 2^w = q2^r$ for some integer $r \geq 0$. By Lemma 5.3, the binary representation of $zq \bmod 2^w$ has $w - 1$ random bits, followed by a 1:

$$zq \bmod 2^w = (\underbrace{b_{w-1},\ldots,b_1}_{w-1},1)_2$$

Therefore, the binary representation of $z(x-y) \bmod 2^w = zq2^r \bmod 2^w$ has $w - r - 1$ random bits, followed by a 1, followed by r 0's:

$$z(x-y) \bmod 2^w = zq2^r \bmod 2^w = (\underbrace{b_{w-r-1},\ldots,b_1}_{w-r-1},1,\underbrace{0,0,\ldots,0}_{r})_2$$

We can now finish the proof: If $r > w - d$, then the d higher order bits of $z(x - y) \bmod 2^w$ contain both 0's and 1's, so the probability that $z(x -$

y) mod 2^w looks like (5.2) or (5.3) is 0. If $r = w - d$, then the probability of looking like (5.2) is 0, but the probability of looking like (5.3) is $1/2^{d-1} = 2/2^d$ (since we must have $b_1,\ldots,b_{d-1} = 1,\ldots,1$). If $r < w - d$, then we must have $b_{w-r-1},\ldots,b_{w-r-d} = 0,\ldots,0$ or $b_{w-r-1},\ldots,b_{w-r-d} = 1,\ldots,1$. The probability of each of these cases is $1/2^d$ and they are mutually exclusive, so the probability of either of these cases is $2/2^d$. This completes the proof. □

5.1.2 Summary

The following theorem summarizes the performance of a ChainedHashTable data structure:

Theorem 5.1. *A ChainedHashTable implements the USet interface. Ignoring the cost of calls to* grow(), *a ChainedHashTable supports the operations* add(x), remove(x), *and* find(x) *in $O(1)$ expected time per operation.*

Furthermore, beginning with an empty ChainedHashTable, any sequence of m add(x) *and* remove(x) *operations results in a total of $O(m)$ time spent during all calls to* grow().

5.2 LinearHashTable: Linear Probing

The ChainedHashTable data structure uses an array of lists, where the ith list stores all elements x such that hash(x) = i. An alternative, called *open addressing* is to store the elements directly in an array, t, with each array location in t storing at most one value. This approach is taken by the LinearHashTable described in this section. In some places, this data structure is described as *open addressing with linear probing.*

The main idea behind a LinearHashTable is that we would, ideally, like to store the element x with hash value i = hash(x) in the table location t[i]. If we cannot do this (because some element is already stored there) then we try to store it at location t[(i + 1) mod t.length]; if that's not possible, then we try t[(i+2) mod t.length], and so on, until we find a place for x.

There are three types of entries stored in t:

1. data values: actual values in the USet that we are representing;
2. null values: at array locations where no data has ever been stored; and
3. del values: at array locations where data was once stored but that has since been deleted.

In addition to the counter, n, that keeps track of the number of elements in the LinearHashTable, a counter, q, keeps track of the number of elements of Types 1 and 3. That is, q is equal to n plus the number of del values in t. To make this work efficiently, we need t to be considerably larger than q, so that there are lots of null values in t. The operations on a LinearHashTable therefore maintain the invariant that t.length ≥ 2q.

To summarize, a LinearHashTable contains an array, t, that stores data elements, and integers n and q that keep track of the number of data elements and non-null values of t, respectively. Because many hash functions only work for table sizes that are a power of 2, we also keep an integer d and maintain the invariant that t.length $= 2^{d}$.

```
LinearHashTable
T[] t;    // the table
int n;    // the size
int d;    // t.length = 2^d
int q;    // number of non-null entries in t
```

The find(x) operation in a LinearHashTable is simple. We start at array entry t[i] where i = hash(x) and search entries t[i], t[(i + 1) mod t.length], t[(i + 2) mod t.length], and so on, until we find an index i′ such that, either, t[i′] = x, or t[i′] = null. In the former case we return t[i′]. In the latter case, we conclude that x is not contained in the hash table and return null.

```
LinearHashTable
T find(T x) {
  int i = hash(x);
  while (t[i] != null) {
    if (t[i] != del && x.equals(t[i])) return t[i];
    i = (i == t.length-1) ? 0 : i + 1; // increment i
```

```
  }
  return null;
}
```

The add(x) operation is also fairly easy to implement. After checking that x is not already stored in the table (using find(x)), we search t[i], t[(i+1) mod t.length], t[(i+2) mod t.length], and so on, until we find a null or del and store x at that location, increment n, and q, if appropriate.

```
LinearHashTable
boolean add(T x) {
  if (find(x) != null) return false;
  if (2*(q+1) > t.length) resize(); // max 50% occupancy
  int i = hash(x);
  while (t[i] != null && t[i] != del)
    i = (i == t.length-1) ? 0 : i + 1; // increment i
  if (t[i] == null) q++;
  n++;
  t[i] = x;
  return true;
}
```

By now, the implementation of the remove(x) operation should be obvious. We search t[i], t[(i + 1) mod t.length], t[(i + 2) mod t.length], and so on until we find an index i′ such that t[i′] = x or t[i′] = null. In the former case, we set t[i′] = del and return true. In the latter case we conclude that x was not stored in the table (and therefore cannot be deleted) and return false.

```
LinearHashTable
T remove(T x) {
  int i = hash(x);
  while (t[i] != null) {
    T y = t[i];
    if (y != del && x.equals(y)) {
      t[i] = del;
      n--;
      if (8*n < t.length) resize(); // min 12.5% occupancy
      return y;
```

```
    }
    i = (i == t.length-1) ? 0 : i + 1;   // increment i
  }
  return null;
}
```

The correctness of the find(x), add(x), and remove(x) methods is easy to verify, though it relies on the use of del values. Notice that none of these operations ever sets a non-null entry to null. Therefore, when we reach an index i′ such that t[i′] = null, this is a proof that the element, x, that we are searching for is not stored in the table; t[i′] has always been null, so there is no reason that a previous add(x) operation would have proceeded beyond index i′.

The resize() method is called by add(x) when the number of non-null entries exceeds t.length/2 or by remove(x) when the number of data entries is less than t.length/8. The resize() method works like the resize() methods in other array-based data structures. We find the smallest non-negative integer d such that $2^d \geq 3n$. We reallocate the array t so that it has size 2^d, and then we insert all the elements in the old version of t into the newly-resized copy of t. While doing this, we reset q equal to n since the newly-allocated t contains no del values.

```
LinearHashTable
void resize() {
  d = 1;
  while ((1<<d) < 3*n) d++;
  T[] told = t;
  t = newArray(1<<d);
  q = n;
  // insert everything from told
  for (int k = 0; k < told.length; k++) {
    if (told[k] != null && told[k] != del) {
      int i = hash(told[k]);
      while (t[i] != null)
        i = (i == t.length-1) ? 0 : i + 1;
      t[i] = told[k];
    }
  }
```

```
}
```

5.2.1 Analysis of Linear Probing

Notice that each operation, add(x), remove(x), or find(x), finishes as soon as (or before) it discovers the first null entry in t. The intuition behind the analysis of linear probing is that, since at least half the elements in t are equal to null, an operation should not take long to complete because it will very quickly come across a null entry. We shouldn't rely too heavily on this intuition, though, because it would lead us to (the incorrect) conclusion that the expected number of locations in t examined by an operation is at most 2.

For the rest of this section, we will assume that all hash values are independently and uniformly distributed in $\{0,\dots,\mathtt{t.length}-1\}$. This is not a realistic assumption, but it will make it possible for us to analyze linear probing. Later in this section we will describe a method, called tabulation hashing, that produces a hash function that is "good enough" for linear probing. We will also assume that all indices into the positions of t are taken modulo t.length, so that t[i] is really a shorthand for t[i mod t.length].

We say that a *run of length k that starts at* i occurs when all the table entries $\mathtt{t}[\mathtt{i}], \mathtt{t}[\mathtt{i}+1],\dots,\mathtt{t}[\mathtt{i}+k-1]$ are non-null and $\mathtt{t}[\mathtt{i}-1]=\mathtt{t}[\mathtt{i}+k]=\mathtt{null}$. The number of non-null elements of t is exactly q and the add(x) method ensures that, at all times, $\mathtt{q}\le\mathtt{t.length}/2$. There are q elements $\mathtt{x}_1,\dots,\mathtt{x}_\mathtt{q}$ that have been inserted into t since the last rebuild() operation. By our assumption, each of these has a hash value, $\mathtt{hash}(\mathtt{x}_j)$, that is uniform and independent of the rest. With this setup, we can prove the main lemma required to analyze linear probing.

Lemma 5.4. *Fix a value* $\mathtt{i}\in\{0,\dots,\mathtt{t.length}-1\}$. *Then the probability that a run of length k starts at* i *is* $O(c^k)$ *for some constant* $0<c<1$.

Proof. If a run of length k starts at i, then there are exactly k elements $\mathtt{x}_j$ such that $\mathtt{hash}(\mathtt{x}_j)\in\{\mathtt{i},\dots,\mathtt{i}+k-1\}$. The probability that this occurs is exactly

$$p_k=\binom{\mathtt{q}}{k}\left(\frac{k}{\mathtt{t.length}}\right)^k\left(\frac{\mathtt{t.length}-k}{\mathtt{t.length}}\right)^{\mathtt{q}-k} ,$$

since, for each choice of k elements, these k elements must hash to one of the k locations and the remaining $\mathtt{q}-k$ elements must hash to the other $\mathtt{t.length}-k$ table locations.[1]

In the following derivation we will cheat a little and replace $r!$ with $(r/e)^r$. Stirling's Approximation (Section 1.3.2) shows that this is only a factor of $O(\sqrt{r})$ from the truth. This is just done to make the derivation simpler; Exercise 5.4 asks the reader to redo the calculation more rigorously using Stirling's Approximation in its entirety.

The value of p_k is maximized when t.length is minimum, and the data structure maintains the invariant that $\mathtt{t.length} \geq 2\mathtt{q}$, so

$$\begin{aligned}
p_k &\le \binom{\mathtt{q}}{k}\left(\frac{k}{2\mathtt{q}}\right)^k\left(\frac{2\mathtt{q}-k}{2\mathtt{q}}\right)^{\mathtt{q}-k} \\
&= \left(\frac{\mathtt{q}!}{(\mathtt{q}-k)!k!}\right)\left(\frac{k}{2\mathtt{q}}\right)^k\left(\frac{2\mathtt{q}-k}{2\mathtt{q}}\right)^{\mathtt{q}-k} \\
&\approx \left(\frac{\mathtt{q}^{\mathtt{q}}}{(\mathtt{q}-k)^{\mathtt{q}-k}k^k}\right)\left(\frac{k}{2\mathtt{q}}\right)^k\left(\frac{2\mathtt{q}-k}{2\mathtt{q}}\right)^{\mathtt{q}-k} && \text{[Stirling's approximation]} \\
&= \left(\frac{\mathtt{q}^k\mathtt{q}^{\mathtt{q}-k}}{(\mathtt{q}-k)^{\mathtt{q}-k}k^k}\right)\left(\frac{k}{2\mathtt{q}}\right)^k\left(\frac{2\mathtt{q}-k}{2\mathtt{q}}\right)^{\mathtt{q}-k} \\
&= \left(\frac{\mathtt{q}k}{2\mathtt{q}k}\right)^k\left(\frac{\mathtt{q}(2\mathtt{q}-k)}{2\mathtt{q}(\mathtt{q}-k)}\right)^{\mathtt{q}-k} \\
&= \left(\frac{1}{2}\right)^k\left(\frac{(2\mathtt{q}-k)}{2(\mathtt{q}-k)}\right)^{\mathtt{q}-k} \\
&= \left(\frac{1}{2}\right)^k\left(1+\frac{k}{2(\mathtt{q}-k)}\right)^{\mathtt{q}-k} \\
&\le \left(\frac{\sqrt{e}}{2}\right)^k .
\end{aligned}$$

(In the last step, we use the inequality $(1+1/x)^x \le e$, which holds for all $x>0$.) Since $\sqrt{e}/2 < 0.824360636 < 1$, this completes the proof. □

Using Lemma 5.4 to prove upper-bounds on the expected running time of find(x), add(x), and remove(x) is now fairly straightforward. Consider the simplest case, where we execute find(x) for some value x that

[1]Note that p_k is greater than the probability that a run of length k starts at i, since the definition of p_k does not include the requirement $\mathtt{t}[\mathtt{i}-1]=\mathtt{t}[\mathtt{i}+k]=\mathtt{null}$.

has never been stored in the `LinearHashTable`. In this case, $\mathtt{i} = \mathtt{hash(x)}$ is a random value in $\{0,\ldots,\mathtt{t.length}-1\}$ independent of the contents of `t`. If `i` is part of a run of length k, then the time it takes to execute the `find(x)` operation is at most $O(1+k)$. Thus, the expected running time can be upper-bounded by

$$O\left(1+\left(\frac{1}{\mathtt{t.length}}\right)\sum_{i=1}^{\mathtt{t.length}}\sum_{k=0}^{\infty}k\Pr\{\mathtt{i}\text{ is part of a run of length }k\}\right) .$$

Note that each run of length k contributes to the inner sum k times for a total contribution of k^2, so the above sum can be rewritten as

$$\begin{aligned}
&O\left(1+\left(\frac{1}{\mathtt{t.length}}\right)\sum_{i=1}^{\mathtt{t.length}}\sum_{k=0}^{\infty}k^2\Pr\{\mathtt{i}\text{ starts a run of length }k\}\right)\\
&\le O\left(1+\left(\frac{1}{\mathtt{t.length}}\right)\sum_{i=1}^{\mathtt{t.length}}\sum_{k=0}^{\infty}k^2 p_k\right)\\
&= O\left(1+\sum_{k=0}^{\infty}k^2 p_k\right)\\
&= O\left(1+\sum_{k=0}^{\infty}k^2\cdot O(c^k)\right)\\
&= O(1) .
\end{aligned}$$

The last step in this derivation comes from the fact that $\sum_{k=0}^{\infty}k^2\cdot O(c^k)$ is an exponentially decreasing series.[2] Therefore, we conclude that the expected running time of the `find(x)` operation for a value `x` that is not contained in a `LinearHashTable` is $O(1)$.

If we ignore the cost of the `resize()` operation, then the above analysis gives us all we need to analyze the cost of operations on a `LinearHashTable`.

First of all, the analysis of `find(x)` given above applies to the `add(x)` operation when `x` is not contained in the table. To analyze the `find(x)` operation when `x` is contained in the table, we need only note that this

[2] In the terminology of many calculus texts, this sum passes the ratio test: There exists a positive integer k_0 such that, for all $k\ge k_0$, $\frac{(k+1)^2c^{k+1}}{k^2c^k}<1$.

is the same as the cost of the add(x) operation that previously added x to the table. Finally, the cost of a remove(x) operation is the same as the cost of a find(x) operation.

In summary, if we ignore the cost of calls to resize(), all operations on a LinearHashTable run in $O(1)$ expected time. Accounting for the cost of resize can be done using the same type of amortized analysis performed for the ArrayStack data structure in Section 2.1.

5.2.2 Summary

The following theorem summarizes the performance of the LinearHashTable data structure:

Theorem 5.2. *A LinearHashTable implements the USet interface. Ignoring the cost of calls to* resize()*, a LinearHashTable supports the operations* add(x)*,* remove(x)*, and* find(x) *in $O(1)$ expected time per operation.*

Furthermore, beginning with an empty LinearHashTable, any sequence of m add(x) *and* remove(x) *operations results in a total of $O(m)$ time spent during all calls to* resize()*.*

5.2.3 Tabulation Hashing

While analyzing the LinearHashTable structure, we made a very strong assumption: That for any set of elements, $\{x_1,\ldots,x_n\}$, the hash values $\mathrm{hash}(x_1),\ldots,\mathrm{hash}(x_n)$ are independently and uniformly distributed over the set $\{0,\ldots,\mathrm{t.length}-1\}$. One way to achieve this is to store a giant array, tab, of length 2^w, where each entry is a random w-bit integer, independent of all the other entries. In this way, we could implement hash(x) by extracting a d-bit integer from tab[x.hashCode()]:

```
LinearHashTable
int idealHash(T x) {
  return tab[x.hashCode() >>> w-d];
}
```

Unfortunately, storing an array of size 2^w is prohibitive in terms of memory usage. The approach used by *tabulation hashing* is to, instead, treat w-bit integers as being comprised of w/r integers, each having only r bits. In this way, tabulation hashing only needs w/r arrays each of length 2^r. All the entries in these arrays are independent w-bit integers. To obtain the value of hash(x) we split x.hashCode() up into w/r r-bit integers and use these as indices into these arrays. We then combine all these values with the bitwise exclusive-or operator to obtain hash(x). The following code shows how this works when w = 32 and r = 4:

LinearHashTable

```
int hash(T x) {
  int h = x.hashCode();
  return (tab[0][h&0xff]
           ^ tab[1][(h>>>8)&0xff]
           ^ tab[2][(h>>>16)&0xff]
           ^ tab[3][(h>>>24)&0xff])
          >>> (w-d);
}
```

In this case, tab is a two-dimensional array with four columns and $2^{32/4} = 256$ rows.

One can easily verify that, for any x, hash(x) is uniformly distributed over $\{0,\ldots,2^d - 1\}$. With a little work, one can even verify that any pair of values have independent hash values. This implies tabulation hashing could be used in place of multiplicative hashing for the ChainedHashTable implementation.

However, it is not true that any set of n distinct values gives a set of n independent hash values. Nevertheless, when tabulation hashing is used, the bound of Theorem 5.2 still holds. References for this are provided at the end of this chapter.

5.3 Hash Codes

The hash tables discussed in the previous section are used to associate data with integer keys consisting of w bits. In many cases, we have keys that are not integers. They may be strings, objects, arrays, or other compound structures. To use hash tables for these types of data, we must map these data types to w-bit hash codes. Hash code mappings should have the following properties:

1. If x and y are equal, then x.hashCode() and y.hashCode() are equal.
2. If x and y are not equal, then the probability that x.hashCode() = y.hashCode() should be small (close to $1/2^{w}$).

The first property ensures that if we store x in a hash table and later look up a value y equal to x, then we will find x—as we should. The second property minimizes the loss from converting our objects to integers. It ensures that unequal objects usually have different hash codes and so are likely to be stored at different locations in our hash table.

5.3.1 Hash Codes for Primitive Data Types

Small primitive data types like `char`, `byte`, `int`, and `float` are usually easy to find hash codes for. These data types always have a binary representation and this binary representation usually consists of w or fewer bits. (For example, in Java, `byte` is an 8-bit type and `float` is a 32-bit type.) In these cases, we just treat these bits as the representation of an integer in the range $\{0,\ldots,2^{w}-1\}$. If two values are different, they get different hash codes. If they are the same, they get the same hash code.

A few primitive data types are made up of more than w bits, usually cw bits for some constant integer c. (Java's `long` and `double` types are examples of this with $c = 2$.) These data types can be treated as compound objects made of c parts, as described in the next section.

5.3.2 Hash Codes for Compound Objects

For a compound object, we want to create a hash code by combining the individual hash codes of the object's constituent parts. This is not as easy as it sounds. Although one can find many hacks for this (for example, combining the hash codes with bitwise exclusive-or operations), many of these hacks turn out to be easy to foil (see Exercises 5.7–5.9). However, if one is willing to do arithmetic with 2w bits of precision, then there are simple and robust methods available. Suppose we have an object made up of several parts $P_0,\ldots,P_{r-1}$ whose hash codes are $\mathtt{x}_0,\ldots,\mathtt{x}_{r-1}$. Then we can choose mutually independent random $\mathtt{w}$-bit integers $\mathtt{z}_0,\ldots,\mathtt{z}_{r-1}$ and a random $2\mathtt{w}$-bit odd integer $\mathtt{z}$ and compute a hash code for our object with

$$h(\mathtt{x}_0,\ldots,\mathtt{x}_{r-1}) = \left(\left(\mathtt{z}\sum_{i=0}^{r-1}\mathtt{z}_i\mathtt{x}_i\right)\bmod 2^{2\mathtt{w}}\right)\operatorname{div} 2^{\mathtt{w}} \enspace .$$

Note that this hash code has a final step (multiplying by $\mathtt{z}$ and dividing by $2^{\mathtt{w}}$) that uses the multiplicative hash function from Section 5.1.1 to take the $2\mathtt{w}$-bit intermediate result and reduce it to a $\mathtt{w}$-bit final result. Here is an example of this method applied to a simple compound object with three parts x0, x1, and x2:

```
                         Point3D
int hashCode() {
  // random numbers from rand.org
  long[] z = {0x2058cc50L, 0xcb19137eL, 0x2cb6b6fdL};
  long zz = 0xbea0107e5067d19dL;

  // convert (unsigned) hashcodes to long
  long h0 = x0.hashCode() & ((1L<<32)-1);
  long h1 = x1.hashCode() & ((1L<<32)-1);
  long h2 = x2.hashCode() & ((1L<<32)-1);

  return (int)(((z[0]*h0 + z[1]*h1 + z[2]*h2)*zz)
               >>> 32);
}
```

The following theorem shows that, in addition to being straightforward to implement, this method is provably good:

Theorem 5.3. *Let* $\mathtt{x}_0,\ldots,\mathtt{x}_{r-1}$ *and* $\mathtt{y}_0,\ldots,\mathtt{y}_{r-1}$ *each be sequences of* $\mathtt{w}$ *bit integers in* $\{0,\ldots,2^{\mathtt{w}}-1\}$ *and assume* $\mathtt{x}_i \neq \mathtt{y}_i$ *for at least one index* $i\in\{0,\ldots,r-1\}$*. Then*

$$\Pr\{h(\mathtt{x}_0,\ldots,\mathtt{x}_{r-1}) = h(\mathtt{y}_0,\ldots,\mathtt{y}_{r-1})\} \le 3/2^{\mathtt{w}} \enspace .$$

Proof. We will first ignore the final multiplicative hashing step and see how that step contributes later. Define:

$$h'(\mathtt{x}_0,\ldots,\mathtt{x}_{r-1}) = \left(\sum_{j=0}^{r-1}\mathtt{z}_j\mathtt{x}_j\right)\bmod 2^{2\mathtt{w}} \enspace .$$

Suppose that $h'(\mathtt{x}_0,\ldots,\mathtt{x}_{r-1}) = h'(\mathtt{y}_0,\ldots,\mathtt{y}_{r-1})$. We can rewrite this as:

$$\mathtt{z}_i(\mathtt{x}_i - \mathtt{y}_i) \bmod 2^{2\mathtt{w}} = t \tag{5.4}$$

where

$$t = \left(\sum_{j=0}^{i-1} \mathtt{z}_j(\mathtt{y}_j - \mathtt{x}_j) + \sum_{j=i+1}^{r-1} \mathtt{z}_j(\mathtt{y}_j - \mathtt{x}_j)\right) \bmod 2^{2\mathtt{w}}$$

If we assume, without loss of generality that $\mathtt{x}_i > \mathtt{y}_i$, then (5.4) becomes

$$\mathtt{z}_i(\mathtt{x}_i - \mathtt{y}_i) = t \ , \tag{5.5}$$

since each of $\mathtt{z}_i$ and $(\mathtt{x}_i - \mathtt{y}_i)$ is at most $2^{\mathtt{w}} - 1$, so their product is at most $2^{2\mathtt{w}} - 2^{\mathtt{w}+1} + 1 < 2^{2\mathtt{w}} - 1$. By assumption, $\mathtt{x}_i - \mathtt{y}_i \neq 0$, so (5.5) has at most one solution in $\mathtt{z}_i$. Therefore, since $\mathtt{z}_i$ and t are independent ($\mathtt{z}_0,\ldots,\mathtt{z}_{r-1}$ are mutually independent), the probability that we select $\mathtt{z}_i$ so that $h'(\mathtt{x}_0,\ldots,\mathtt{x}_{r-1}) = h'(\mathtt{y}_0,\ldots,\mathtt{y}_{r-1})$ is at most $1/2^{\mathtt{w}}$.

The final step of the hash function is to apply multiplicative hashing to reduce our 2w-bit intermediate result $h'(\mathtt{x}_0,\ldots,\mathtt{x}_{r-1})$ to a w-bit final result $h(\mathtt{x}_0,\ldots,\mathtt{x}_{r-1})$. By Theorem 5.3, if $h'(\mathtt{x}_0,\ldots,\mathtt{x}_{r-1}) \neq h'(\mathtt{y}_0,\ldots,\mathtt{y}_{r-1})$, then $\Pr\{h(\mathtt{x}_0,\ldots,\mathtt{x}_{r-1}) = h(\mathtt{y}_0,\ldots,\mathtt{y}_{r-1})\} \leq 2/2^{\mathtt{w}}$.

To summarize,

$$\begin{aligned}
&\Pr\left\{\begin{array}{l} h(\mathtt{x}_0,\ldots,\mathtt{x}_{r-1}) \\ \quad = h(\mathtt{y}_0,\ldots,\mathtt{y}_{r-1}) \end{array}\right\} \\
&= \Pr\left\{\begin{array}{l} h'(\mathtt{x}_0,\ldots,\mathtt{x}_{r-1}) = h'(\mathtt{y}_0,\ldots,\mathtt{y}_{r-1}) \text{ or} \\ h'(\mathtt{x}_0,\ldots,\mathtt{x}_{r-1}) \neq h'(\mathtt{y}_0,\ldots,\mathtt{y}_{r-1}) \\ \quad \text{and } \mathtt{z}h'(\mathtt{x}_0,\ldots,\mathtt{x}_{r-1}) \operatorname{div} 2^{\mathtt{w}} = \mathtt{z}h'(\mathtt{y}_0,\ldots,\mathtt{y}_{r-1}) \operatorname{div} 2^{\mathtt{w}} \end{array}\right\} \\
&\leq 1/2^{\mathtt{w}} + 2/2^{\mathtt{w}} = 3/2^{\mathtt{w}} \ .
\end{aligned}$$

□

5.3.3 Hash Codes for Arrays and Strings

The method from the previous section works well for objects that have a fixed, constant, number of components. However, it breaks down when we want to use it with objects that have a variable number of components, since it requires a random w-bit integer $\mathtt{z}_i$ for each component. We could use a pseudorandom sequence to generate as many $\mathtt{z}_i$'s as we need, but then the $\mathtt{z}_i$'s are not mutually independent, and it becomes difficult to prove that the pseudorandom numbers don't interact badly with the hash function we are using. In particular, the values of t and z_i in the proof of Theorem 5.3 are no longer independent.

A more rigorous approach is to base our hash codes on polynomials over prime fields; these are just regular polynomials that are evaluated modulo some prime number, p. This method is based on the following theorem, which says that polynomials over prime fields behave pretty-much like usual polynomials:

Theorem 5.4. *Let* p *be a prime number, and let* $f(\mathrm{z}) = \mathrm{x}_0\mathrm{z}^0 + \mathrm{x}_1\mathrm{z}^1 + \cdots + \mathrm{x}_{r-1}\mathrm{z}^{r-1}$ *be a non-trivial polynomial with coefficients* $\mathrm{x}_i \in \{0,\ldots,\mathrm{p}-1\}$*. Then the equation* $f(\mathrm{z}) \bmod \mathrm{p} = 0$ *has at most* $r-1$ *solutions for* $\mathrm{z} \in \{0,\ldots,p-1\}$*.*

To use Theorem 5.4, we hash a sequence of integers $\mathrm{x}_0,\ldots,\mathrm{x}_{r-1}$ with each $\mathrm{x}_i \in \{0,\ldots,\mathrm{p}-2\}$ using a random integer $\mathrm{z} \in \{0,\ldots,\mathrm{p}-1\}$ via the formula

$$h(\mathrm{x}_0,\ldots,\mathrm{x}_{r-1}) = \left(\mathrm{x}_0\mathrm{z}^0 + \cdots + \mathrm{x}_{r-1}\mathrm{z}^{r-1} + (\mathrm{p}-1)\mathrm{z}^r\right) \bmod \mathrm{p} \enspace .$$

Note the extra $(\mathrm{p}-1)\mathrm{z}^r$ term at the end of the formula. It helps to think of $(\mathrm{p}-1)$ as the last element, x_r, in the sequence $\mathrm{x}_0,\ldots,\mathrm{x}_r$. Note that this element differs from every other element in the sequence (each of which is in the set $\{0,\ldots,\mathrm{p}-2\}$). We can think of $\mathrm{p}-1$ as an end-of-sequence marker.

The following theorem, which considers the case of two sequences of the same length, shows that this hash function gives a good return for the small amount of randomization needed to choose z:

Theorem 5.5. *Let* $\mathrm{p} > 2^{\mathrm{w}}+1$ *be a prime, let* $\mathrm{x}_0,\ldots,\mathrm{x}_{r-1}$ *and* $\mathrm{y}_0,\ldots,\mathrm{y}_{r-1}$ *each be sequences of* w*-bit integers in* $\{0,\ldots,2^{\mathrm{w}}-1\}$*, and assume* $\mathrm{x}_i \neq \mathrm{y}_i$ *for at least one index* $i \in \{0,\ldots,r-1\}$*. Then*

$$\Pr\{h(\mathrm{x}_0,\ldots,\mathrm{x}_{r-1}) = h(\mathrm{y}_0,\ldots,\mathrm{y}_{r-1})\} \le (r-1)/\mathrm{p}\} \enspace .$$

Proof. The equation $h(\mathrm{x}_0,\ldots,\mathrm{x}_{r-1}) = h(\mathrm{y}_0,\ldots,\mathrm{y}_{r-1})$ can be rewritten as

$$\left((\mathrm{x}_0-\mathrm{y}_0)\mathrm{z}^0 + \cdots + (\mathrm{x}_{r-1}-\mathrm{y}_{r-1})\mathrm{z}^{r-1}\right) \bmod \mathrm{p} = 0. \tag{5.6}$$

Since $\mathrm{x}_\mathrm{i} \neq \mathrm{y}_\mathrm{i}$, this polynomial is non-trivial. Therefore, by Theorem 5.4, it has at most $r-1$ solutions in z. The probability that we pick z to be one of these solutions is therefore at most $(r-1)/\mathrm{p}$. □

Note that this hash function also deals with the case in which two sequences have different lengths, even when one of the sequences is a prefix of the other. This is because this function effectively hashes the infinite sequence

$$\mathtt{x}_0,\ldots,\mathtt{x}_{r-1},\mathtt{p}-1,0,0,\ldots\ .$$

This guarantees that if we have two sequences of length r and r' with $r > r'$, then these two sequences differ at index $i = r$. In this case, (5.6) becomes

$$\left(\sum_{i=0}^{i=r'-1}(\mathtt{x}_i-\mathtt{y}_i)\mathtt{z}^i+(\mathtt{x}_{r'}-\mathtt{p}+1)\mathtt{z}^{r'}+\sum_{i=r'+1}^{i=r-1}\mathtt{x}_i\mathtt{z}^i+(\mathtt{p}-1)\mathtt{z}^r\right)\bmod \mathtt{p}=0\ ,$$

which, by Theorem 5.4, has at most r solutions in $\mathtt{z}$. This combined with Theorem 5.5 suffice to prove the following more general theorem:

Theorem 5.6. *Let* $\mathtt{p} > 2^{\mathtt{w}}+1$ *be a prime, let* $\mathtt{x}_0,\ldots,\mathtt{x}_{r-1}$ *and* $\mathtt{y}_0,\ldots,\mathtt{y}_{r'-1}$ *be distinct sequences of* $\mathtt{w}$*-bit integers in* $\{0,\ldots,2^{\mathtt{w}}-1\}$*. Then*

$$\Pr\{h(\mathtt{x}_0,\ldots,\mathtt{x}_{r-1})=h(\mathtt{y}_0,\ldots,\mathtt{y}_{r-1})\}\le\max\{r,r'\}/\mathtt{p}\ .$$

The following example code shows how this hash function is applied to an object that contains an array, `x`, of values:

GeomVector

```
int hashCode() {
  long p = (1L<<32)-5;    // prime: 2^32 - 5
  long z = 0x64b6055aL;   // 32 bits from random.org
  int z2 = 0x5067d19d;    // random odd 32 bit number
  long s = 0;
  long zi = 1;
  for (int i = 0; i < x.length; i++) {
    // reduce to 31 bits
    long xi = (x[i].hashCode() * z2) >>> 1;
    s = (s + zi * xi) % p;
    zi = (zi * z) % p;
  }
  s = (s + zi * (p-1)) % p;
  return (int)s;
}
```

The preceding code sacrifices some collision probability for implementation convenience. In particular, it applies the multiplicative hash function from Section 5.1.1, with $d = 31$ to reduce x[i].hashCode() to a 31-bit value. This is so that the additions and multiplications that are done modulo the prime $p = 2^{32} - 5$ can be carried out using unsigned 63-bit arithmetic. Thus the probability of two different sequences, the longer of which has length r, having the same hash code is at most

$$2/2^{31} + r/(2^{32} - 5)$$

rather than the $r/(2^{32} - 5)$ specified in Theorem 5.6.

5.4 Discussion and Exercises

Hash tables and hash codes represent an enormous and active field of research that is just touched upon in this chapter. The online Bibliography on Hashing [10] contains nearly 2000 entries.

A variety of different hash table implementations exist. The one described in Section 5.1 is known as *hashing with chaining* (each array entry contains a chain (List) of elements). Hashing with chaining dates back to an internal IBM memorandum authored by H. P. Luhn and dated January 1953. This memorandum also seems to be one of the earliest references to linked lists.

An alternative to hashing with chaining is that used by *open addressing* schemes, where all data is stored directly in an array. These schemes include the LinearHashTable structure of Section 5.2. This idea was also proposed, independently, by a group at IBM in the 1950s. Open addressing schemes must deal with the problem of *collision resolution*: the case where two values hash to the same array location. Different strategies exist for collision resolution; these provide different performance guarantees and often require more sophisticated hash functions than the ones described here.

Yet another category of hash table implementations are the so-called *perfect hashing* methods. These are methods in which find(x) operations take $O(1)$ time in the worst-case. For static data sets, this can be accomplished by finding *perfect hash functions* for the data; these are functions that map each piece of data to a unique array location. For data that changes over time, perfect hashing methods include *FKS two-level hash tables* [31, 24] and *cuckoo hashing* [57].

The hash functions presented in this chapter are probably among the most practical methods currently known that can be proven to work well for any set of data. Other provably good methods date back to the pioneering work of Carter and Wegman who introduced the notion of *universal hashing* and described several hash functions for different scenarios [14]. Tabulation hashing, described in Section 5.2.3, is due to Carter and Wegman [14], but its analysis, when applied to linear probing (and several other hash table schemes) is due to Pătraşcu and Thorup [60].

The idea of *multiplicative hashing* is very old and seems to be part of the hashing folklore [48, Section 6.4]. However, the idea of choosing the multiplier $\mathtt{z}$ to be a random *odd* number, and the analysis in Section 5.1.1 is due to Dietzfelbinger *et al.* [23]. This version of multiplicative hashing is one of the simplest, but its collision probability of $2/2^{\mathtt{d}}$ is a factor of two larger than what one could expect with a random function from $2^{\mathtt{w}} \to 2^{\mathtt{d}}$. The *multiply-add hashing* method uses the function

$$h(\mathtt{x}) = ((\mathtt{z}\mathtt{x} + b) \bmod 2^{2\mathtt{w}}) \operatorname{div} 2^{2\mathtt{w}-\mathtt{d}}$$

where $\mathtt{z}$ and $\mathtt{b}$ are each randomly chosen from $\{0,\ldots,2^{2\mathtt{w}}-1\}$. Multiply-add hashing has a collision probability of only $1/2^{\mathtt{d}}$ [21], but requires $2\mathtt{w}$-bit precision arithmetic.

There are a number of methods of obtaining hash codes from fixed-length sequences of $\mathtt{w}$-bit integers. One particularly fast method [11] is the function

$$\begin{aligned} &h(\mathtt{x}_0,\ldots,\mathtt{x}_{r-1}) \\ &\quad = \left(\textstyle\sum_{i=0}^{r/2-1}((\mathtt{x}_{2i} + \mathtt{a}_{2i}) \bmod 2^{\mathtt{w}})((\mathtt{x}_{2i+1} + \mathtt{a}_{2i+1}) \bmod 2^{\mathtt{w}})\right) \bmod 2^{2\mathtt{w}} \end{aligned}$$

where r is even and $\mathtt{a}_0,\ldots,\mathtt{a}_{r-1}$ are randomly chosen from $\{0,\ldots,2^{\mathtt{w}}\}$. This yields a $2\mathtt{w}$-bit hash code that has collision probability $1/2^{\mathtt{w}}$. This can be reduced to a $\mathtt{w}$-bit hash code using multiplicative (or multiply-add) hashing. This method is fast because it requires only $r/2$ $2\mathtt{w}$-bit multiplications whereas the method described in Section 5.3.2 requires r multiplications. (The mod operations occur implicitly by using $\mathtt{w}$ and $2\mathtt{w}$-bit arithmetic for the additions and multiplications, respectively.)

The method from Section 5.3.3 of using polynomials over prime fields to hash variable-length arrays and strings is due to Dietzfelbinger *et al.* [22]. Due to its use of the mod operator which relies on a costly machine instruction, it is, unfortunately, not very fast. Some variants of this method choose the prime p to be one of the form $2^w - 1$, in which case the mod operator can be replaced with addition (+) and bitwise-and (&) operations [47, Section 3.6]. Another option is to apply one of the fast methods for fixed-length strings to blocks of length c for some constant $c > 1$ and then apply the prime field method to the resulting sequence of $\lceil r/c \rceil$ hash codes.

Exercise 5.1. A certain university assigns each of its students student numbers the first time they register for any course. These numbers are sequential integers that started at 0 many years ago and are now in the millions. Suppose we have a class of one hundred first year students and we want to assign them hash codes based on their student numbers. Does it make more sense to use the first two digits or the last two digits of their student number? Justify your answer.

Exercise 5.2. Consider the hashing scheme in Section 5.1.1, and suppose $n = 2^d$ and $d \le w/2$.

1. Show that, for any choice of the muliplier, z, there exists n values that all have the same hash code. (Hint: This is easy, and doesn't require any number theory.)
2. Given the multiplier, z, describe n values that all have the same hash code. (Hint: This is harder, and requires some basic number theory.)

Exercise 5.3. Prove that the bound $2/2^d$ in Lemma 5.1 is the best possible bound by showing that, if $x = 2^{w-d-2}$ and $y = 3x$, then $\Pr\{\mathtt{hash}(x) = \mathtt{hash}(y)\} = 2/2^d$. (Hint look at the binary representations of zx and z3x and use the fact that $z3x = zx + 2zx$.)

Exercise 5.4. Reprove Lemma 5.4 using the full version of Stirling's Approximation given in Section 1.3.2.

Exercise 5.5. Consider the following simplified version of the code for adding an element x to a `LinearHashTable`, which simply stores x in the first null array entry it finds. Explain why this could be very slow by giving an example of a sequence of $O(n)$ add(x), remove(x), and find(x) operations that would take on the order of n^2 time to execute.

LinearHashTable
```
boolean addSlow(T x) {
  if (2*(q+1) > t.length) resize(); // max 50% occupancy
  int i = hash(x);
  while (t[i] != null) {
    if (t[i] != del && x.equals(t[i])) return false;
    i = (i == t.length-1) ? 0 : i + 1; // increment i
  }
  t[i] = x;
  n++; q++;
  return true;
}
```

Exercise 5.6. Early versions of the Java hashCode() method for the String class worked by not using all of the characters found in long strings. For example, for a sixteen character string, the hash code was computed using only the eight even-indexed characters. Explain why this was a very bad idea by giving an example of large set of strings that all have the same hash code.

Exercise 5.7. Suppose you have an object made up of two w-bit integers, x and y. Show why $x \oplus y$ does not make a good hash code for your object. Give an example of a large set of objects that would all have hash code 0.

Exercise 5.8. Suppose you have an object made up of two w-bit integers, x and y. Show why $x + y$ does not make a good hash code for your object. Give an example of a large set of objects that would all have the same hash code.

Exercise 5.9. Suppose you have an object made up of two w-bit integers, x and y. Suppose that the hash code for your object is defined by some deterministic function $h(x, y)$ that produces a single w-bit integer. Prove that there exists a large set of objects that have the same hash code.

Exercise 5.10. Let $p = 2^w - 1$ for some positive integer w. Explain why, for a positive integer x

$$(x \bmod 2^{\mathsf{w}}) + (x \operatorname{div} 2^{\mathsf{w}}) \equiv x \bmod (2^{\mathsf{w}} - 1) \ .$$

(This gives an algorithm for computing $x \bmod (2^{\mathsf{w}} - 1)$ by repeatedly setting

$$\mathsf{x} = \mathsf{x}\&((1{<<}\mathsf{w}) - 1) + \mathsf{x}{>>>}\mathsf{w}$$

until $\mathsf{x} \le 2^{\mathsf{w}} - 1$.)

Exercise 5.11. Find some commonly used hash table implementation such as the (Java Collection Framework `HashMap` or the `HashTable` or `LinearHashTable` implementations in this book, and design a program that stores integers in this data structure so that there are integers, `x`, such that `find(x)` takes linear time. That is, find a set of `n` integers for which there are c`n` elements that hash to the same table location.

Depending on how good the implementation is, you may be able to do this just by inspecting the code for the implementation, or you may have to write some code that does trial insertions and searches, timing how long it takes to add and find particular values. (This can be, and has been, used to launch denial of service attacks on web servers [17].)

Chapter 6

Binary Trees

This chapter introduces one of the most fundamental structures in computer science: binary trees. The use of the word *tree* here comes from the fact that, when we draw them, the resultant drawing often resembles the trees found in a forest. There are many ways of ways of defining binary trees. Mathematically, a *binary tree* is a connected, undirected, finite graph with no cycles, and no vertex of degree greater than three.

For most computer science applications, binary trees are *rooted:* A special node, r, of degree at most two is called the *root* of the tree. For every node, u ≠ r, the second node on the path from u to r is called the *parent* of u. Each of the other nodes adjacent to u is called a *child* of u. Most of the binary trees we are interested in are *ordered*, so we distinguish between the *left child* and *right child* of u.

In illustrations, binary trees are usually drawn from the root downward, with the root at the top of the drawing and the left and right children respectively given by left and right positions in the drawing (Figure 6.1). For example, Figure 6.2.a shows a binary tree with nine nodes.

Because binary trees are so important, a certain terminology has developed for them: The *depth* of a node, u, in a binary tree is the length of the path from u to the root of the tree. If a node, w, is on the path from u to r, then w is called an *ancestor* of u and u a *descendant* of w. The *subtree* of a node, u, is the binary tree that is rooted at u and contains all of u's descendants. The *height* of a node, u, is the length of the longest path from u to one of its descendants. The *height* of a tree is the height of its root. A node, u, is a *leaf* if it has no children.

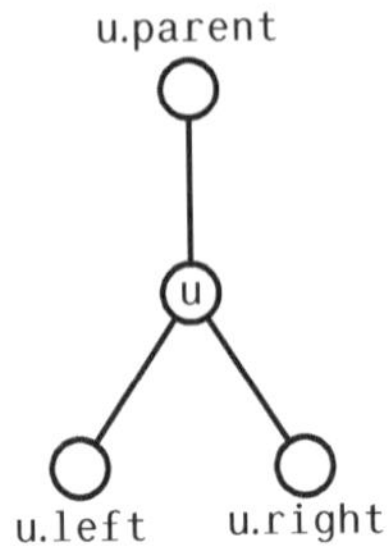

Figure 6.1: The parent, left child, and right child of the node u in a BinaryTree.

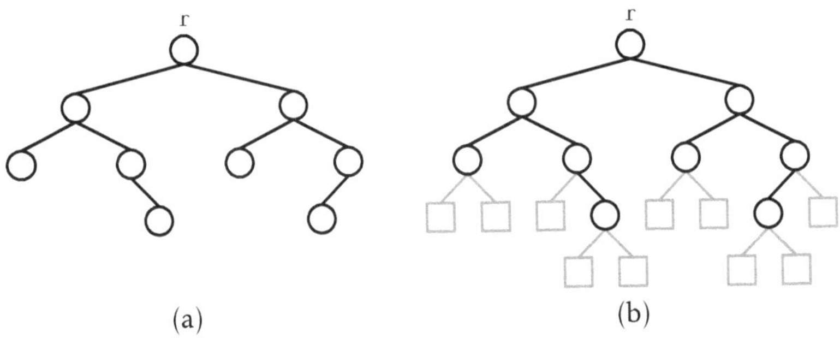

Figure 6.2: A binary tree with (a) nine real nodes and (b) ten external nodes.

We sometimes think of the tree as being augmented with *external nodes*. Any node that does not have a left child has an external node as its left child, and, correspondingly, any node that does not have a right child has an external node as its right child (see Figure 6.2.b). It is easy to verify, by induction, that a binary tree with $n \geq 1$ real nodes has $n+1$ external nodes.

6.1 BinaryTree: A Basic Binary Tree

The simplest way to represent a node, u, in a binary tree is to explicitly store the (at most three) neighbours of u:

BinaryTree
```
class BTNode<Node extends BTNode<Node>> {
  Node left;
  Node right;
  Node parent;
}
```

When one of these three neighbours is not present, we set it to `nil`. In this way, both external nodes of the tree and the parent of the root correspond to the value `nil`.

The binary tree itself can then be represented by a reference to its root node, r:

BinaryTree
```
Node r;
```

We can compute the depth of a node, u, in a binary tree by counting the number of steps on the path from u to the root:

BinaryTree
```
int depth(Node u) {
  int d = 0;
  while (u != r) {
    u = u.parent;
    d++;
```

```
  }
  return d;
}
```

6.1.1 Recursive Algorithms

Using recursive algorithms makes it very easy to compute facts about binary trees. For example, to compute the size of (number of nodes in) a binary tree rooted at node u, we recursively compute the sizes of the two subtrees rooted at the children of u, sum up these sizes, and add one:

BinaryTree
```
int size(Node u) {
  if (u == nil) return 0;
  return 1 + size(u.left) + size(u.right);
}
```

To compute the height of a node u, we can compute the height of u's two subtrees, take the maximum, and add one:

BinaryTree
```
int height(Node u) {
  if (u == nil) return -1;
  return 1 + max(height(u.left), height(u.right));
}
```

6.1.2 Traversing Binary Trees

The two algorithms from the previous section both use recursion to visit all the nodes in a binary tree. Each of them visits the nodes of the binary tree in the same order as the following code:

BinaryTree
```
void traverse(Node u) {
  if (u == nil) return;
  traverse(u.left);
  traverse(u.right);
}
```

Using recursion this way produces very short, simple code, but it can also be problematic. The maximum depth of the recursion is given by the maximum depth of a node in the binary tree, i.e., the tree's height. If the height of the tree is very large, then this recursion could very well use more stack space than is available, causing a crash.

To traverse a binary tree without recursion, you can use an algorithm that relies on where it came from to determine where it will go next. See Figure 6.3. If we arrive at a node u from u.parent, then the next thing to do is to visit u.left. If we arrive at u from u.left, then the next thing to do is to visit u.right. If we arrive at u from u.right, then we are done visiting u's subtree, and so we return to u.parent. The following code implements this idea, with code included for handling the cases where any of u.left, u.right, or u.parent is nil:

BinaryTree

```
void traverse2() {
  Node u = r, prev = nil, next;
  while (u != nil) {
    if (prev == u.parent) {
      if (u.left != nil) next = u.left;
      else if (u.right != nil) next = u.right;
      else next = u.parent;
    } else if (prev == u.left) {
      if (u.right != nil) next = u.right;
      else next = u.parent;
    } else {
      next = u.parent;
    }
    prev = u;
    u = next;
  }
}
```

The same facts that can be computed with recursive algorithms can also be computed in this way, without recursion. For example, to compute the size of the tree we keep a counter, n, and increment n whenever visiting a node for the first time:

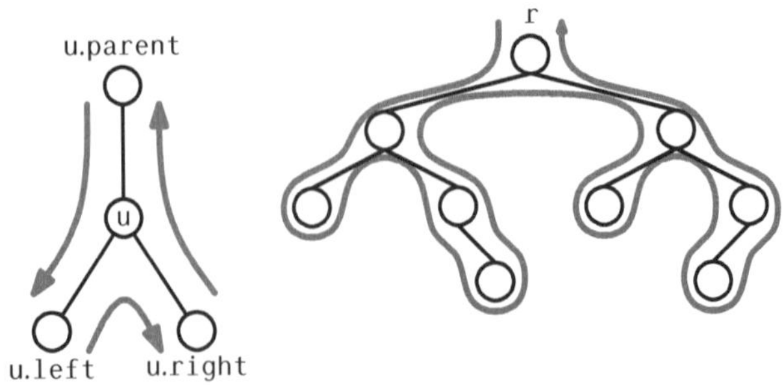

Figure 6.3: The three cases that occur at node u when traversing a binary tree non-recursively, and the resultant traversal of the tree.

BinaryTree
```
int size2() {
  Node u = r, prev = nil, next;
  int n = 0;
  while (u != nil) {
    if (prev == u.parent) {
      n++;
      if (u.left != nil) next = u.left;
      else if (u.right != nil) next = u.right;
      else next = u.parent;
    } else if (prev == u.left) {
      if (u.right != nil) next = u.right;
      else next = u.parent;
    } else {
      next = u.parent;
    }
    prev = u;
    u = next;
  }
  return n;
}
```

In some implementations of binary trees, the parent field is not used. When this is the case, a non-recursive implementation is still possible, but the implementation has to use a List (or Stack) to keep track of the path from the current node to the root.

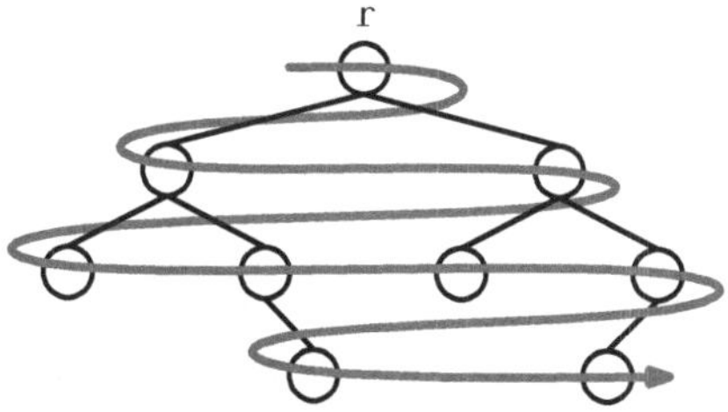

Figure 6.4: During a breadth-first traversal, the nodes of a binary tree are visited level-by-level, and left-to-right within each level.

A special kind of traversal that does not fit the pattern of the above functions is the *breadth-first traversal*. In a breadth-first traversal, the nodes are visited level-by-level starting at the root and moving down, visiting the nodes at each level from left to right (see Figure 6.4). This is similar to the way that we would read a page of English text. Breadth-first traversal is implemented using a queue, q, that initially contains only the root, r. At each step, we extract the next node, u, from q, process u and add u.left and u.right (if they are non-nil) to q:

BinaryTree
```
void bfTraverse() {
  Queue<Node> q = new LinkedList<Node>();
  if (r != nil) q.add(r);
  while (!q.isEmpty()) {
    Node u = q.remove();
    if (u.left != nil) q.add(u.left);
    if (u.right != nil) q.add(u.right);
  }
}
```

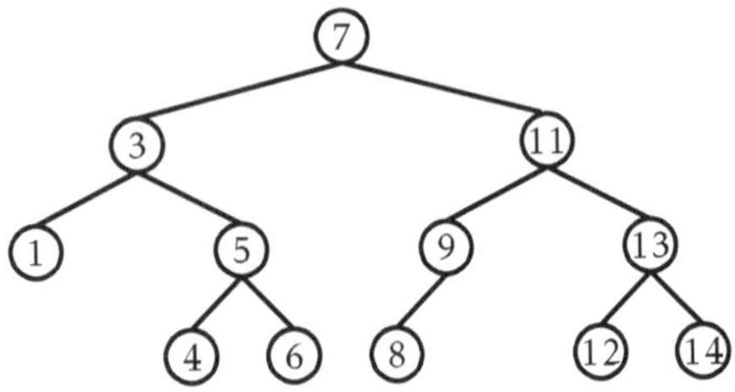

Figure 6.5: A binary search tree.

6.2 BinarySearchTree: An Unbalanced Binary Search Tree

A BinarySearchTree is a special kind of binary tree in which each node, u, also stores a data value, u.x, from some total order. The data values in a binary search tree obey the *binary search tree property*: For a node, u, every data value stored in the subtree rooted at u.left is less than u.x and every data value stored in the subtree rooted at u.right is greater than u.x. An example of a BinarySearchTree is shown in Figure 6.5.

6.2.1 Searching

The binary search tree property is extremely useful because it allows us to quickly locate a value, x, in a binary search tree. To do this we start searching for x at the root, r. When examining a node, u, there are three cases:

1. If x < u.x, then the search proceeds to u.left;
2. If x > u.x, then the search proceeds to u.right;
3. If x = u.x, then we have found the node u containing x.

The search terminates when Case 3 occurs or when u = nil. In the former case, we found x. In the latter case, we conclude that x is not in the binary search tree.

```
BinarySearchTree
T findEQ(T x) {
  Node u = r;
  while (u != nil) {
    int comp = compare(x, u.x);
    if (comp < 0)
      u = u.left;
    else if (comp > 0)
      u = u.right;
    else
      return u.x;
  }
  return null;
}
```

Two examples of searches in a binary search tree are shown in Figure 6.6. As the second example shows, even if we don't find x in the tree, we still gain some valuable information. If we look at the last node, u, at which Case 1 occurred, we see that u.x is the smallest value in the tree that is greater than x. Similarly, the last node at which Case 2 occurred contains the largest value in the tree that is less than x. Therefore, by keeping track of the last node, z, at which Case 1 occurs, a BinarySearchTree can implement the find(x) operation that returns the smallest value stored in the tree that is greater than or equal to x:

```
BinarySearchTree
T find(T x) {
  Node w = r, z = nil;
  while (w != nil) {
    int comp = compare(x, w.x);
    if (comp < 0) {
      z = w;
      w = w.left;
    } else if (comp > 0) {
      w = w.right;
    } else {
      return w.x;
    }
```

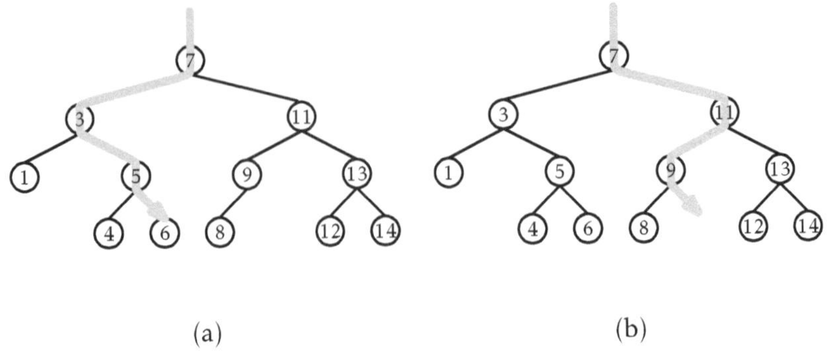

Figure 6.6: An example of (a) a successful search (for 6) and (b) an unsuccessful search (for 10) in a binary search tree.

```
  }
  return z == nil ? null : z.x;
}
```

6.2.2 Addition

To add a new value, x, to a BinarySearchTree, we first search for x. If we find it, then there is no need to insert it. Otherwise, we store x at a leaf child of the last node, p, encountered during the search for x. Whether the new node is the left or right child of p depends on the result of comparing x and p.x.

BinarySearchTree

```
boolean add(T x) {
  Node p = findLast(x);
  return addChild(p, newNode(x));
}
```

BinarySearchTree

```
Node findLast(T x) {
  Node w = r, prev = nil;
  while (w != nil) {
```

```
    prev = w;
    int comp = compare(x, w.x);
    if (comp < 0) {
      w = w.left;
    } else if (comp > 0) {
      w = w.right;
    } else {
      return w;
    }
  }
  return prev;
}
```

```
BinarySearchTree
boolean addChild(Node p, Node u) {
  if (p == nil) {
    r = u;              // inserting into empty tree
  } else {
    int comp = compare(u.x, p.x);
    if (comp < 0) {
      p.left = u;
    } else if (comp > 0) {
      p.right = u;
    } else {
      return false;    // u.x is already in the tree
    }
    u.parent = p;
  }
  n++;
  return true;
}
```

An example is shown in Figure 6.7. The most time-consuming part of this process is the initial search for x, which takes an amount of time proportional to the height of the newly added node u. In the worst case, this is equal to the height of the BinarySearchTree.

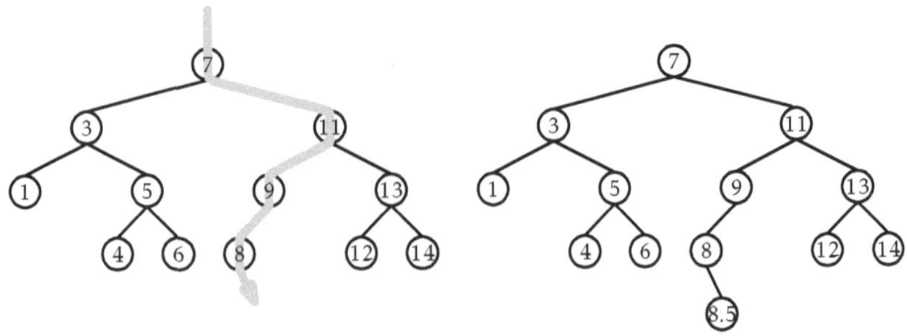

Figure 6.7: Inserting the value 8.5 into a binary search tree.

6.2.3 Removal

Deleting a value stored in a node, u, of a BinarySearchTree is a little more difficult. If u is a leaf, then we can just detach u from its parent. Even better: If u has only one child, then we can splice u from the tree by having u.parent adopt u's child (see Figure 6.8):

```
BinarySearchTree
void splice(Node u) {
  Node s, p;
  if (u.left != nil) {
    s = u.left;
  } else {
    s = u.right;
  }
  if (u == r) {
    r = s;
    p = nil;
  } else {
    p = u.parent;
    if (p.left == u) {
      p.left = s;
    } else {
      p.right = s;
    }
  }
  if (s != nil) {
```

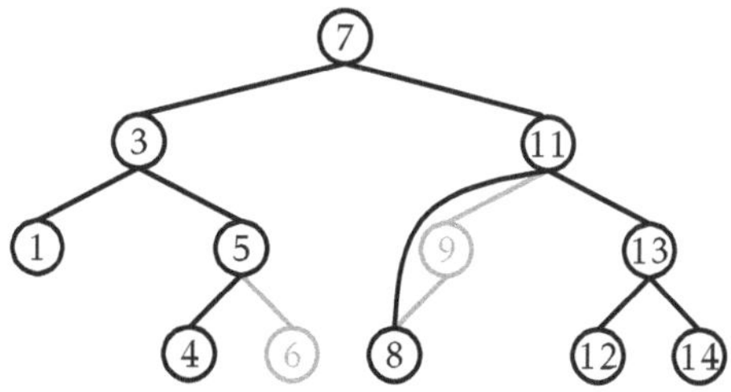

Figure 6.8: Removing a leaf (6) or a node with only one child (9) is easy.

```
      s.parent = p;
    }
    n--;
}
```

Things get tricky, though, when u has two children. In this case, the simplest thing to do is to find a node, w, that has less than two children and such that w.x can replace u.x. To maintain the binary search tree property, the value w.x should be close to the value of u.x. For example, choosing w such that w.x is the smallest value greater than u.x will work. Finding the node w is easy; it is the smallest value in the subtree rooted at u.right. This node can be easily removed because it has no left child (see Figure 6.9).

```
BinarySearchTree
void remove(Node u) {
  if (u.left == nil || u.right == nil) {
    splice(u);
  } else {
    Node w = u.right;
    while (w.left != nil)
      w = w.left;
    u.x = w.x;
    splice(w);
  }
}
```

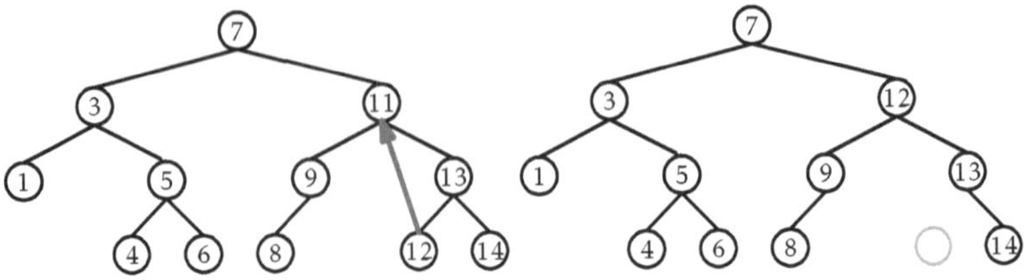

Figure 6.9: Deleting a value (11) from a node, u, with two children is done by replacing u's value with the smallest value in the right subtree of u.

6.2.4 Summary

The find(x), add(x), and remove(x) operations in a BinarySearchTree each involve following a path from the root of the tree to some node in the tree. Without knowing more about the shape of the tree it is difficult to say much about the length of this path, except that it is less than n, the number of nodes in the tree. The following (unimpressive) theorem summarizes the performance of the BinarySearchTree data structure:

Theorem 6.1. *BinarySearchTree implements the SSet interface and supports the operations* add(x), remove(x), *and* find(x) *in* $O(n)$ *time per operation.*

Theorem 6.1 compares poorly with Theorem 4.1, which shows that the SkiplistSSet structure can implement the SSet interface with $O(\log n)$ expected time per operation. The problem with the BinarySearchTree structure is that it can become *unbalanced*. Instead of looking like the tree in Figure 6.5 it can look like a long chain of n nodes, all but the last having exactly one child.

There are a number of ways of avoiding unbalanced binary search trees, all of which lead to data structures that have $O(\log n)$ time operations. In Chapter 7 we show how $O(\log n)$ *expected* time operations can be achieved with randomization. In Chapter 8 we show how $O(\log n)$ *amortized* time operations can be achieved with partial rebuilding operations. In Chapter 9 we show how $O(\log n)$ *worst-case* time operations can be achieved by simulating a tree that is not binary: one in which nodes can have up to four children.

6.3 Discussion and Exercises

Binary trees have been used to model relationships for thousands of years. One reason for this is that binary trees naturally model (pedigree) family trees. These are the family trees in which the root is a person, the left and right children are the person's parents, and so on, recursively. In more recent centuries binary trees have also been used to model species trees in biology, where the leaves of the tree represent extant species and the internal nodes of the tree represent *speciation events* in which two populations of a single species evolve into two separate species.

Binary search trees appear to have been discovered independently by several groups in the 1950s [48, Section 6.2.2]. Further references to specific kinds of binary search trees are provided in subsequent chapters.

When implementing a binary tree from scratch, there are several design decisions to be made. One of these is the question of whether or not each node stores a pointer to its parent. If most of the operations simply follow a root-to-leaf path, then parent pointers are unnecessary, waste space, and are a potential source of coding errors. On the other hand, the lack of parent pointers means that tree traversals must be done recursively or with the use of an explicit stack. Some other methods (like inserting or deleting into some kinds of balanced binary search trees) are also complicated by the lack of parent pointers.

Another design decision is concerned with how to store the parent, left child, and right child pointers at a node. In the implementation given here, these pointers are stored as separate variables. Another option is to store them in an array, p, of length 3, so that u.p[0] is the left child of u, u.p[1] is the right child of u, and u.p[2] is the parent of u. Using an array this way means that some sequences of `if` statements can be simplified into algebraic expressions.

An example of such a simplification occurs during tree traversal. If a traversal arrives at a node u from u.p[i], then the next node in the traversal is u.p[(i + 1) mod 3]. Similar examples occur when there is left-right symmetry. For example, the sibling of u.p[i] is u.p[(i + 1) mod 2]. This trick works whether u.p[i] is a left child (i = 0) or a right child (i = 1) of u. In some cases this means that some complicated code that would otherwise need to have both a left version and right version can be written only once. See the methods `rotateLeft(u)` and `rotateRight(u)` on page 163 for an example.

Exercise 6.1. Prove that a binary tree having $n \geq 1$ nodes has $n-1$ edges.

Exercise 6.2. Prove that a binary tree having $n \geq 1$ real nodes has $n+1$ external nodes.

Exercise 6.3. Prove that, if a binary tree, T, has at least one leaf, then either (a) T's root has at most one child or (b) T has more than one leaf.

Exercise 6.4. Implement a non-recursive method, `size2(u)`, that computes the size of the subtree rooted at node `u`.

Exercise 6.5. Write a non-recursive method, `height2(u)`, that computes the height of node `u` in a `BinaryTree`.

Exercise 6.6. A binary tree is *size-balanced* if, for every node `u`, the size of the subtrees rooted at `u.left` and `u.right` differ by at most one. Write a recursive method, `isBalanced()`, that tests if a binary tree is balanced. Your method should run in $O(n)$ time. (Be sure to test your code on some large trees with different shapes; it is easy to write a method that takes much longer than $O(n)$ time.)

A *pre-order* traversal of a binary tree is a traversal that visits each node, `u`, before any of its children. An *in-order* traversal visits `u` after visiting all the nodes in `u`'s left subtree but before visiting any of the nodes in `u`'s right subtree. A *post-order* traversal visits `u` only after visiting all other nodes in `u`'s subtree. The pre/in/post-order numbering of a tree labels the nodes of a tree with the integers $0,\ldots,n-1$ in the order that they are encountered by a pre/in/post-order traversal. See Figure 6.10 for an example.

Exercise 6.7. Create a subclass of `BinaryTree` whose nodes have fields for storing pre-order, post-order, and in-order numbers. Write recursive methods `preOrderNumber()`, `inOrderNumber()`, and `postOrderNumbers()` that assign these numbers correctly. These methods should each run in $O(n)$ time.

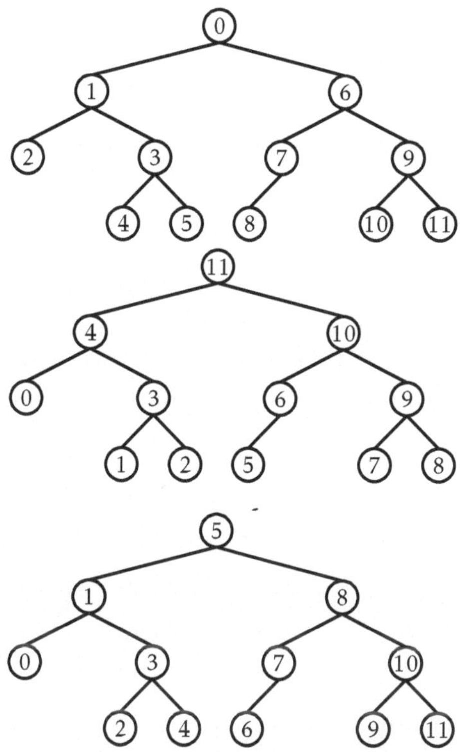

Figure 6.10: Pre-order, post-order, and in-order numberings of a binary tree.

Exercise 6.8. Implement the non-recursive functions `nextPreOrder(u)`, `nextInOrder(u)`, and `nextPostOrder(u)` that return the node that follows u in a pre-order, in-order, or post-order traversal, respectively. These functions should take amortized constant time; if we start at any node u and repeatedly call one of these functions and assign the return value to u until u = `null`, then the cost of all these calls should be $O(n)$.

Exercise 6.9. Suppose we are given a binary tree with pre-, post-, and in-order numbers assigned to the nodes. Show how these numbers can be used to answer each of the following questions in constant time:

1. Given a node u, determine the size of the subtree rooted at u.

2. Given a node u, determine the depth of u.

3. Given two nodes u and w, determine if u is an ancestor of w

Exercise 6.10. Suppose you are given a list of nodes with pre-order and in-order numbers assigned. Prove that there is at most one possible tree with this pre-order/in-order numbering and show how to construct it.

Exercise 6.11. Show that the shape of any binary tree on n nodes can be represented using at most $2(n-1)$ bits. (Hint: think about recording what happens during a traversal and then playing back that recording to reconstruct the tree.)

Exercise 6.12. Illustrate what happens when we add the values 3.5 and then 4.5 to the binary search tree in Figure 6.5.

Exercise 6.13. Illustrate what happens when we remove the values 3 and then 5 from the binary search tree in Figure 6.5.

Exercise 6.14. Implement a `BinarySearchTree` method, `getLE(x)`, that returns a list of all items in the tree that are less than or equal to x. The running time of your method should be $O(n' + h)$ where n' is the number of items less than or equal to x and h is the height of the tree.

Exercise 6.15. Describe how to add the elements $\{1,\ldots,n\}$ to an initially empty `BinarySearchTree` in such a way that the resulting tree has height $n-1$. How many ways are there to do this?

Exercise 6.16. If we have some `BinarySearchTree` and perform the operations `add(x)` followed by `remove(x)` (with the same value of `x`) do we necessarily return to the original tree?

Exercise 6.17. Can a `remove(x)` operation increase the height of any node in a `BinarySearchTree`? If so, by how much?

Exercise 6.18. Can an `add(x)` operation increase the height of any node in a `BinarySearchTree`? Can it increase the height of the tree? If so, by how much?

Exercise 6.19. Design and implement a version of `BinarySearchTree` in which each node, `u`, maintains values `u.size` (the size of the subtree rooted at `u`), `u.depth` (the depth of `u`), and `u.height` (the height of the subtree rooted at `u`).

These values should be maintained, even during calls to the `add(x)` and `remove(x)` operations, but this should not increase the cost of these operations by more than a constant factor.

Chapter 7

Random Binary Search Trees

In this chapter, we present a binary search tree structure that uses randomization to achieve $O(\log n)$ expected time for all operations.

7.1 Random Binary Search Trees

Consider the two binary search trees shown in Figure 7.1, each of which has $n = 15$ nodes. The one on the left is a list and the other is a perfectly balanced binary search tree. The one on the left has a height of $n - 1 = 14$ and the one on the right has a height of three.

Imagine how these two trees could have been constructed. The one on the left occurs if we start with an empty `BinarySearchTree` and add the sequence

$$\langle 0,1,2,3,4,5,6,7,8,9,10,11,12,13,14\rangle \ .$$

No other sequence of additions will create this tree (as you can prove by induction on n). On the other hand, the tree on the right can be created by the sequence

$$\langle 7,3,11,1,5,9,13,0,2,4,6,8,10,12,14\rangle \ .$$

Other sequences work as well, including

$$\langle 7,3,1,5,0,2,4,6,11,9,13,8,10,12,14\rangle \ ,$$

and

$$\langle 7,3,1,11,5,0,2,4,6,9,13,8,10,12,14\rangle \ .$$

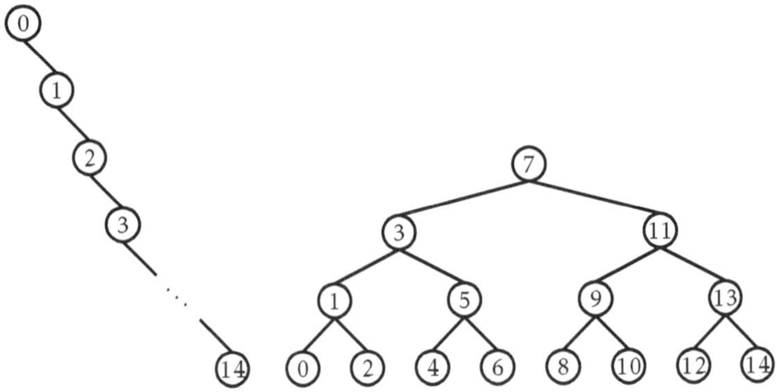

Figure 7.1: Two binary search trees containing the integers $0,\ldots,14$.

In fact, there are 21,964,800 addition sequences that generate the tree on the right and only one that generates the tree on the left.

The above example gives some anecdotal evidence that, if we choose a random permutation of $0,\ldots,14$, and add it into a binary search tree, then we are more likely to get a very balanced tree (the right side of Figure 7.1) than we are to get a very unbalanced tree (the left side of Figure 7.1).

We can formalize this notion by studying random binary search trees. A *random binary search tree* of size n is obtained in the following way: Take a random permutation, $x_0,\ldots,x_{n-1}$, of the integers $0,\ldots,n-1$ and add its elements, one by one, into a `BinarySearchTree`. By *random permutation* we mean that each of the possible $n!$ permutations (orderings) of $0,\ldots,n-1$ is equally likely, so that the probability of obtaining any particular permutation is $1/n!$.

Note that the values $0,\ldots,n-1$ could be replaced by any ordered set of n elements without changing any of the properties of the random binary search tree. The element $x \in \{0,\ldots,n-1\}$ is simply standing in for the element of rank x in an ordered set of size n.

Before we can present our main result about random binary search trees, we must take some time for a short digression to discuss a type of number that comes up frequently when studying randomized structures. For a non-negative integer, k, the k-th *harmonic number*, denoted H_k, is

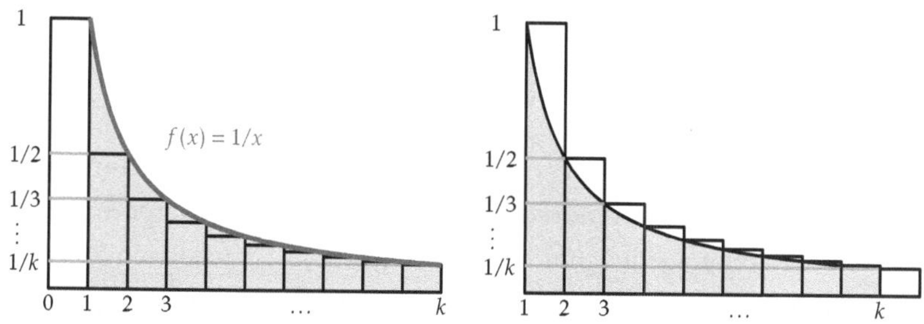

Figure 7.2: The kth harmonic number $H_k = \sum_{i=1}^{k} 1/i$ is upper- and lower-bounded by two integrals. The value of these integrals is given by the area of the shaded region, while the value of H_k is given by the area of the rectangles.

defined as

$$H_k = 1 + 1/2 + 1/3 + \cdots + 1/k \ .$$

The harmonic number H_k has no simple closed form, but it is very closely related to the natural logarithm of k. In particular,

$$\ln k < H_k \le \ln k + 1 \ .$$

Readers who have studied calculus might notice that this is because the integral $\int_1^k (1/x)\,\mathrm{d}x = \ln k$. Keeping in mind that an integral can be interpreted as the area between a curve and the x-axis, the value of H_k can be lower-bounded by the integral $\int_1^k (1/x)\,\mathrm{d}x$ and upper-bounded by $1 + \int_1^k (1/x)\,\mathrm{d}x$. (See Figure 7.2 for a graphical explanation.)

Lemma 7.1. *In a random binary search tree of size* n, *the following statements hold:*

1. *For any* $\mathtt{x} \in \{0,\ldots,\mathtt{n}-1\}$, *the expected length of the search path for* x *is* $H_{\mathtt{x}+1} + H_{\mathtt{n}-\mathtt{x}} - O(1)$.[1]

2. *For any* $\mathtt{x} \in (-1,n) \setminus \{0,\ldots,\mathtt{n}-1\}$, *the expected length of the search path for* x *is* $H_{\lceil \mathtt{x} \rceil} + H_{\mathtt{n}-\lceil \mathtt{x} \rceil}$.

[1]The expressions $\mathtt{x}+1$ and $\mathtt{n}-\mathtt{x}$ can be interpreted respectively as the number of elements in the tree less than or equal to x and the number of elements in the tree greater than or equal to x.

We will prove Lemma 7.1 in the next section. For now, consider what the two parts of Lemma 7.1 tell us. The first part tells us that if we search for an element in a tree of size $\mathtt{n}$, then the expected length of the search path is at most $2\ln n + O(1)$. The second part tells us the same thing about searching for a value not stored in the tree. When we compare the two parts of the lemma, we see that it is only slightly faster to search for something that is in the tree compared to something that is not.

7.1.1 Proof of Lemma 7.1

The key observation needed to prove Lemma 7.1 is the following: The search path for a value $\mathtt{x}$ in the open interval $(-1,\mathtt{n})$ in a random binary search tree, T, contains the node with key $i < \mathtt{x}$ if, and only if, in the random permutation used to create T, i appears before any of $\{i+1, i+2, \ldots, \lfloor \mathtt{x} \rfloor\}$.

To see this, refer to Figure 7.3 and notice that until some value in $\{i, i+1, \ldots, \lfloor \mathtt{x} \rfloor\}$ is added, the search paths for each value in the open interval $(i-1, \lfloor \mathtt{x} \rfloor + 1)$ are identical. (Remember that for two values to have different search paths, there must be some element in the tree that compares differently with them.) Let j be the first element in $\{i, i+1, \ldots, \lfloor \mathtt{x} \rfloor\}$ to appear in the random permutation. Notice that j is now and will always be on the search path for $\mathtt{x}$. If $j \neq i$ then the node $\mathtt{u}_j$ containing j is created before the node $\mathtt{u}_i$ that contains i. Later, when i is added, it will be added to the subtree rooted at $\mathtt{u}_j$.left, since $i < j$. On the other hand, the search path for $\mathtt{x}$ will never visit this subtree because it will proceed to $\mathtt{u}_j$.right after visiting $\mathtt{u}_j$.

Similarly, for $i > \mathtt{x}$, i appears in the search path for $\mathtt{x}$ if and only if i appears before any of $\{\lceil \mathtt{x} \rceil, \lceil \mathtt{x} \rceil + 1, \ldots, i-1\}$ in the random permutation used to create T.

Notice that, if we start with a random permutation of $\{0, \ldots, \mathtt{n}\}$, then the subsequences containing only $\{i, i+1, \ldots, \lfloor \mathtt{x} \rfloor\}$ and $\{\lceil \mathtt{x} \rceil, \lceil \mathtt{x} \rceil + 1, \ldots, i-1\}$ are also random permutations of their respective elements. Each element, then, in the subsets $\{i, i+1, \ldots, \lfloor \mathtt{x} \rfloor\}$ and $\{\lceil \mathtt{x} \rceil, \lceil \mathtt{x} \rceil + 1, \ldots, i-1\}$ is equally likely to appear before any other in its subset in the random permutation used

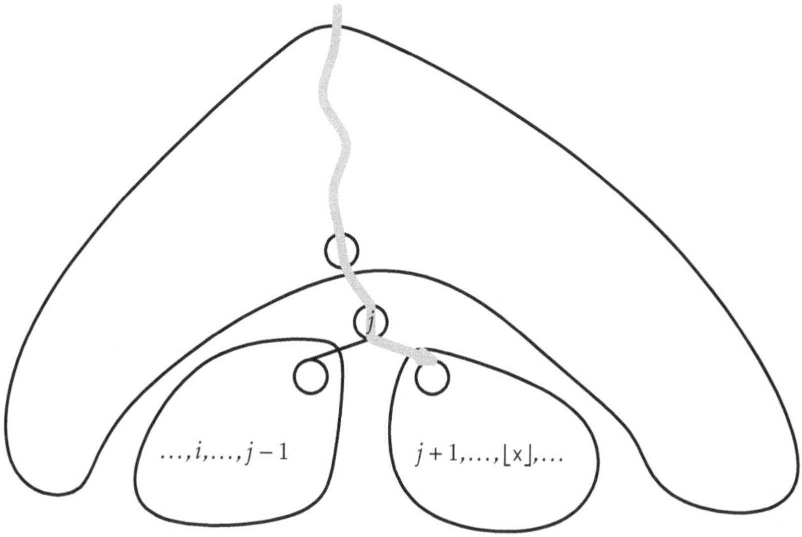

Figure 7.3: The value $i < x$ is on the search path for x if and only if i is the first element among $\{i, i+1, \ldots, \lfloor x \rfloor\}$ added to the tree.

to create T. So we have

$$\Pr\{i \text{ is on the search path for } x\} = \begin{cases} 1/(\lfloor x \rfloor - i + 1) & \text{if } i < x \\ 1/(i - \lceil x \rceil + 1) & \text{if } i > x \end{cases} .$$

With this observation, the proof of Lemma 7.1 involves some simple calculations with harmonic numbers:

Proof of Lemma 7.1. Let I_i be the indicator random variable that is equal to one when i appears on the search path for x and zero otherwise. Then the length of the search path is given by

$$\sum_{i \in \{0,\ldots,n-1\} \setminus \{x\}} I_i$$

so, if $x \in \{0, \ldots, n-1\}$, the expected length of the search path is given by

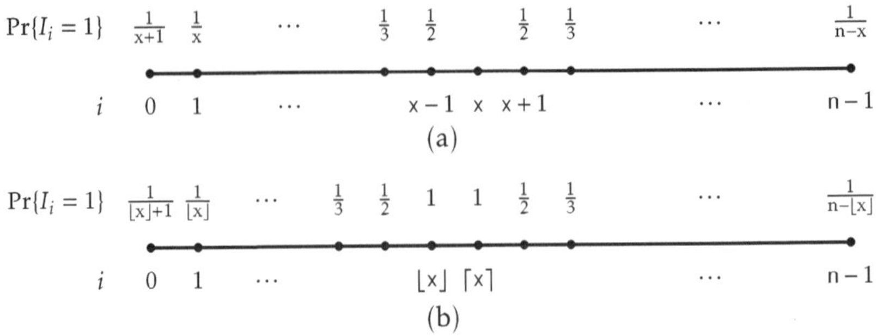

Figure 7.4: The probabilities of an element being on the search path for x when (a) x is an integer and (b) when x is not an integer.

(see Figure 7.4.a)

$$
\begin{aligned}
\mathrm{E}\left[\sum_{i=0}^{x-1} I_i + \sum_{i=x+1}^{n-1} I_i\right] &= \sum_{i=0}^{x-1} \mathrm{E}[I_i] + \sum_{i=x+1}^{n-1} \mathrm{E}[I_i] \\
&= \sum_{i=0}^{x-1} 1/(\lfloor x\rfloor - i + 1) + \sum_{i=x+1}^{n-1} 1/(i - \lceil x\rceil + 1) \\
&= \sum_{i=0}^{x-1} 1/(x - i + 1) + \sum_{i=x+1}^{n-1} 1/(i - x + 1) \\
&= \frac{1}{2} + \frac{1}{3} + \cdots + \frac{1}{x+1} \\
&\quad + \frac{1}{2} + \frac{1}{3} + \cdots + \frac{1}{n-x} \\
&= H_{x+1} + H_{n-x} - 2 \ .
\end{aligned}
$$

The corresponding calculations for a search value $x \in (-1, n) \setminus \{0, \ldots, n-1\}$ are almost identical (see Figure 7.4.b). □

7.1.2 Summary

The following theorem summarizes the performance of a random binary search tree:

Theorem 7.1. *A random binary search tree can be constructed in* $O(n \log n)$ *time. In a random binary search tree, the* find(x) *operation takes* $O(\log n)$ *expected time.*

We should emphasize again that the expectation in Theorem 7.1 is with respect to the random permutation used to create the random binary search tree. In particular, it does not depend on a random choice of x; it is true for every value of x.

7.2 Treap: A Randomized Binary Search Tree

The problem with random binary search trees is, of course, that they are not dynamic. They don't support the add(x) or remove(x) operations needed to implement the SSet interface. In this section we describe a data structure called a Treap that uses Lemma 7.1 to implement the SSet interface.[2]

A node in a Treap is like a node in a BinarySearchTree in that it has a data value, x, but it also contains a unique numerical *priority*, p, that is assigned at random:

Treap
```
class Node<T> extends BSTNode<Node<T>,T> {
  int p;
}
```

In addition to being a binary search tree, the nodes in a Treap also obey the *heap property*:

- (Heap Property) At every node u, except the root, u.parent.p $<$ u.p.

In other words, each node has a priority smaller than that of its two children. An example is shown in Figure 7.5.

The heap and binary search tree conditions together ensure that, once the key (x) and priority (p) for each node are defined, the shape of the Treap is completely determined. The heap property tells us that the node

[2]The names Treap comes from the fact that this data structure is simultaneously a binary search **tree** (Section 6.2) and a **heap** (Chapter 10).

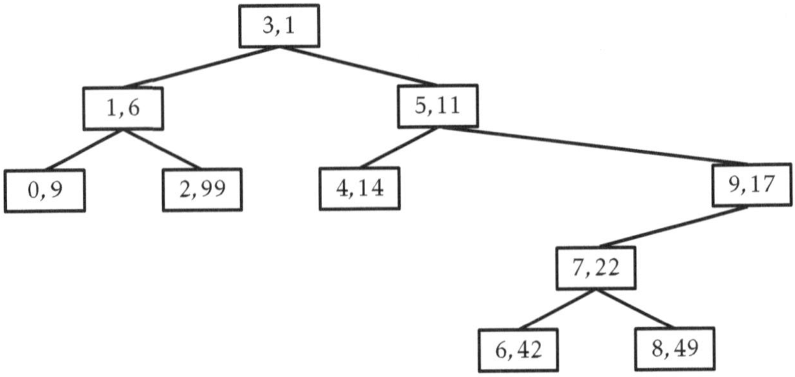

Figure 7.5: An example of a Treap containing the integers 0,...,9. Each node, u, is illustrated as a box containing u.x, u.p.

with minimum priority has to be the root, r, of the Treap. The binary search tree property tells us that all nodes with keys smaller than r.x are stored in the subtree rooted at r.left and all nodes with keys larger than r.x are stored in the subtree rooted at r.right.

The important point about the priority values in a Treap is that they are unique and assigned at random. Because of this, there are two equivalent ways we can think about a Treap. As defined above, a Treap obeys the heap and binary search tree properties. Alternatively, we can think of a Treap as a BinarySearchTree whose nodes were added in increasing order of priority. For example, the Treap in Figure 7.5 can be obtained by adding the sequence of (x, p) values

$$\langle (3,1),(1,6),(0,9),(5,11),(4,14),(9,17),(7,22),(6,42),(8,49),(2,99)\rangle$$

into a BinarySearchTree.

Since the priorities are chosen randomly, this is equivalent to taking a random permutation of the keys—in this case the permutation is

$$\langle 3,1,0,5,9,4,7,6,8,2\rangle$$

—and adding these to a BinarySearchTree. But this means that the shape of a treap is identical to that of a random binary search tree. In particular, if we replace each key x by its rank,[3] then Lemma 7.1 applies. Restating Lemma 7.1 in terms of Treaps, we have:

Lemma 7.2. *In a Treap that stores a set S of n keys, the following statements hold:*

1. *For any $x \in S$, the expected length of the search path for x is $H_{r(x)+1} + H_{n-r(x)} - O(1)$.*
2. *For any $x \notin S$, the expected length of the search path for x is $H_{r(x)} + H_{n-r(x)}$.*

Here, $r(x)$ denotes the rank of x in the set $S \cup \{x\}$.

Again, we emphasize that the expectation in Lemma 7.2 is taken over the random choices of the priorities for each node. It does not require any assumptions about the randomness in the keys.

Lemma 7.2 tells us that Treaps can implement the `find(x)` operation efficiently. However, the real benefit of a Treap is that it can support the `add(x)` and `delete(x)` operations. To do this, it needs to perform rotations in order to maintain the heap property. Refer to Figure 7.6. A *rotation* in a binary search tree is a local modification that takes a parent u of a node w and makes w the parent of u, while preserving the binary search tree property. Rotations come in two flavours: *left* or *right* depending on whether w is a right or left child of u, respectively.

The code that implements this has to handle these two possibilities and be careful of a boundary case (when u is the root), so the actual code is a little longer than Figure 7.6 would lead a reader to believe:

BinarySearchTree
```
void rotateLeft(Node u) {
  Node w = u.right;
  w.parent = u.parent;
  if (w.parent != nil) {
    if (w.parent.left == u) {
      w.parent.left = w;
    } else {
```

[3]The rank of an element x in a set S of elements is the number of elements in S that are less than x.

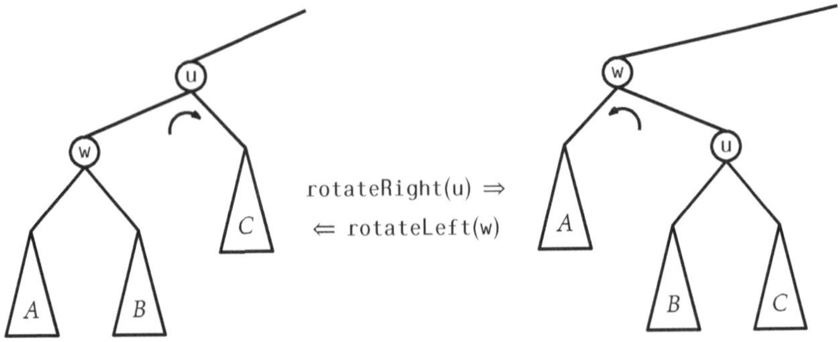

Figure 7.6: Left and right rotations in a binary search tree.

```
      w.parent.right = w;
    }
  }
  u.right = w.left;
  if (u.right != nil) {
    u.right.parent = u;
  }
  u.parent = w;
  w.left = u;
  if (u == r) { r = w; r.parent = nil; }
}
void rotateRight(Node u) {
  Node w = u.left;
  w.parent = u.parent;
  if (w.parent != nil) {
    if (w.parent.left == u) {
      w.parent.left = w;
    } else {
      w.parent.right = w;
    }
  }
  u.left = w.right;
  if (u.left != nil) {
    u.left.parent = u;
  }
  u.parent = w;
  w.right = u;
```

```
  if (u == r) { r = w; r.parent = nil; }
}
```

In terms of the Treap data structure, the most important property of a rotation is that the depth of w decreases by one while the depth of u increases by one.

Using rotations, we can implement the add(x) operation as follows: We create a new node, u, assign u.x = x, and pick a random value for u.p. Next we add u using the usual add(x) algorithm for a BinarySearchTree, so that u is now a leaf of the Treap. At this point, our Treap satisfies the binary search tree property, but not necessarily the heap property. In particular, it may be the case that u.parent.p > u.p. If this is the case, then we perform a rotation at node w=u.parent so that u becomes the parent of w. If u continues to violate the heap property, we will have to repeat this, decreasing u's depth by one every time, until u either becomes the root or u.parent.p < u.p.

```
Treap
boolean add(T x) {
  Node<T> u = newNode();
  u.x = x;
  u.p = rand.nextInt();
  if (super.add(u)) {
    bubbleUp(u);
    return true;
  }
  return false;
}
void bubbleUp(Node<T> u) {
  while (u.parent != nil && u.parent.p > u.p) {
    if (u.parent.right == u) {
      rotateLeft(u.parent);
    } else {
      rotateRight(u.parent);
    }
  }
  if (u.parent == nil) {
    r = u;
  }
```

```
}
```

An example of an add(x) operation is shown in Figure 7.7.

The running time of the add(x) operation is given by the time it takes to follow the search path for x plus the number of rotations performed to move the newly-added node, u, up to its correct location in the Treap. By Lemma 7.2, the expected length of the search path is at most $2\ln n + O(1)$. Furthermore, each rotation decreases the depth of u. This stops if u becomes the root, so the expected number of rotations cannot exceed the expected length of the search path. Therefore, the expected running time of the add(x) operation in a Treap is $O(\log n)$. (Exercise 7.5 asks you to show that the expected number of rotations performed during an addition is actually only $O(1)$.)

The remove(x) operation in a Treap is the opposite of the add(x) operation. We search for the node, u, containing x, then perform rotations to move u downwards until it becomes a leaf, and then we splice u from the Treap. Notice that, to move u downwards, we can perform either a left or right rotation at u, which will replace u with u.right or u.left, respectively. The choice is made by the first of the following that apply:

1. If u.left and u.right are both null, then u is a leaf and no rotation is performed.

2. If u.left (or u.right) is null, then perform a right (or left, respectively) rotation at u.

3. If u.left.p < u.right.p (or u.left.p > u.right.p), then perform a right rotation (or left rotation, respectively) at u.

These three rules ensure that the Treap doesn't become disconnected and that the heap property is restored once u is removed.

Treap

```
boolean remove(T x) {
  Node<T> u = findLast(x);
  if (u != nil && compare(u.x, x) == 0) {
    trickleDown(u);
    splice(u);
    return true;
```

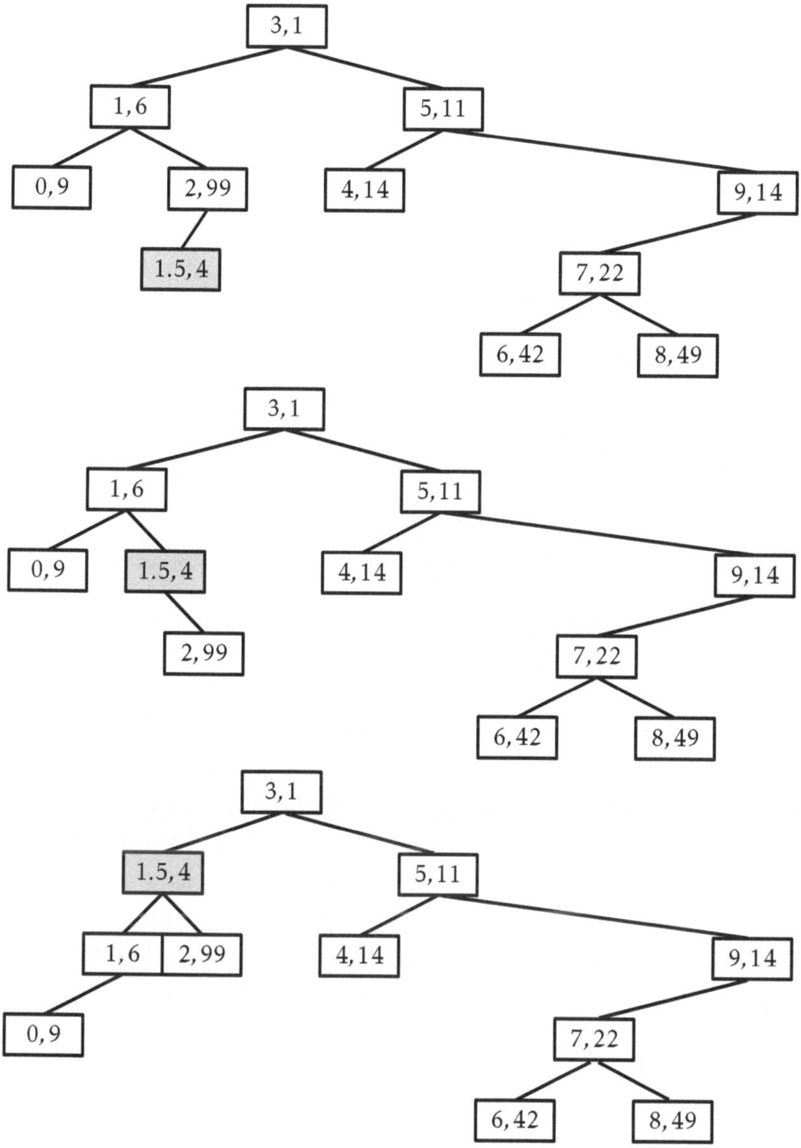

Figure 7.7: Adding the value 1.5 into the Treap from Figure 7.5.

```
  }
  return false;
}
void trickleDown(Node<T> u) {
  while (u.left != nil || u.right != nil) {
    if (u.left == nil) {
      rotateLeft(u);
    } else if (u.right == nil) {
      rotateRight(u);
    } else if (u.left.p < u.right.p) {
      rotateRight(u);
    } else {
      rotateLeft(u);
    }
    if (r == u) {
      r = u.parent;
    }
  }
}
```

An example of the remove(x) operation is shown in Figure 7.8.

The trick to analyze the running time of the remove(x) operation is to notice that this operation reverses the add(x) operation. In particular, if we were to reinsert x, using the same priority u.p, then the add(x) operation would do exactly the same number of rotations and would restore the Treap to exactly the same state it was in before the remove(x) operation took place. (Reading from bottom-to-top, Figure 7.8 illustrates the addition of the value 9 into a Treap.) This means that the expected running time of the remove(x) on a Treap of size n is proportional to the expected running time of the add(x) operation on a Treap of size n−1. We conclude that the expected running time of remove(x) is $O(\log n)$.

7.2.1 Summary

The following theorem summarizes the performance of the Treap data structure:

Theorem 7.2. *A Treap implements the SSet interface. A Treap supports the operations* add(x), remove(x), *and* find(x) *in* $O(\log n)$ *expected time per*

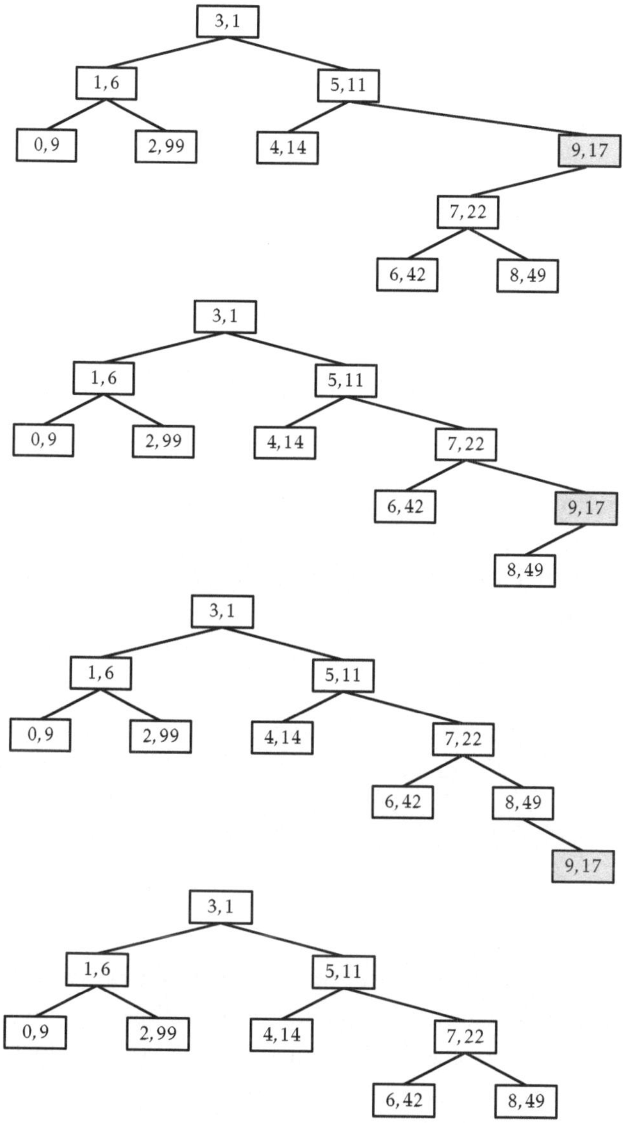

Figure 7.8: Removing the value 9 from the Treap in Figure 7.5.

operation.

It is worth comparing the Treap data structure to the SkiplistSSet data structure. Both implement the SSet operations in $O(\log n)$ expected time per operation. In both data structures, add(x) and remove(x) involve a search and then a constant number of pointer changes (see Exercise 7.5 below). Thus, for both these structures, the expected length of the search path is the critical value in assessing their performance. In a SkiplistSSet, the expected length of a search path is

$$2\log n + O(1) \ ,$$

In a Treap, the expected length of a search path is

$$2\ln n + O(1) \approx 1.386\log n + O(1) \ .$$

Thus, the search paths in a Treap are considerably shorter and this translates into noticeably faster operations on Treaps than Skiplists. Exercise 4.7 in Chapter 4 shows how the expected length of the search path in a Skiplist can be reduced to

$$e\ln n + O(1) \approx 1.884\log n + O(1)$$

by using biased coin tosses. Even with this optimization, the expected length of search paths in a SkiplistSSet is noticeably longer than in a Treap.

7.3 Discussion and Exercises

Random binary search trees have been studied extensively. Devroye [19] gives a proof of Lemma 7.1 and related results. There are much stronger results in the literature as well, the most impressive of which is due to Reed [64], who shows that the expected height of a random binary search tree is

$$\alpha\ln n - \beta\ln\ln n + O(1)$$

where $\alpha \approx 4.31107$ is the unique solution on the interval $[2,\infty)$ of the equation $\alpha\ln((2e/\alpha)) = 1$ and $\beta = \frac{3}{2\ln(\alpha/2)}$. Furthermore, the variance of the height is constant.

The name Treap was coined by Seidel and Aragon [67] who discussed Treaps and some of their variants. However, their basic structure was studied much earlier by Vuillemin [76] who called them Cartesian trees.

One possible space-optimization of the Treap data structure is the elimination of the explicit storage of the priority p in each node. Instead, the priority of a node, u, is computed by hashing u's address in memory (in 32-bit Java, this is equivalent to hashing u.hashCode()). Although a number of hash functions will probably work well for this in practice, for the important parts of the proof of Lemma 7.1 to remain valid, the hash function should be randomized and have the *min-wise independent property*: For any distinct values $x_1,\ldots,x_k$, each of the hash values $h(x_1),\ldots,h(x_k)$ should be distinct with high probability and, for each $i \in \{1,\ldots,k\}$,

$$\Pr\{h(x_i) = \min\{h(x_1),\ldots,h(x_k)\}\} \leq c/k$$

for some constant c. One such class of hash functions that is easy to implement and fairly fast is *tabulation hashing* (Section 5.2.3).

Another Treap variant that doesn't store priorities at each node is the randomized binary search tree of Martínez and Roura [51]. In this variant, every node, u, stores the size, u.size, of the subtree rooted at u. Both the add(x) and remove(x) algorithms are randomized. The algorithm for adding x to the subtree rooted at u does the following:

1. With probability 1/(size(u)+1), the value x is added the usual way, as a leaf, and rotations are then done to bring x up to the root of this subtree.

2. Otherwise (with probability 1 − 1/(size(u) + 1)), the value x is recursively added into one of the two subtrees rooted at u.left or u.right, as appropriate.

The first case corresponds to an add(x) operation in a Treap where x's node receives a random priority that is smaller than any of the size(u) priorities in u's subtree, and this case occurs with exactly the same probability.

Removing a value x from a randomized binary search tree is similar to the process of removing from a Treap. We find the node, u, that contains x and then perform rotations that repeatedly increase the depth of u until it becomes a leaf, at which point we can splice it from the tree. The choice of whether to perform a left or right rotation at each step is randomized.

1. With probability u.left.size/(u.size − 1), we perform a right rotation at u, making u.left the root of the subtree that was formerly rooted at u.

2. With probability u.right.size/(u.size − 1), we perform a left rotation at u, making u.right the root of the subtree that was formerly rooted at u.

Again, we can easily verify that these are exactly the same probabilities that the removal algorithm in a Treap will perform a left or right rotation of u.

Randomized binary search trees have the disadvantage, compared to treaps, that when adding and removing elements they make many random choices, and they must maintain the sizes of subtrees. One advantage of randomized binary search trees over treaps is that subtree sizes can serve another useful purpose, namely to provide access by rank in $O(\log n)$ expected time (see Exercise 7.10). In comparison, the random priorities stored in treap nodes have no use other than keeping the treap balanced.

Exercise 7.1. Illustrate the addition of 4.5 (with priority 7) and then 7.5 (with priority 20) on the Treap in Figure 7.5.

Exercise 7.2. Illustrate the removal of 5 and then 7 on the Treap in Figure 7.5.

Exercise 7.3. Prove the assertion that there are 21,964,800 sequences that generate the tree on the right hand side of Figure 7.1. (Hint: Give a recursive formula for the number of sequences that generate a complete binary tree of height h and evaluate this formula for $h = 3$.)

Exercise 7.4. Design and implement the permute(a) method that takes as input an array, a, that contains n distinct values and randomly permutes a. The method should run in $O(n)$ time and you should prove that each of the n! possible permutations of a is equally probable.

Exercise 7.5. Use both parts of Lemma 7.2 to prove that the expected number of rotations performed by an add(x) operation (and hence also a remove(x) operation) is $O(1)$.

Exercise 7.6. Modify the Treap implementation given here so that it does not explicitly store priorities. Instead, it should simulate them by hashing the hashCode() of each node.

Exercise 7.7. Suppose that a binary search tree stores, at each node, u, the height, u.height, of the subtree rooted at u, and the size, u.size of the subtree rooted at u.

1. Show how, if we perform a left or right rotation at u, then these two quantities can be updated, in constant time, for all nodes affected by the rotation.

2. Explain why the same result is not possible if we try to also store the depth, u.depth, of each node u.

Exercise 7.8. Design and implement an algorithm that constructs a Treap from a sorted array, a, of n elements. This method should run in $O(\mathtt{n})$ worst-case time and should construct a Treap that is indistinguishable from one in which the elements of a were added one at a time using the add(x) method.

Exercise 7.9. This exercise works out the details of how one can efficiently search a Treap given a pointer that is close to the node we are searching for.

1. Design and implement a Treap implementation in which each node keeps track of the minimum and maximum values in its subtree.

2. Using this extra information, add a fingerFind(x,u) method that executes the find(x) operation with the help of a pointer to the node u (which is hopefully not far from the node that contains x). This operation should start at u and walk upwards until it reaches a node w such that $\mathtt{w.min} \le \mathtt{x} \le \mathtt{w.max}$. From that point onwards, it should perform a standard search for x starting from w. (One can show that fingerFind(x,u) takes $O(1 + \log r)$ time, where r is the number of elements in the treap whose value is between x and u.x.)

3. Extend your implementation into a version of a treap that starts all its find(x) operations from the node most recently found by find(x).

Exercise 7.10. Design and implement a version of a Treap that includes a get(i) operation that returns the key with rank i in the Treap. (Hint: Have each node, u, keep track of the size of the subtree rooted at u.)

Exercise 7.11. Implement a TreapList, an implementation of the List interface as a treap. Each node in the treap should store a list item, and an in-order traversal of the treap finds the items in the same order that they occur in the list. All the List operations get(i), set(i,x), add(i,x) and remove(i) should run in $O(\log n)$ expected time.

Exercise 7.12. Design and implement a version of a Treap that supports the split(x) operation. This operation removes all values from the Treap that are greater than x and returns a second Treap that contains all the removed values.
Example: the code t2 = t.split(x) removes from t all values greater than x and returns a new Treap t2 containing all these values. The split(x) operation should run in $O(\log n)$ expected time.
Warning: For this modification to work properly and still allow the size() method to run in constant time, it is necessary to implement the modifications in Exercise 7.10.

Exercise 7.13. Design and implement a version of a Treap that supports the absorb(t2) operation, which can be thought of as the inverse of the split(x) operation. This operation removes all values from the Treap t2 and adds them to the receiver. This operation presupposes that the smallest value in t2 is greater than the largest value in the receiver. The absorb(t2) operation should run in $O(\log n)$ expected time.

Exercise 7.14. Implement Martinez's randomized binary search trees, as discussed in this section. Compare the performance of your implementation with that of the Treap implementation.

Chapter 8

Scapegoat Trees

In this chapter, we study a binary search tree data structure, the ScapegoatTree. This structure is based on the common wisdom that, when something goes wrong, the first thing people tend to do is find someone to blame (the *scapegoat*). Once blame is firmly established, we can leave the scapegoat to fix the problem.

A ScapegoatTree keeps itself balanced by *partial rebuilding operations*. During a partial rebuilding operation, an entire subtree is deconstructed and rebuilt into a perfectly balanced subtree. There are many ways of rebuilding a subtree rooted at node u into a perfectly balanced tree. One of the simplest is to traverse u's subtree, gathering all its nodes into an array, a, and then to recursively build a balanced subtree using a. If we let m = a.length/2, then the element a[m] becomes the root of the new subtree, a[0],...,a[m − 1] get stored recursively in the left subtree and a[m + 1],...,a[a.length − 1] get stored recursively in the right subtree.

```
ScapegoatTree
void rebuild(Node<T> u) {
  int ns = size(u);
  Node<T> p = u.parent;
  Node<T>[] a =  Array.newInstance(Node.class, ns);
  packIntoArray(u, a, 0);
  if (p == nil) {
    r = buildBalanced(a, 0, ns);
    r.parent = nil;
  } else if (p.right == u) {
    p.right = buildBalanced(a, 0, ns);
```

```
    p.right.parent = p;
  } else {
    p.left = buildBalanced(a, 0, ns);
    p.left.parent = p;
  }
}
int packIntoArray(Node<T> u, Node<T>[] a, int i) {
  if (u == nil) {
    return i;
  }
  i = packIntoArray(u.left, a, i);
  a[i++] = u;
  return packIntoArray(u.right, a, i);
}
Node<T> buildBalanced(Node<T>[] a, int i, int ns) {
  if (ns == 0)
    return nil;
  int m = ns / 2;
  a[i + m].left = buildBalanced(a, i, m);
  if (a[i + m].left != nil)
    a[i + m].left.parent = a[i + m];
  a[i + m].right = buildBalanced(a, i + m + 1, ns - m - 1);
  if (a[i + m].right != nil)
    a[i + m].right.parent = a[i + m];
  return a[i + m];
}
```

A call to `rebuild(u)` takes $O(\mathtt{size(u)})$ time. The resulting subtree has minimum height; there is no tree of smaller height that has `size(u)` nodes.

8.1 ScapegoatTree: A Binary Search Tree with Partial Rebuilding

A ScapegoatTree is a BinarySearchTree that, in addition to keeping track of the number, n, of nodes in the tree also keeps a counter, q, that maintains an upper-bound on the number of nodes.

ScapegoatTree

```
int q;
```

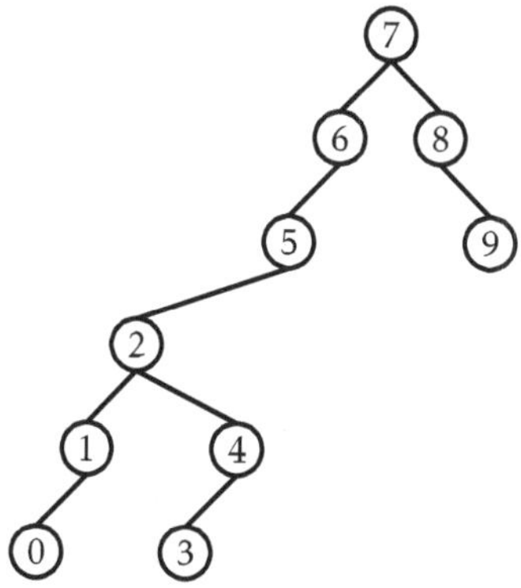

Figure 8.1: A ScapegoatTree with 10 nodes and height 5.

At all times, n and q obey the following inequalities:

$$q/2 \leq n \leq q \ .$$

In addition, a ScapegoatTree has logarithmic height; at all times, the height of the scapegoat tree does not exceed:

$$\log_{3/2} q \leq \log_{3/2} 2n < \log_{3/2} n + 2 \ . \tag{8.1}$$

Even with this constraint, a ScapegoatTree can look surprisingly unbalanced. The tree in Figure 8.1 has $q = n = 10$ and height $5 < \log_{3/2} 10 \approx 5.679$.

Implementing the find(x) operation in a ScapegoatTree is done using the standard algorithm for searching in a BinarySearchTree (see Section 6.2). This takes time proportional to the height of the tree which, by (8.1) is $O(\log n)$.

To implement the add(x) operation, we first increment n and q and then use the usual algorithm for adding x to a binary search tree; we search for x and then add a new leaf u with u.x = x. At this point, we may get lucky and the depth of u might not exceed $\log_{3/2} q$. If so, then we leave well enough alone and don't do anything else.

Unfortunately, it will sometimes happen that $\text{depth}(u) > \log_{3/2} q$. In this case, we need to reduce the height. This isn't a big job; there is only one node, namely u, whose depth exceeds $\log_{3/2} q$. To fix u, we walk from u back up to the root looking for a *scapegoat*, w. The scapegoat, w, is a very unbalanced node. It has the property that

$$\frac{\texttt{size(w.child)}}{\texttt{size(w)}} > \frac{2}{3}\ , \tag{8.2}$$

where w.child is the child of w on the path from the root to u. We'll very shortly prove that a scapegoat exists. For now, we can take it for granted. Once we've found the scapegoat w, we completely destroy the subtree rooted at w and rebuild it into a perfectly balanced binary search tree. We know, from (8.2), that, even before the addition of u, w's subtree was not a complete binary tree. Therefore, when we rebuild w, the height decreases by at least 1 so that height of the ScapegoatTree is once again at most $\log_{3/2} q$.

ScapegoatTree

```
boolean add(T x) {
  // first do basic insertion keeping track of depth
  Node<T> u = newNode(x);
  int d = addWithDepth(u);
  if (d > log32(q)) {
    // depth exceeded, find scapegoat
    Node<T> w = u.parent;
    while (3*size(w) <= 2*size(w.parent))
      w = w.parent;
    rebuild(w.parent);
  }
  return d >= 0;
}
```

If we ignore the cost of finding the scapegoat w and rebuilding the subtree rooted at w, then the running time of add(x) is dominated by the initial search, which takes $O(\log q) = O(\log n)$ time. We will account for the cost of finding the scapegoat and rebuilding using amortized analysis in the next section.

The implementation of remove(x) in a ScapegoatTree is very simple. We search for x and remove it using the usual algorithm for removing a node from a BinarySearchTree. (Note that this can never increase the

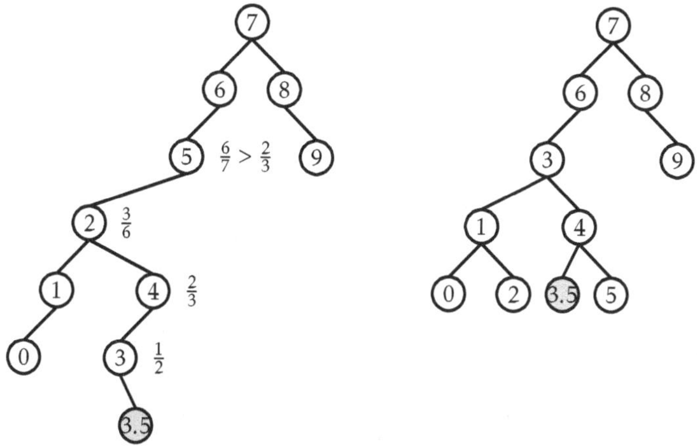

Figure 8.2: Inserting 3.5 into a ScapegoatTree increases its height to 6, which violates (8.1) since $6 > \log_{3/2} 11 \approx 5.914$. A scapegoat is found at the node containing 5.

height of the tree.) Next, we decrement n, but leave q unchanged. Finally, we check if q > 2n and, if so, then we *rebuild the entire tree* into a perfectly balanced binary search tree and set q = n.

```
ScapegoatTree
boolean remove(T x) {
  if (super.remove(x)) {
    if (2*n < q) {
      rebuild(r);
      q = n;
    }
    return true;
  }
  return false;
}
```

Again, if we ignore the cost of rebuilding, the running time of the remove(x) operation is proportional to the height of the tree, and is therefore $O(\log n)$.

8.1.1 Analysis of Correctness and Running-Time

In this section, we analyze the correctness and amortized running time of operations on a ScapegoatTree. We first prove the correctness by showing that, when the add(x) operation results in a node that violates Condition (8.1), then we can always find a scapegoat:

Lemma 8.1. *Let* u *be a node of depth $h > \log_{3/2} \mathtt{q}$ in a* ScapegoatTree. *Then there exists a node* w *on the path from* u *to the root such that*

$$\frac{\mathtt{size(w)}}{\mathtt{size(parent(w))}} > 2/3 \ .$$

Proof. Suppose, for the sake of contradiction, that this is not the case, and

$$\frac{\mathtt{size(w)}}{\mathtt{size(parent(w))}} \le 2/3 \ .$$

for all nodes w on the path from u to the root. Denote the path from the root to u as $\mathtt{r} = \mathtt{u}_0, \ldots, \mathtt{u}_h = \mathtt{u}$. Then, we have $\mathtt{size(u_0)} = \mathtt{n}$, $\mathtt{size(u_1)} \le \frac{2}{3}\mathtt{n}$, $\mathtt{size(u_2)} \le \frac{4}{9}\mathtt{n}$ and, more generally,

$$\mathtt{size(u}_i\mathtt{)} \le \left(\frac{2}{3}\right)^i \mathtt{n} \ .$$

But this gives a contradiction, since $\mathtt{size(u)} \ge 1$, hence

$$1 \le \mathtt{size(u)} \le \left(\frac{2}{3}\right)^h \mathtt{n} < \left(\frac{2}{3}\right)^{\log_{3/2} \mathtt{q}} \mathtt{n} \le \left(\frac{2}{3}\right)^{\log_{3/2} \mathtt{n}} \mathtt{n} = \left(\frac{1}{\mathtt{n}}\right) \mathtt{n} = 1 \ . \qquad \square$$

Next, we analyze the parts of the running time that are not yet accounted for. There are two parts: The cost of calls to size(u) when searching for scapegoat nodes, and the cost of calls to rebuild(w) when we find a scapegoat w. The cost of calls to size(u) can be related to the cost of calls to rebuild(w), as follows:

Lemma 8.2. *During a call to* add(x) *in a* ScapegoatTree, *the cost of finding the scapegoat* w *and rebuilding the subtree rooted at* w *is* $O(\mathtt{size(w)})$.

Proof. The cost of rebuilding the scapegoat node w, once we find it, is $O(\mathtt{size(w)})$. When searching for the scapegoat node, we call size(u) on a sequence of nodes $\mathtt{u}_0,\ldots,\mathtt{u}_k$ until we find the scapegoat $\mathtt{u}_k = \mathtt{w}$. However, since $\mathtt{u}_k$ is the first node in this sequence that is a scapegoat, we know that

$$\mathtt{size}(\mathtt{u}_i) < \frac{2}{3}\mathtt{size}(\mathtt{u}_{i+1})$$

for all $i \in \{0,\ldots,k-2\}$. Therefore, the cost of all calls to $\mathtt{size(u)}$ is

$$\begin{aligned}
O\left(\sum_{i=0}^{k}\mathtt{size}(\mathtt{u}_{k-i})\right) &= O\left(\mathtt{size}(\mathtt{u}_k) + \sum_{i=0}^{k-1}\mathtt{size}(\mathtt{u}_{k-i-1})\right) \\
&= O\left(\mathtt{size}(\mathtt{u}_k) + \sum_{i=0}^{k-1}\left(\frac{2}{3}\right)^i\mathtt{size}(\mathtt{u}_k)\right) \\
&= O\left(\mathtt{size}(\mathtt{u}_k)\left(1 + \sum_{i=0}^{k-1}\left(\frac{2}{3}\right)^i\right)\right) \\
&= O(\mathtt{size}(\mathtt{u}_k)) = O(\mathtt{size}(\mathtt{w})) \enspace ,
\end{aligned}$$

where the last line follows from the fact that the sum is a geometrically decreasing series. □

All that remains is to prove an upper-bound on the cost of all calls to $\mathtt{rebuild(u)}$ during a sequence of m operations:

Lemma 8.3. *Starting with an empty* ScapegoatTree *any sequence of m* $\mathtt{add(x)}$ *and* $\mathtt{remove(x)}$ *operations causes at most $O(m\log m)$ time to be used by* $\mathtt{rebuild(u)}$ *operations.*

Proof. To prove this, we will use a *credit scheme*. We imagine that each node stores a number of credits. Each credit can pay for some constant, c, units of time spent rebuilding. The scheme gives out a total of $O(m\log m)$ credits and every call to $\mathtt{rebuild(u)}$ is paid for with credits stored at u.

During an insertion or deletion, we give one credit to each node on the path to the inserted node, or deleted node, u. In this way we hand out at most $\log_{3/2}\mathtt{q} \le \log_{3/2} m$ credits per operation. During a deletion we also store an additional credit "on the side." Thus, in total we give out at most $O(m\log m)$ credits. All that remains is to show that these credits are sufficient to pay for all calls to $\mathtt{rebuild(u)}$.

If we call $\texttt{rebuild}(\mathtt{u})$ during an insertion, it is because $\mathtt{u}$ is a scapegoat. Suppose, without loss of generality, that

$$\frac{\mathtt{size}(\mathtt{u.left})}{\mathtt{size}(\mathtt{u})} > \frac{2}{3} \ .$$

Using the fact that

$$\mathtt{size}(\mathtt{u}) = 1 + \mathtt{size}(\mathtt{u.left}) + \mathtt{size}(\mathtt{u.right})$$

we deduce that

$$\frac{1}{2}\mathtt{size}(\mathtt{u.left}) > \mathtt{size}(\mathtt{u.right})$$

and therefore

$$\mathtt{size}(\mathtt{u.left}) - \mathtt{size}(\mathtt{u.right}) > \frac{1}{2}\mathtt{size}(\mathtt{u.left}) > \frac{1}{3}\mathtt{size}(\mathtt{u}) \ .$$

Now, the last time a subtree containing $\mathtt{u}$ was rebuilt (or when $\mathtt{u}$ was inserted, if a subtree containing $\mathtt{u}$ was never rebuilt), we had

$$\mathtt{size}(\mathtt{u.left}) - \mathtt{size}(\mathtt{u.right}) \le 1 \ .$$

Therefore, the number of $\mathtt{add}(\mathtt{x})$ or $\mathtt{remove}(\mathtt{x})$ operations that have affected $\mathtt{u.left}$ or $\mathtt{u.right}$ since then is at least

$$\frac{1}{3}\mathtt{size}(\mathtt{u}) - 1 \ .$$

and there are therefore at least this many credits stored at $\mathtt{u}$ that are available to pay for the $O(\mathtt{size}(\mathtt{u}))$ time it takes to call $\texttt{rebuild}(\mathtt{u})$.

If we call $\texttt{rebuild}(\mathtt{u})$ during a deletion, it is because $\mathtt{q} > 2\mathtt{n}$. In this case, we have $\mathtt{q} - \mathtt{n} > \mathtt{n}$ credits stored "on the side," and we use these to pay for the $O(\mathtt{n})$ time it takes to rebuild the root. This completes the proof. □

8.1.2 Summary

The following theorem summarizes the performance of the ScapegoatTree data structure:

Theorem 8.1. *A* ScapegoatTree *implements the* SSet *interface. Ignoring the cost of* rebuild(u) *operations, a* ScapegoatTree *supports the operations* add(x), remove(x), *and* find(x) *in* $O(\log n)$ *time per operation.*

Furthermore, beginning with an empty ScapegoatTree*, any sequence of* m add(x) *and* remove(x) *operations results in a total of* $O(m \log m)$ *time spent during all calls to* rebuild(u).

8.2 Discussion and Exercises

The term *scapegoat tree* is due to Galperin and Rivest [33], who define and analyze these trees. However, the same structure was discovered earlier by Andersson [5, 7], who called them *general balanced trees* since they can have any shape as long as their height is small.

Experimenting with the ScapegoatTree implementation will reveal that it is often considerably slower than the other SSet implementations in this book. This may be somewhat surprising, since height bound of

$$\log_{3/2} q \approx 1.709 \log n + O(1)$$

is better than the expected length of a search path in a Skiplist and not too far from that of a Treap. The implementation could be optimized by storing the sizes of subtrees explicitly at each node or by reusing already computed subtree sizes (Exercises 8.5 and 8.6). Even with these optimizations, there will always be sequences of add(x) and delete(x) operation for which a ScapegoatTree takes longer than other SSet implementations.

This gap in performance is due to the fact that, unlike the other SSet implementations discussed in this book, a ScapegoatTree can spend a lot of time restructuring itself. Exercise 8.3 asks you to prove that there are sequences of n operations in which a ScapegoatTree will spend on the order of $n \log n$ time in calls to rebuild(u). This is in contrast to other SSet implementations discussed in this book, which only make $O(n)$ structural changes during a sequence of n operations. This is, unfortunately, a necessary consequence of the fact that a ScapegoatTree does all its restructuring by calls to rebuild(u) [20].

Despite their lack of performance, there are applications in which a

ScapegoatTree could be the right choice. This would occur any time there is additional data associated with nodes that cannot be updated in constant time when a rotation is performed, but that can be updated during a rebuild(u) operation. In such cases, the ScapegoatTree and related structures based on partial rebuilding may work. An example of such an application is outlined in Exercise 8.11.

Exercise 8.1. Illustrate the addition of the values 1.5 and then 1.6 on the ScapegoatTree in Figure 8.1.

Exercise 8.2. Illustrate what happens when the sequence 1,5,2,4,3 is added to an empty ScapegoatTree, and show where the credits described in the proof of Lemma 8.3 go, and how they are used during this sequence of additions.

Exercise 8.3. Show that, if we start with an empty ScapegoatTree and call add(x) for x = $1,2,3,\ldots,$n, then the total time spent during calls to rebuild(u) is at least $cn\log n$ for some constant $c > 0$.

Exercise 8.4. The ScapegoatTree, as described in this chapter, guarantees that the length of the search path does not exceed $\log_{3/2} q$.

1. Design, analyze, and implement a modified version of ScapegoatTree where the length of the search path does not exceed $\log_b q$, where b is a parameter with $1 < b < 2$.

2. What does your analysis and/or your experiments say about the amortized cost of find(x), add(x) and remove(x) as a function of n and b?

Exercise 8.5. Modify the add(x) method of the ScapegoatTree so that it does not waste any time recomputing the sizes of subtrees that have already been computed. This is possible because, by the time the method wants to compute size(w), it has already computed one of size(w.left) or size(w.right). Compare the performance of your modified implementation with the implementation given here.

Exercise 8.6. Implement a second version of the ScapegoatTree data structure that explicitly stores and maintains the sizes of the subtree rooted at each node. Compare the performance of the resulting implementation with that of the original ScapegoatTree implementation as well as the implementation from Exercise 8.5.

Exercise 8.7. Reimplement the rebuild(u) method discussed at the beginning of this chapter so that it does not require the use of an array to store the nodes of the subtree being rebuilt. Instead, it should use recursion to first connect the nodes into a linked list and then convert this linked list into a perfectly balanced binary tree. (There are very elegant recursive implementations of both steps.)

Exercise 8.8. Analyze and implement a WeightBalancedTree. This is a tree in which each node u, except the root, maintains the *balance invariant* that size(u) $\leq$ (2/3)size(u.parent). The add(x) and remove(x) operations are identical to the standard BinarySearchTree operations, except that any time the balance invariant is violated at a node u, the subtree rooted at u.parent is rebuilt. Your analysis should show that operations on a WeightBalancedTree run in $O(\log n)$ amortized time.

Exercise 8.9. Analyze and implement a CountdownTree. In a CountdownTree each node u keeps a *timer* u.t. The add(x) and remove(x) operations are exactly the same as in a standard BinarySearchTree except that, whenever one of these operations affects u's subtree, u.t is decremented. When u.t = 0 the entire subtree rooted at u is rebuilt into a perfectly balanced binary search tree. When a node u is involved in a rebuilding operation (either because u is rebuilt or one of u's ancestors is rebuilt) u.t is reset to size(u)/3.

Your analysis should show that operations on a CountdownTree run in $O(\log n)$ amortized time. (Hint: First show that each node u satisfies some version of a balance invariant.)

Exercise 8.10. Analyze and implement a DynamiteTree. In a DynamiteTree each node u keeps tracks of the size of the subtree rooted at u in a variable u.size. The add(x) and remove(x) operations are exactly the same as in a standard BinarySearchTree except that, whenever one of these operations affects a node u's subtree, u *explodes* with probability 1/u.size. When u explodes, its entire subtree is rebuilt into a perfectly balanced binary search tree.

Your analysis should show that operations on a `DynamiteTree` run in $O(\log n)$ expected time.

Exercise 8.11. Design and implement a Sequence data structure that maintains a sequence (list) of elements. It supports these operations:

- `addAfter(e)`: Add a new element after the element e in the sequence. Return the newly added element. (If e is null, the new element is added at the beginning of the sequence.)
- `remove(e)`: Remove e from the sequence.
- `testBefore(e1,e2)`: return `true` if and only if e1 comes before e2 in the sequence.

The first two operations should run in $O(\log n)$ amortized time. The third operation should run in constant time.

The Sequence data structure can be implemented by storing the elements in something like a `ScapegoatTree`, in the same order that they occur in the sequence. To implement `testBefore(e1,e2)` in constant time, each element e is labelled with an integer that encodes the path from the root to e. In this way, `testBefore(e1,e2)` can be implemented by comparing the labels of e1 and e2.

Chapter 9

Red-Black Trees

In this chapter, we present red-black trees, a version of binary search trees with logarithmic height. Red-black trees are one of the most widely used data structures. They appear as the primary search structure in many library implementations, including the Java Collections Framework and several implementations of the C++ Standard Template Library. They are also used within the Linux operating system kernel. There are several reasons for the popularity of red-black trees:

1. A red-black tree storing n values has height at most $2\log n$.
2. The add(x) and remove(x) operations on a red-black tree run in $O(\log n)$ *worst-case* time.
3. The amortized number of rotations performed during an add(x) or remove(x) operation is constant.

The first two of these properties already put red-black trees ahead of skiplists, treaps, and scapegoat trees. Skiplists and treaps rely on randomization and their $O(\log n)$ running times are only expected. Scapegoat trees have a guaranteed bound on their height, but add(x) and remove(x) only run in $O(\log n)$ amortized time. The third property is just icing on the cake. It tells us that that the time needed to add or remove an element x is dwarfed by the time it takes to find x.[1]

However, the nice properties of red-black trees come with a price: implementation complexity. Maintaining a bound of $2\log n$ on the height

[1]Note that skiplists and treaps also have this property in the expected sense. See Exercises 4.6 and 7.5.

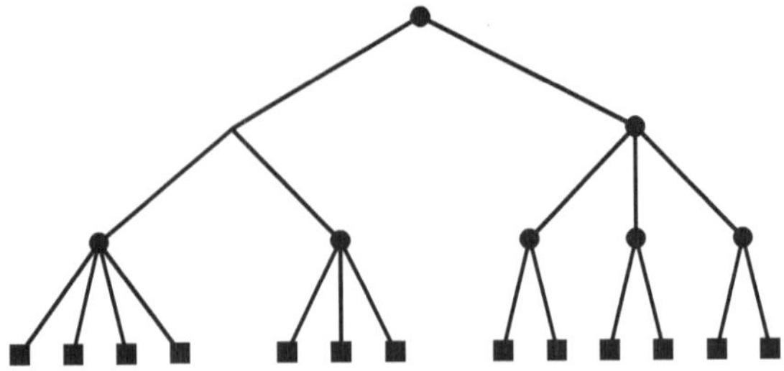

Figure 9.1: A 2-4 tree of height 3.

is not easy. It requires a careful analysis of a number of cases. We must ensure that the implementation does exactly the right thing in each case. One misplaced rotation or change of colour produces a bug that can be very difficult to understand and track down.

Rather than jumping directly into the implementation of red-black trees, we will first provide some background on a related data structure: 2-4 trees. This will give some insight into how red-black trees were discovered and why efficiently maintaining them is even possible.

9.1 2-4 Trees

A 2-4 tree is a rooted tree with the following properties:

Property 9.1 (height)**.** All leaves have the same depth.

Property 9.2 (degree)**.** Every internal node has 2, 3, or 4 children.

An example of a 2-4 tree is shown in Figure 9.1. The properties of 2-4 trees imply that their height is logarithmic in the number of leaves:

Lemma 9.1. *A 2-4 tree with* n *leaves has height at most* $\log \mathtt{n}$.

Proof. The lower-bound of 2 on the number of children of an internal node implies that, if the height of a 2-4 tree is h, then it has at least 2^h leaves. In other words,

$$\mathtt{n} \geq 2^h .$$

Taking logarithms on both sides of this inequality gives $h \leq \log \mathtt{n}$. □

9.1.1 Adding a Leaf

Adding a leaf to a 2-4 tree is easy (see Figure 9.2). If we want to add a leaf u as the child of some node w on the second-last level, then we simply make u a child of w. This certainly maintains the height property, but could violate the degree property; if w had four children prior to adding u, then w now has five children. In this case, we *split* w into two nodes, w and w′, having two and three children, respectively. But now w′ has no parent, so we recursively make w′ a child of w's parent. Again, this may cause w's parent to have too many children in which case we split it. This process goes on until we reach a node that has fewer than four children, or until we split the root, r, into two nodes r and r′. In the latter case, we make a new root that has r and r′ as children. This simultaneously increases the depth of all leaves and so maintains the height property.

Since the height of the 2-4 tree is never more than $\log n$, the process of adding a leaf finishes after at most $\log n$ steps.

9.1.2 Removing a Leaf

Removing a leaf from a 2-4 tree is a little more tricky (see Figure 9.3). To remove a leaf u from its parent w, we just remove it. If w had only two children prior to the removal of u, then w is left with only one child and violates the degree property.

To correct this, we look at w's sibling, w′. The node w′ is sure to exist since w's parent had at least two children. If w′ has three or four children, then we take one of these children from w′ and give it to w. Now w has two children and w′ has two or three children and we are done.

On the other hand, if w′ has only two children, then we *merge* w and w′ into a single node, w, that has three children. Next we recursively remove w′ from the parent of w′. This process ends when we reach a node, u, where u or its sibling has more than two children, or when we reach the root. In the latter case, if the root is left with only one child, then we delete the root and make its child the new root. Again, this simultaneously decreases the height of every leaf and therefore maintains the height property.

Again, since the height of the tree is never more than $\log n$, the process

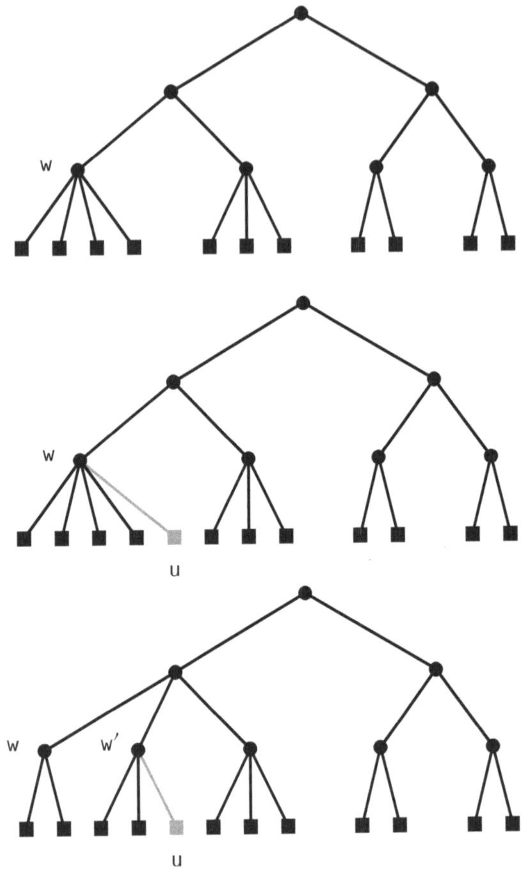

Figure 9.2: Adding a leaf to a 2-4 Tree. This process stops after one split because w.parent has a degree of less than 4 before the addition.

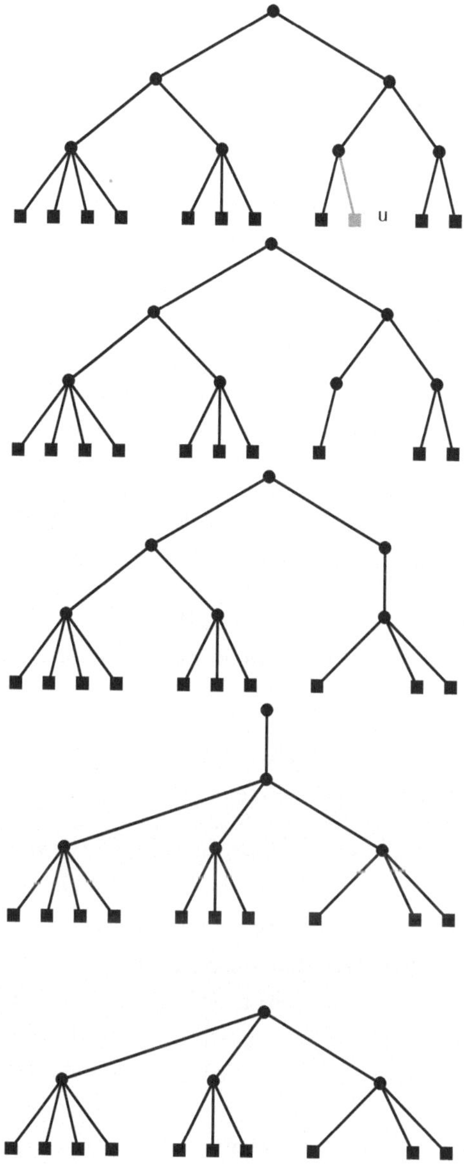

Figure 9.3: Removing a leaf from a 2-4 Tree. This process goes all the way to the root because each of u's ancestors and their siblings have only two children.

of removing a leaf finishes after at most $\log n$ steps.

9.2 RedBlackTree: A Simulated 2-4 Tree

A red-black tree is a binary search tree in which each node, u, has a *colour* which is either *red* or *black*. Red is represented by the value 0 and black by the value 1.

```
RedBlackTree
class Node<T> extends BSTNode<Node<T>,T> {
  byte colour;
}
```

Before and after any operation on a red-black tree, the following two properties are satisfied. Each property is defined both in terms of the colours red and black, and in terms of the numeric values 0 and 1.

Property 9.3 (black-height). There are the same number of black nodes on every root to leaf path. (The sum of the colours on any root to leaf path is the same.)

Property 9.4 (no-red-edge). No two red nodes are adjacent. (For any node u, except the root, u.colour + u.parent.colour ≥ 1.)

Notice that we can always colour the root, r, of a red-black tree black without violating either of these two properties, so we will assume that the root is black, and the algorithms for updating a red-black tree will maintain this. Another trick that simplifies red-black trees is to treat the external nodes (represented by nil) as black nodes. This way, every real node, u, of a red-black tree has exactly two children, each with a well-defined colour. An example of a red-black tree is shown in Figure 9.4.

9.2.1 Red-Black Trees and 2-4 Trees

At first it might seem surprising that a red-black tree can be efficiently updated to maintain the black-height and no-red-edge properties, and it seems unusual to even consider these as useful properties. However,

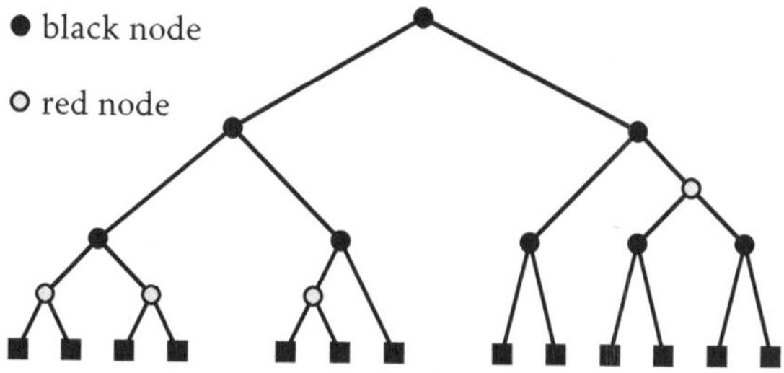

Figure 9.4: An example of a red-black tree with black-height 3. External (nil) nodes are drawn as squares.

red-black trees were designed to be an efficient simulation of 2-4 trees as binary trees.

Refer to Figure 9.5. Consider any red-black tree, T, having n nodes and perform the following transformation: Remove each red node u and connect u's two children directly to the (black) parent of u. After this transformation we are left with a tree T' having only black nodes.

Every internal node in T' has two, three, or four children: A black node that started out with two black children will still have two black children after this transformation. A black node that started out with one red and one black child will have three children after this transformation. A black node that started out with two red children will have four children after this transformation. Furthermore, the black-height property now guarantees that every root-to-leaf path in T' has the same length. In other words, T' is a 2-4 tree!

The 2-4 tree T' has $n+1$ leaves that correspond to the $n+1$ external nodes of the red-black tree. Therefore, this tree has height at most $\log(n+1)$. Now, every root to leaf path in the 2-4 tree corresponds to a path from the root of the red-black tree T to an external node. The first and last node in this path are black and at most one out of every two internal nodes is red, so this path has at most $\log(n+1)$ black nodes and at most $\log(n+1)-1$ red nodes. Therefore, the longest path from the root to any *internal* node in T is at most

$$2\log(n+1)-2 \leq 2\log n \enspace ,$$

for any $n \geq 1$. This proves the most important property of red-black trees:

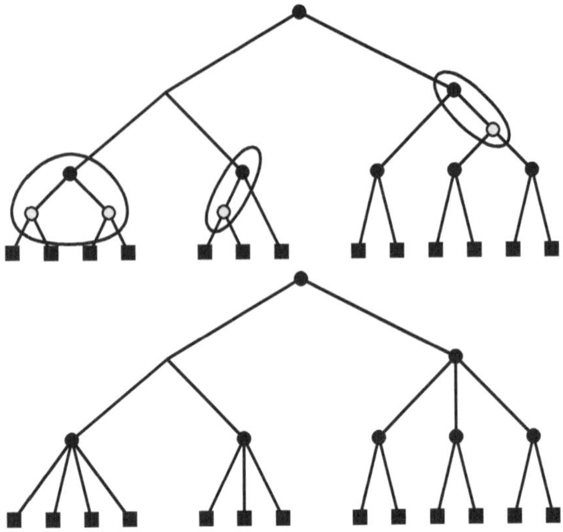

Figure 9.5: Every red-black tree has a corresponding 2-4 tree.

Lemma 9.2. *The height of red-black tree with* n *nodes is at most* $2\log n$.

Now that we have seen the relationship between 2-4 trees and red-black trees, it is not hard to believe that we can efficiently maintain a red-black tree while adding and removing elements.

We have already seen that adding an element in a BinarySearchTree can be done by adding a new leaf. Therefore, to implement add(x) in a red-black tree we need a method of simulating splitting a node with five children in a 2-4 tree. A 2-4 tree node with five children is represented by a black node that has two red children, one of which also has a red child. We can "split" this node by colouring it red and colouring its two children black. An example of this is shown in Figure 9.6.

Similarly, implementing remove(x) requires a method of merging two nodes and borrowing a child from a sibling. Merging two nodes is the inverse of a split (shown in Figure 9.6), and involves colouring two (black) siblings red and colouring their (red) parent black. Borrowing from a sibling is the most complicated of the procedures and involves both rotations and recolouring nodes.

Of course, during all of this we must still maintain the no-red-edge

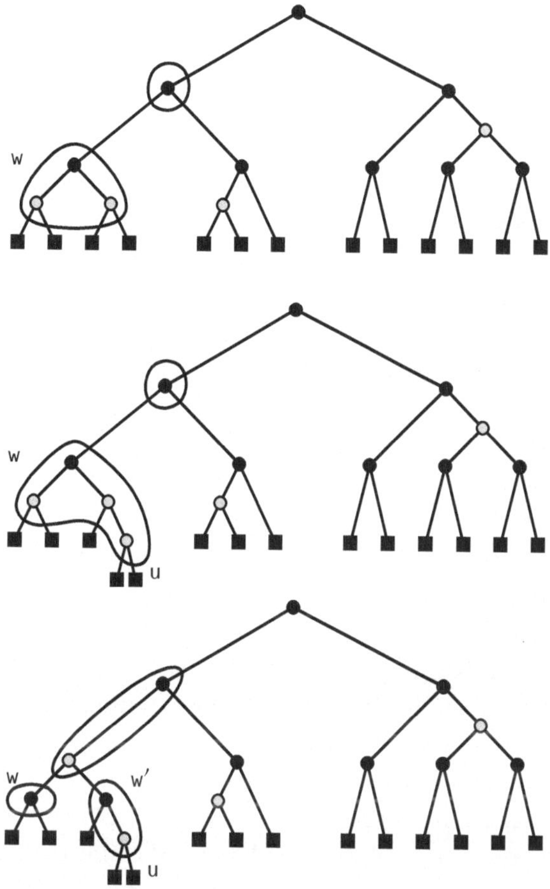

Figure 9.6: Simulating a 2-4 tree split operation during an addition in a red-black tree. (This simulates the 2-4 tree addition shown in Figure 9.2.)

property and the black-height property. While it is no longer surprising that this can be done, there are a large number of cases that have to be considered if we try to do a direct simulation of a 2-4 tree by a red-black tree. At some point, it just becomes simpler to disregard the underlying 2-4 tree and work directly towards maintaining the properties of the red-black tree.

9.2.2 Left-Leaning Red-Black Trees

No single definition of red-black trees exists. Rather, there is a family of structures that manage to maintain the black-height and no-red-edge properties during `add(x)` and `remove(x)` operations. Different structures do this in different ways. Here, we implement a data structure that we call a `RedBlackTree`. This structure implements a particular variant of red-black trees that satisfies an additional property:

Property 9.5 (left-leaning)**.** At any node `u`, if `u.left` is black, then `u.right` is black.

Note that the red-black tree shown in Figure 9.4 does not satisfy the left-leaning property; it is violated by the parent of the red node in the rightmost path.

The reason for maintaining the left-leaning property is that it reduces the number of cases encountered when updating the tree during `add(x)` and `remove(x)` operations. In terms of 2-4 trees, it implies that every 2-4 tree has a unique representation: A node of degree two becomes a black node with two black children. A node of degree three becomes a black node whose left child is red and whose right child is black. A node of degree four becomes a black node with two red children.

Before we describe the implementation of `add(x)` and `remove(x)` in detail, we first present some simple subroutines used by these methods that are illustrated in Figure 9.7. The first two subroutines are for manipulating colours while preserving the black-height property. The `pushBlack(u)` method takes as input a black node `u` that has two red children and colours `u` red and its two children black. The `pullBlack(u)` method reverses this operation:

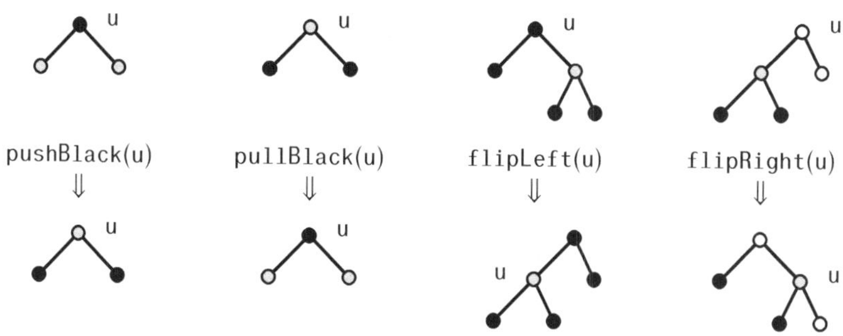

Figure 9.7: Flips, pulls and pushes

```
                              RedBlackTree
void pushBlack(Node<T> u) {
  u.colour--;
  u.left.colour++;
  u.right.colour++;
}
void pullBlack(Node<T> u) {
  u.colour++;
  u.left.colour--;
  u.right.colour--;
}
```

The `flipLeft(u)` method swaps the colours of u and `u.right` and then performs a left rotation at u. This method reverses the colours of these two nodes as well as their parent-child relationship:

```
                              RedBlackTree
void flipLeft(Node<T> u) {
  swapColors(u, u.right);
  rotateLeft(u);
}
```

The `flipLeft(u)` operation is especially useful in restoring the left-leaning property at a node u that violates it (because `u.left` is black and `u.right` is red). In this special case, we can be assured that this operation preserves both the black-height and no-red-edge properties. The flipRight(u) operation is symmetric with flipLeft(u), when the roles of left and right are reversed.

RedBlackTree
```
void flipRight(Node<T> u) {
  swapColors(u, u.left);
  rotateRight(u);
}
```

9.2.3 Addition

To implement add(x) in a RedBlackTree, we perform a standard BinarySearchTree insertion to add a new leaf, u, with u.x = x and set u.colour = red. Note that this does not change the black height of any node, so it does not violate the black-height property. It may, however, violate the left-leaning property (if u is the right child of its parent), and it may violate the no-red-edge property (if u's parent is red). To restore these properties, we call the method addFixup(u).

RedBlackTree
```
boolean add(T x) {
  Node<T> u = newNode(x);
  u.colour = red;
  boolean added = add(u);
  if (added)
    addFixup(u);
  return added;
}
```

Illustrated in Figure 9.8, the addFixup(u) method takes as input a node u whose colour is red and which may violate the no-red-edge property and/or the left-leaning property. The following discussion is probably impossible to follow without referring to Figure 9.8 or recreating it on a piece of paper. Indeed, the reader may wish to study this figure before continuing.

If u is the root of the tree, then we can colour u black to restore both properties. If u's sibling is also red, then u's parent must be black, so both the left-leaning and no-red-edge properties already hold.

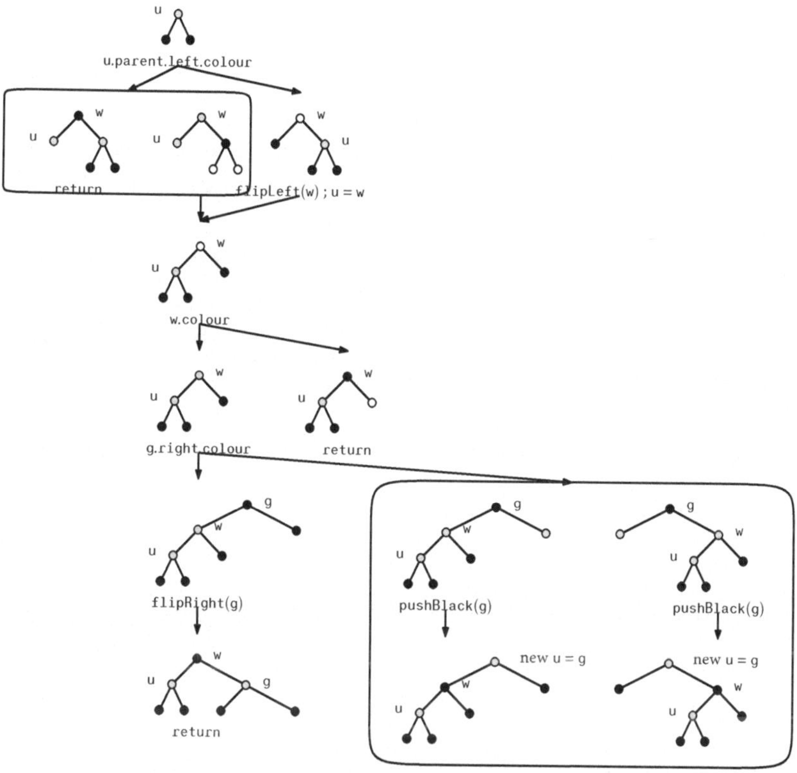

Figure 9.8: A single round in the process of fixing Property 2 after an insertion.

Otherwise, we first determine if u's parent, w, violates the left-leaning property and, if so, perform a flipLeft(w) operation and set u = w. This leaves us in a well-defined state: u is the left child of its parent, w, so w now satisfies the left-leaning property. All that remains is to ensure the no-red-edge property at u. We only have to worry about the case in which w is red, since otherwise u already satisfies the no-red-edge property.

Since we are not done yet, u is red and w is red. The no-red-edge property (which is only violated by u and not by w) implies that u's grandparent g exists and is black. If g's right child is red, then the left-leaning property ensures that both g's children are red, and a call to pushBlack(g) makes g red and w black. This restores the no-red-edge property at u, but may cause it to be violated at g, so the whole process starts over with u = g.

If g's right child is black, then a call to flipRight(g) makes w the (black) parent of g and gives w two red children, u and g. This ensures that u satisfies the no-red-edge property and g satisfies the left-leaning property. In this case we can stop.

RedBlackTree

```
void addFixup(Node<T> u) {
  while (u.colour == red) {
    if (u == r) { // u is the root - done
      u.colour = black;
      return;
    }
    Node<T> w = u.parent;
    if (w.left.colour == black) { // ensure left-leaning
      flipLeft(w);
      u = w;
      w = u.parent;
    }
    if (w.colour == black)
      return; // no red-red edge = done
    Node<T> g = w.parent; // grandparent of u
    if (g.right.colour == black) {
      flipRight(g);
      return;
    } else {
      pushBlack(g);
```

```
            u = g;
        }
    }
}
```

The insertFixup(u) method takes constant time per iteration and each iteration either finishes or moves u closer to the root. Therefore, the insertFixup(u) method finishes after $O(\log n)$ iterations in $O(\log n)$ time.

9.2.4 Removal

The remove(x) operation in a RedBlackTree is the most complicated to implement, and this is true of all known red-black tree variants. Just like the remove(x) operation in a BinarySearchTree, this operation boils down to finding a node w with only one child, u, and splicing w out of the tree by having w.parent adopt u.

The problem with this is that, if w is black, then the black-height property will now be violated at w.parent. We may avoid this problem, temporarily, by adding w.colour to u.colour. Of course, this introduces two other problems: (1) if u and w both started out black, then u.colour + w.colour = 2 (double black), which is an invalid colour. If w was red, then it is replaced by a black node u, which may violate the left-leaning property at u.parent. Both of these problems can be resolved with a call to the removeFixup(u) method.

```
RedBlackTree
boolean remove(T x) {
  Node<T> u = findLast(x);
  if (u == nil || compare(u.x, x) != 0)
    return false;
  Node<T> w = u.right;
  if (w == nil) {
    w = u;
    u = w.left;
  } else {
    while (w.left != nil)
      w = w.left;
```

```
      u.x = w.x;
      u = w.right;
    }
    splice(w);
    u.colour += w.colour;
    u.parent = w.parent;
    removeFixup(u);
    return true;
  }
```

The removeFixup(u) method takes as its input a node u whose colour is black (1) or double-black (2). If u is double-black, then removeFixup(u) performs a series of rotations and recolouring operations that move the double-black node up the tree until it can be eliminated. During this process, the node u changes until, at the end of this process, u refers to the root of the subtree that has been changed. The root of this subtree may have changed colour. In particular, it may have gone from red to black, so the removeFixup(u) method finishes by checking if u's parent violates the left-leaning property and, if so, fixing it.

```
RedBlackTree
void removeFixup(Node<T> u) {
  while (u.colour > black) {
    if (u == r) {
      u.colour = black;
    } else if (u.parent.left.colour == red) {
      u = removeFixupCase1(u);
    } else if (u == u.parent.left) {
      u = removeFixupCase2(u);
    } else {
      u = removeFixupCase3(u);
    }
  }
  if (u != r) { // restore left-leaning property if needed
    Node<T> w = u.parent;
    if (w.right.colour == red && w.left.colour == black) {
      flipLeft(w);
    }
  }
```

```
}
```

The removeFixup(u) method is illustrated in Figure 9.9. Again, the following text will be difficult, if not impossible, to follow without referring to Figure 9.9. Each iteration of the loop in removeFixup(u) processes the double-black node u, based on one of four cases:

Case 0: u is the root. This is the easiest case to treat. We recolour u to be black (this does not violate any of the red-black tree properties).

Case 1: u's sibling, v, is red. In this case, u's sibling is the left child of its parent, w (by the left-leaning property). We perform a right-flip at w and then proceed to the next iteration. Note that this action causes w's parent to violate the left-leaning property and the depth of u to increase. However, it also implies that the next iteration will be in Case 3 with w coloured red. When examining Case 3 below, we will see that the process will stop during the next iteration.

```
RedBlackTree
Node<T> removeFixupCase1(Node<T> u) {
  flipRight(u.parent);
  return u;
}
```

Case 2: u's sibling, v, is black, and u is the left child of its parent, w. In this case, we call pullBlack(w), making u black, v red, and darkening the colour of w to black or double-black. At this point, w does not satisfy the left-leaning property, so we call flipLeft(w) to fix this.

At this point, w is red and v is the root of the subtree with which we started. We need to check if w causes the no-red-edge property to be violated. We do this by inspecting w's right child, q. If q is black, then w satisfies the no-red-edge property and we can continue the next iteration with u = v.

Otherwise (q is red), so both the no-red-edge property and the left-leaning properties are violated at q and w, respectively. The left-leaning property is restored with a call to rotateLeft(w), but the no-red-edge property is still violated. At this point, q is the left child of v, w is the left child of q, q and w are both red, and v is black or double-black. A flipRight(v) makes q the parent of both v and w. Following this up by a

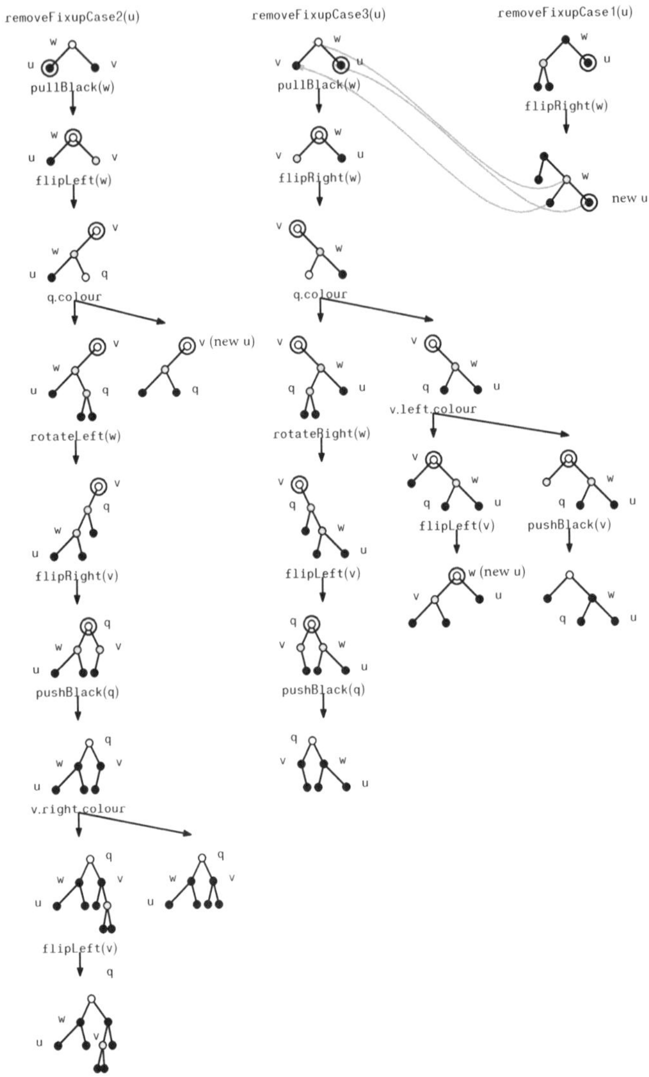

Figure 9.9: A single round in the process of eliminating a double-black node after a removal.

pushBlack(q) makes both v and w black and sets the colour of q back to the original colour of w.

At this point, the double-black node is has been eliminated and the no-red-edge and black-height properties are reestablished. Only one possible problem remains: the right child of v may be red, in which case the left-leaning property would be violated. We check this and perform a flipLeft(v) to correct it if necessary.

```
RedBlackTree
Node<T> removeFixupCase2(Node<T> u) {
  Node<T> w = u.parent;
  Node<T> v = w.right;
  pullBlack(w); // w.left
  flipLeft(w); // w is now red
  Node<T> q = w.right;
  if (q.colour == red) { // q-w is red-red
    rotateLeft(w);
    flipRight(v);
    pushBlack(q);
    if (v.right.colour == red)
      flipLeft(v);
    return q;
  } else {
    return v;
  }
}
```

Case 3: u's sibling is black and u is the right child of its parent, w. This case is symmetric to Case 2 and is handled mostly the same way. The only differences come from the fact that the left-leaning property is asymmetric, so it requires different handling.

As before, we begin with a call to pullBlack(w), which makes v red and u black. A call to flipRight(w) promotes v to the root of the subtree. At this point w is red, and the code branches two ways depending on the colour of w's left child, q.

If q is red, then the code finishes up exactly the same way as Case 2 does, but is even simpler since there is no danger of v not satisfying the left-leaning property.

The more complicated case occurs when q is black. In this case, we examine the colour of v's left child. If it is red, then v has two red children and its extra black can be pushed down with a call to pushBlack(v). At this point, v now has w's original colour, and we are done.

If v's left child is black, then v violates the left-leaning property, and we restore this with a call to flipLeft(v). We then return the node v so that the next iteration of removeFixup(u) then continues with u = v.

```
RedBlackTree
Node<T> removeFixupCase3(Node<T> u) {
  Node<T> w = u.parent;
  Node<T> v = w.left;
  pullBlack(w);
  flipRight(w); // w is now red
  Node<T> q = w.left;
  if (q.colour == red) { // q-w is red-red
    rotateRight(w);
    flipLeft(v);
    pushBlack(q);
    return q;
  } else {
    if (v.left.colour == red) {
      pushBlack(v); // both v's children are red
      return v;
    } else { // ensure left-leaning
      flipLeft(v);
      return w;
    }
  }
}
```

Each iteration of removeFixup(u) takes constant time. Cases 2 and 3 either finish or move u closer to the root of the tree. Case 0 (where u is the root) always terminates and Case 1 leads immediately to Case 3, which also terminates. Since the height of the tree is at most $2\log n$, we conclude that there are at most $O(\log n)$ iterations of removeFixup(u), so removeFixup(u) runs in $O(\log n)$ time.

9.3 Summary

The following theorem summarizes the performance of the `RedBlackTree` data structure:

Theorem 9.1. *A `RedBlackTree` implements the `SSet` interface and supports the operations* `add(x)`, `remove(x)`, *and* `find(x)` *in* $O(\log n)$ *worst-case time per operation.*

Not included in the above theorem is the following extra bonus:

Theorem 9.2. *Beginning with an empty `RedBlackTree`, any sequence of m* `add(x)` *and* `remove(x)` *operations results in a total of $O(m)$ time spent during all calls* `addFixup(u)` *and* `removeFixup(u)`.

We only sketch a proof of Theorem 9.2. By comparing `addFixup(u)` and `removeFixup(u)` with the algorithms for adding or removing a leaf in a 2-4 tree, we can convince ourselves that this property is inherited from a 2-4 tree. In particular, if we can show that the total time spent splitting, merging, and borrowing in a 2-4 tree is $O(m)$, then this implies Theorem 9.2.

The proof of this theorem for 2-4 trees uses the potential method of amortized analysis.[2] Define the potential of an internal node u in a 2-4 tree as

$$\Phi(\mathtt{u}) = \begin{cases} 1 & \text{if u has 2 children} \\ 0 & \text{if u has 3 children} \\ 3 & \text{if u has 4 children} \end{cases}$$

and the potential of a 2-4 tree as the sum of the potentials of its nodes. When a split occurs, it is because a node with four children becomes two nodes, with two and three children. This means that the overall potential drops by $3 - 1 - 0 = 2$. When a merge occurs, two nodes that used to have two children are replaced by one node with three children. The result is a drop in potential of $2 - 0 = 2$. Therefore, for every split or merge, the potential decreases by two.

Next notice that, if we ignore splitting and merging of nodes, there are only a constant number of nodes whose number of children is changed by

[2]See the proofs of Lemma 2.2 and Lemma 3.1 for other applications of the potential method.

the addition or removal of a leaf. When adding a node, one node has its number of children increase by one, increasing the potential by at most three. During the removal of a leaf, one node has its number of children decrease by one, increasing the potential by at most one, and two nodes may be involved in a borrowing operation, increasing their total potential by at most one.

To summarize, each merge and split causes the potential to drop by at least two. Ignoring merging and splitting, each addition or removal causes the potential to rise by at most three, and the potential is always non-negative. Therefore, the number of splits and merges caused by m additions or removals on an initially empty tree is at most $3m/2$. Theorem 9.2 is a consequence of this analysis and the correspondence between 2-4 trees and red-black trees.

9.4 Discussion and Exercises

Red-black trees were first introduced by Guibas and Sedgewick [38]. Despite their high implementation complexity they are found in some of the most commonly used libraries and applications. Most algorithms and data structures textbooks discuss some variant of red-black trees.

Andersson [6] describes a left-leaning version of balanced trees that is similar to red-black trees but has the additional constraint that any node has at most one red child. This implies that these trees simulate 2-3 trees rather than 2-4 trees. They are significantly simpler, though, than the `RedBlackTree` structure presented in this chapter.

Sedgewick [66] describes two versions of left-leaning red-black trees. These use recursion along with a simulation of top-down splitting and merging in 2-4 trees. The combination of these two techniques makes for particularly short and elegant code.

A related, and older, data structure is the *AVL tree* [3]. AVL trees are *height-balanced*: At each node u, the height of the subtree rooted at `u.left` and the subtree rooted at `u.right` differ by at most one. It follows immediately that, if $F(h)$ is the minimum number of leaves in a tree of height h, then $F(h)$ obeys the Fibonacci recurrence

$$F(h) = F(h-1) + F(h-2)$$

with base cases $F(0) = 1$ and $F(1) = 1$. This means $F(h)$ is approximately $\varphi^h/\sqrt{5}$, where $\varphi = (1 + \sqrt{5})/2 \approx 1.61803399$ is the *golden ratio*. (More precisely, $|\varphi^h/\sqrt{5} - F(h)| \leq 1/2$.) Arguing as in the proof of Lemma 9.1, this implies

$$h \leq \log_{\varphi} \mathtt{n} \approx 1.440420088 \log \mathtt{n} \ ,$$

so AVL trees have smaller height than red-black trees. The height balancing can be maintained during add(x) and remove(x) operations by walking back up the path to the root and performing a rebalancing operation at each node u where the height of u's left and right subtrees differ by two. See Figure 9.10.

Andersson's variant of red-black trees, Sedgewick's variant of red-black trees, and AVL trees are all simpler to implement than the RedBlackTree structure defined here. Unfortunately, none of them can guarantee that the amortized time spent rebalancing is $O(1)$ per update. In particular, there is no analogue of Theorem 9.2 for those structures.

Exercise 9.1. Illustrate the 2-4 tree that corresponds to the RedBlackTree in Figure 9.11.

Exercise 9.2. Illustrate the addition of 13, then 3.5, then 3.3 on the RedBlackTree in Figure 9.11.

Exercise 9.3. Illustrate the removal of 11, then 9, then 5 on the RedBlackTree in Figure 9.11.

Exercise 9.4. Show that, for arbitrarily large values of n, there are red-black trees with n nodes that have height $2\log \mathtt{n} - O(1)$.

Exercise 9.5. Consider the operations pushBlack(u) and pullBlack(u). What do these operations do to the underlying 2-4 tree that is being simulated by the red-black tree?

Exercise 9.6. Show that, for arbitrarily large values of n, there exist sequences of add(x) and remove(x) operations that lead to red-black trees with n nodes that have height $2\log \mathtt{n} - O(1)$.

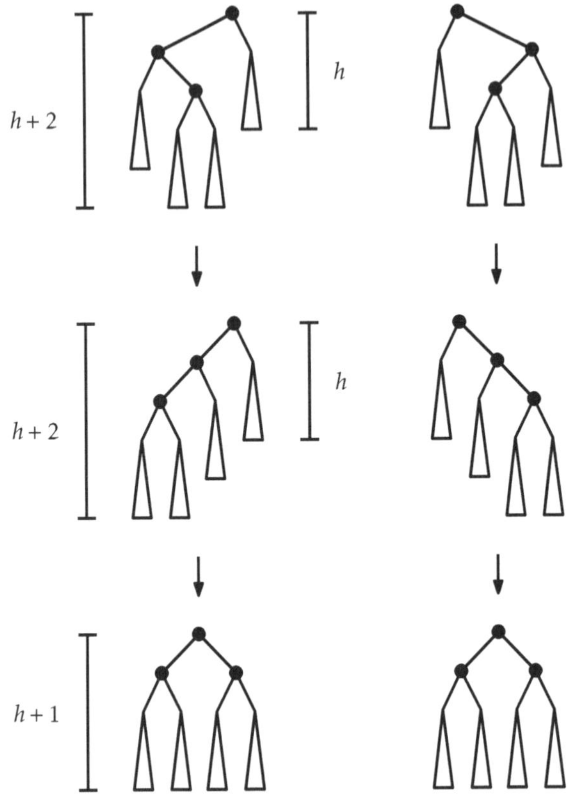

Figure 9.10: Rebalancing in an AVL tree. At most two rotations are required to convert a node whose subtrees have a height of h and $h+2$ into a node whose subtrees each have a height of at most $h+1$.

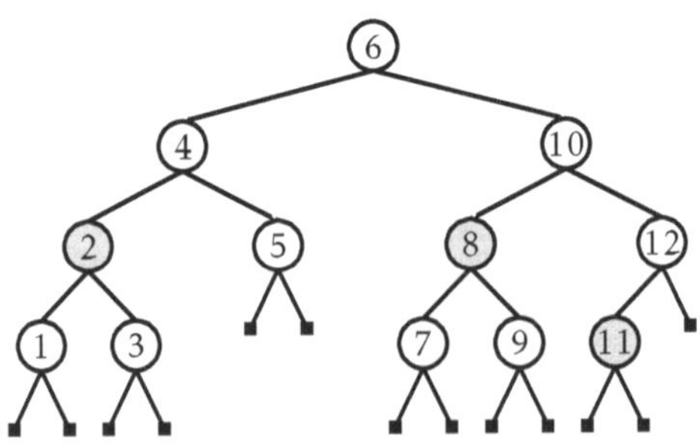

Figure 9.11: A red-black tree on which to practice.

Exercise 9.7. Why does the method remove(x) in the RedBlackTree implementation perform the assignment u.parent = w.parent? Shouldn't this already be done by the call to splice(w)?

Exercise 9.8. Suppose a 2-4 tree, T, has n_ℓ leaves and n_i internal nodes.

1. What is the minimum value of n_i, as a function of n_ℓ?
2. What is the maximum value of n_i, as a function of n_ℓ?
3. If T' is a red-black tree that represents T, then how many red nodes does T' have?

Exercise 9.9. Suppose you are given a binary search tree with n nodes and a height of at most $2\log n - 2$. Is it always possible to colour the nodes red and black so that the tree satisfies the black-height and no-red-edge properties? If so, can it also be made to satisfy the left-leaning property?

Exercise 9.10. Suppose you have two red-black trees T_1 and T_2 that have the same black height, h, and such that the largest key in T_1 is smaller than the smallest key in T_2. Show how to merge T_1 and T_2 into a single red-black tree in $O(h)$ time.

Exercise 9.11. Extend your solution to Exercise 9.10 to the case where the two trees T_1 and T_2 have different black heights, $h_1 \neq h_2$. The running-time should be $O(\max\{h_1, h_2\})$.

Exercise 9.12. Prove that, during an add(x) operation, an AVL tree must perform at most one rebalancing operation (that involves at most two rotations; see Figure 9.10). Give an example of an AVL tree and a remove(x) operation on that tree that requires on the order of $\log n$ rebalancing operations.

Exercise 9.13. Implement an AVLTree class that implements AVL trees as described above. Compare its performance to that of the RedBlackTree implementation. Which implementation has a faster find(x) operation?

Exercise 9.14. Design and implement a series of experiments that compare the relative performance of find(x), add(x), and remove(x) for the SSet implemeentations SkiplistSSet, ScapegoatTree, Treap, and RedBlackTree. Be sure to include multiple test scenarios, including cases where the data is random, already sorted, is removed in random order, is removed in sorted order, and so on.

Chapter 10

Heaps

In this chapter, we discuss two implementations of the extremely useful priority Queue data structure. Both of these structures are a special kind of binary tree called a *heap*, which means "a disorganized pile." This is in contrast to binary search trees that can be thought of as a highly organized pile.

The first heap implementation uses an array to simulate a complete binary tree. This very fast implementation is the basis of one of the fastest known sorting algorithms, namely heapsort (see Section 11.1.3). The second implementation is based on more flexible binary trees. It supports a `meld(h)` operation that allows the priority queue to absorb the elements of a second priority queue `h`.

10.1 `BinaryHeap`: An Implicit Binary Tree

Our first implementation of a (priority) `Queue` is based on a technique that is over four hundred years old. *Eytzinger's method* allows us to represent a complete binary tree as an array by laying out the nodes of the tree in breadth-first order (see Section 6.1.2). In this way, the root is stored at position 0, the root's left child is stored at position 1, the root's right child at position 2, the left child of the left child of the root is stored at position 3, and so on. See Figure 10.1.

If we apply Eytzinger's method to a sufficiently large tree, some patterns emerge. The left child of the node at index `i` is at index `left(i)` =

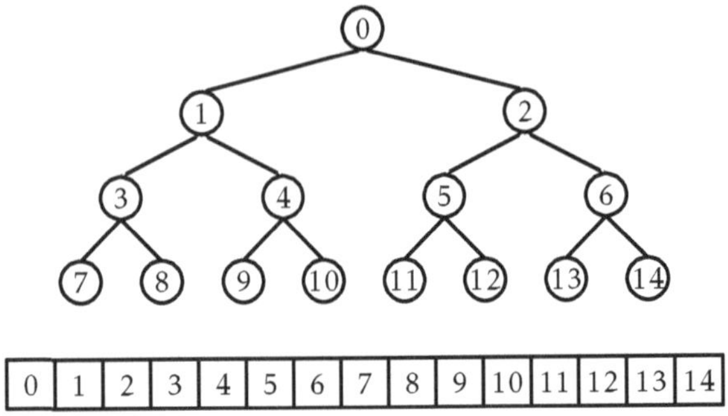

Figure 10.1: Eytzinger's method represents a complete binary tree as an array.

$2i + 1$ and the right child of the node at index i is at index right(i) = $2i + 2$. The parent of the node at index i is at index parent(i) = $(i - 1)/2$.

```
BinaryHeap
int left(int i) {
  return 2*i + 1;
}
int right(int i) {
  return 2*i + 2;
}
int parent(int i) {
  return (i-1)/2;
}
```

A BinaryHeap uses this technique to implicitly represent a complete binary tree in which the elements are *heap-ordered*: The value stored at any index i is not smaller than the value stored at index parent(i), with the exception of the root value, $i = 0$. It follows that the smallest value in the priority Queue is therefore stored at position 0 (the root).

In a BinaryHeap, the n elements are stored in an array a:

```
BinaryHeap
T[] a;
int n;
```

Implementing the add(x) operation is fairly straightforward. As with all array-based structures, we first check to see if a is full (by checking if a.length = n) and, if so, we grow a. Next, we place x at location a[n] and increment n. At this point, all that remains is to ensure that we maintain the heap property. We do this by repeatedly swapping x with its parent until x is no longer smaller than its parent. See Figure 10.2.

BinaryHeap
```
boolean add(T x) {
  if (n + 1 > a.length) resize();
  a[n++] = x;
  bubbleUp(n-1);
  return true;
}
void bubbleUp(int i) {
  int p = parent(i);
  while (i > 0 && compare(a[i], a[p]) < 0) {
    swap(i,p);
    i = p;
    p = parent(i);
  }
}
```

Implementing the remove() operation, which removes the smallest value from the heap, is a little trickier. We know where the smallest value is (at the root), but we need to replace it after we remove it and ensure that we maintain the heap property.

The easiest way to do this is to replace the root with the value a[n − 1], delete that value, and decrement n. Unfortunately, the new root element is now probably not the smallest element, so it needs to be moved downwards. We do this by repeatedly comparing this element to its two children. If it is the smallest of the three then we are done. Otherwise, we swap this element with the smallest of its two children and continue.

BinaryHeap
```
T remove() {
  T x = a[0];
  a[0] = a[--n];
  trickleDown(0);
```

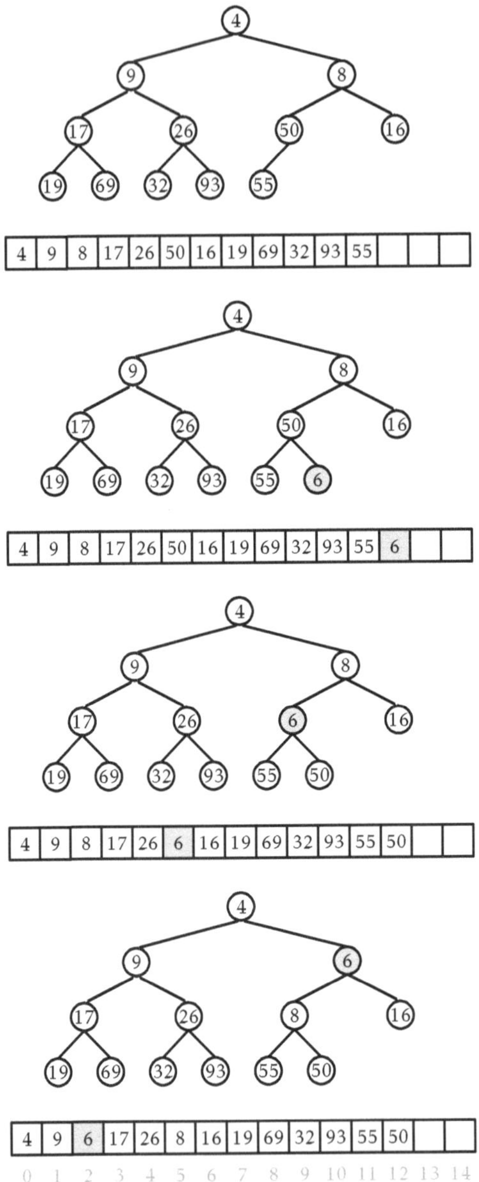

Figure 10.2: Adding the value 6 to a `BinaryHeap`.

```
  if (3*n < a.length) resize();
  return x;
}
void trickleDown(int i) {
  do {
    int j = -1;
    int r = right(i);
    if (r < n && compare(a[r], a[i]) < 0) {
      int l = left(i);
      if (compare(a[l], a[r]) < 0) {
        j = l;
      } else {
        j = r;
      }
    } else {
      int l = left(i);
      if (l < n && compare(a[l], a[i]) < 0) {
        j = l;
      }
    }
    if (j >= 0)  swap(i, j);
    i = j;
  } while (i >= 0);
}
```

As with other array-based structures, we will ignore the time spent in calls to resize(), since these can be accounted for using the amortization argument from Lemma 2.1. The running times of both add(x) and remove() then depend on the height of the (implicit) binary tree. Luckily, this is a *complete* binary tree; every level except the last has the maximum possible number of nodes. Therefore, if the height of this tree is h, then it has at least 2^h nodes. Stated another way

$$n \geq 2^h \ .$$

Taking logarithms on both sides of this equation gives

$$h \leq \log n \ .$$

Therefore, both the add(x) and remove() operation run in $O(\log n)$ time.

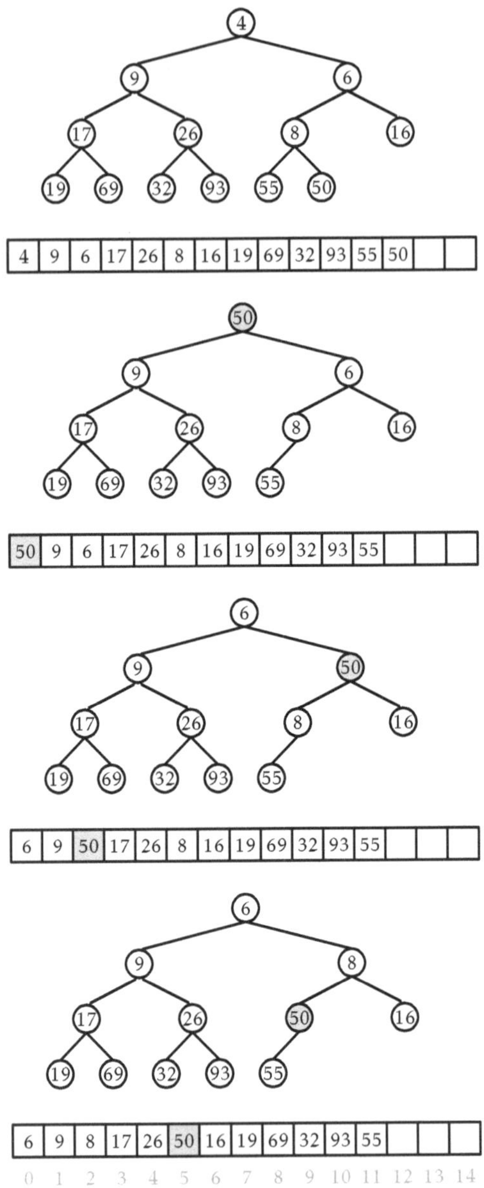

Figure 10.3: Removing the minimum value, 4, from a `BinaryHeap`.

10.1.1 Summary

The following theorem summarizes the performance of a BinaryHeap:

Theorem 10.1. *A BinaryHeap implements the (priority) Queue interface. Ignoring the cost of calls to* resize()*, a BinaryHeap supports the operations* add(x) *and* remove() *in* $O(\log n)$ *time per operation.*

Furthermore, beginning with an empty BinaryHeap, any sequence of m add(x) *and* remove() *operations results in a total of* $O(m)$ *time spent during all calls to* resize().

10.2 MeldableHeap: A Randomized Meldable Heap

In this section, we describe the MeldableHeap, a priority Queue implementation in which the underlying structure is also a heap-ordered binary tree. However, unlike a BinaryHeap in which the underlying binary tree is completely defined by the number of elements, there are no restrictions on the shape of the binary tree that underlies a MeldableHeap; anything goes.

The add(x) and remove() operations in a MeldableHeap are implemented in terms of the merge(h1,h2) operation. This operation takes two heap nodes h1 and h2 and merges them, returning a heap node that is the root of a heap that contains all elements in the subtree rooted at h1 and all elements in the subtree rooted at h2.

The nice thing about a merge(h1,h2) operation is that it can be defined recursively. See Figure 10.4. If either h1 or h2 is nil, then we are merging with an empty set, so we return h2 or h1, respectively. Otherwise, assume h1.x $\leq$ h2.x since, if h1.x $>$ h2.x, then we can reverse the roles of h1 and h2. Then we know that the root of the merged heap will contain h1.x, and we can recursively merge h2 with h1.left or h1.right, as we wish. This is where randomization comes in, and we toss a coin to decide whether to merge h2 with h1.left or h1.right:

MeldableHeap
```
Node<T> merge(Node<T> h1, Node<T> h2) {
  if (h1 == nil) return h2;
```

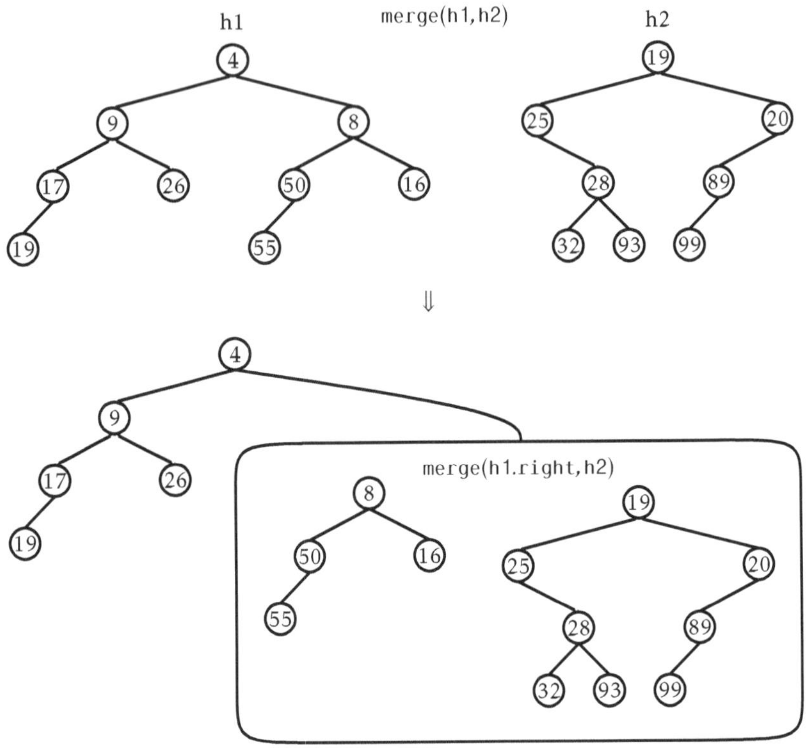

Figure 10.4: Merging h1 and h2 is done by merging h2 with one of h1.left or h1.right.

```
    if (h2 == nil) return h1;
    if (compare(h2.x, h1.x) < 0) return merge(h2, h1);
    // now we know h1.x <= h2.x
    if (rand.nextBoolean()) {
      h1.left = merge(h1.left, h2);
      h1.left.parent = h1;
    } else {
      h1.right = merge(h1.right, h2);
      h1.right.parent = h1;
    }
    return h1;
}
```

In the next section, we show that merge(h1,h2) runs in $O(\log n)$ expected time, where n is the total number of elements in h1 and h2.

With access to a merge(h1,h2) operation, the add(x) operation is easy. We create a new node u containing x and then merge u with the root of our heap:

```
MeldableHeap
boolean add(T x) {
  Node<T> u = newNode();
  u.x = x;
  r = merge(u, r);
  r.parent = nil;
  n++;
  return true;
}
```

This takes $O(\log(n+1)) = O(\log n)$ expected time.

The remove() operation is similarly easy. The node we want to remove is the root, so we just merge its two children and make the result the root:

```
MeldableHeap
T remove() {
  T x = r.x;
  r = merge(r.left, r.right);
  if (r != nil) r.parent = nil;
  n--;
  return x;
}
```

Again, this takes $O(\log n)$ expected time.

Additionally, a MeldableHeap can implement many other operations in $O(\log n)$ expected time, including:

- remove(u): remove the node u (and its key u.x) from the heap.
- absorb(h): add all the elements of the MeldableHeap h to this heap, emptying h in the process.

Each of these operations can be implemented using a constant number of merge(h1,h2) operations that each take $O(\log n)$ expected time.

10.2.1 Analysis of `merge(h1,h2)`

The analysis of `merge(h1,h2)` is based on the analysis of a random walk in a binary tree. A *random walk* in a binary tree starts at the root of the tree. At each step in the random walk, a coin is tossed and, depending on the result of this coin toss, the walk proceeds to the left or to the right child of the current node. The walk ends when it falls off the tree (the current node becomes `nil`).

The following lemma is somewhat remarkable because it does not depend at all on the shape of the binary tree:

Lemma 10.1. *The expected length of a random walk in a binary tree with* $\mathtt{n}$ *nodes is at most* $\log(\mathtt{n}+1)$.

Proof. The proof is by induction on $\mathtt{n}$. In the base case, $\mathtt{n}=0$ and the walk has length $0=\log(\mathtt{n}+1)$. Suppose now that the result is true for all non-negative integers $\mathtt{n}'<\mathtt{n}$.

Let $\mathtt{n}_1$ denote the size of the root's left subtree, so that $\mathtt{n}_2=\mathtt{n}-\mathtt{n}_1-1$ is the size of the root's right subtree. Starting at the root, the walk takes one step and then continues in a subtree of size $\mathtt{n}_1$ or $\mathtt{n}_2$. By our inductive hypothesis, the expected length of the walk is then

$$\mathrm{E}[W]=1+\frac{1}{2}\log(\mathtt{n}_1+1)+\frac{1}{2}\log(\mathtt{n}_2+1) \enspace ,$$

since each of $\mathtt{n}_1$ and $\mathtt{n}_2$ are less than $\mathtt{n}$. Since log is a concave function, $\mathrm{E}[W]$ is maximized when $\mathtt{n}_1=\mathtt{n}_2=(\mathtt{n}-1)/2$. Therefore, the expected number of steps taken by the random walk is

$$\begin{aligned}\mathrm{E}[W]&=1+\frac{1}{2}\log(\mathtt{n}_1+1)+\frac{1}{2}\log(\mathtt{n}_2+1)\\&\le 1+\log((\mathtt{n}-1)/2+1)\\&=1+\log((\mathtt{n}+1)/2)\\&=\log(\mathtt{n}+1) \enspace .\end{aligned}$$

□

We make a quick digression to note that, for readers who know a little about information theory, the proof of Lemma 10.1 can be stated in terms of entropy.

Information Theoretic Proof of Lemma 10.1. Let d_i denote the depth of the ith external node and recall that a binary tree with $\mathtt{n}$ nodes has $\mathtt{n}+1$ external nodes. The probability of the random walk reaching the ith external node is exactly $p_i = 1/2^{d_i}$, so the expected length of the random walk is given by

$$H = \sum_{i=0}^{\mathtt{n}} p_i d_i = \sum_{i=0}^{\mathtt{n}} p_i \log\left(2^{d_i}\right) = \sum_{i=0}^{\mathtt{n}} p_i \log(1/p_i)$$

The right hand side of this equation is easily recognizable as the entropy of a probability distribution over $\mathtt{n}+1$ elements. A basic fact about the entropy of a distribution over $\mathtt{n}+1$ elements is that it does not exceed $\log(\mathtt{n}+1)$, which proves the lemma. □

With this result on random walks, we can now easily prove that the running time of the `merge(h1,h2)` operation is $O(\log \mathtt{n})$.

Lemma 10.2. *If* `h1` *and* `h2` *are the roots of two heaps containing* $\mathtt{n}_1$ *and* $\mathtt{n}_2$ *nodes, respectively, then the expected running time of* `merge(h1,h2)` *is at most* $O(\log \mathtt{n})$*, where* $\mathtt{n} = \mathtt{n}_1 + \mathtt{n}_2$.

Proof. Each step of the merge algorithm takes one step of a random walk, either in the heap rooted at `h1` or the heap rooted at `h2`. The algorithm terminates when either of these two random walks fall out of its corresponding tree (when `h1 = null` or `h2 = null`). Therefore, the expected number of steps performed by the merge algorithm is at most

$$\log(\mathtt{n}_1+1)+\log(\mathtt{n}_2+1) \le 2\log \mathtt{n} \ .$$ □

10.2.2 Summary

The following theorem summarizes the performance of a `MeldableHeap`:

Theorem 10.2. *A* `MeldableHeap` *implements the (priority)* `Queue` *interface. A* `MeldableHeap` *supports the operations* `add(x)` *and* `remove()` *in* $O(\log \mathtt{n})$ *expected time per operation.*

10.3 Discussion and Exercises

The implicit representation of a complete binary tree as an array, or list, seems to have been first proposed by Eytzinger [27]. He used this representation in books containing pedigree family trees of noble families. The BinaryHeap data structure described here was first introduced by Williams [78].

The randomized MeldableHeap data structure described here appears to have first been proposed by Gambin and Malinowski [34]. Other meldable heap implementations exist, including leftist heaps [16, 48, Section 5.3.2], binomial heaps [75], Fibonacci heaps [30], pairing heaps [29], and skew heaps [72], although none of these are as simple as the MeldableHeap structure.

Some of the above structures also support a decreaseKey(u, y) operation in which the value stored at node u is decreased to y. (It is a precondition that $y \le u.x$.) In most of the preceding structures, this operation can be supported in $O(\log n)$ time by removing node u and adding y. However, some of these structures can implement decreaseKey(u, y) more efficiently. In particular, decreaseKey(u, y) takes $O(1)$ amortized time in Fibonacci heaps and $O(\log\log n)$ amortized time in a special version of pairing heaps [25]. This more efficient decreaseKey(u, y) operation has applications in speeding up several graph algorithms, including Dijkstra's shortest path algorithm [30].

Exercise 10.1. Illustrate the addition of the values 7 and then 3 to the BinaryHeap shown at the end of Figure 10.2.

Exercise 10.2. Illustrate the removal of the next two values (6 and 8) on the BinaryHeap shown at the end of Figure 10.3.

Exercise 10.3. Implement the remove(i) method, that removes the value stored in a[i] in a BinaryHeap. This method should run in $O(\log n)$ time. Next, explain why this method is not likely to be useful.

Exercise 10.4. A d-ary tree is a generalization of a binary tree in which each internal node has d children. Using Eytzinger's method it is also possible to represent complete d-ary trees using arrays. Work out the equations that, given an index i, determine the index of i's parent and each of i's d children in this representation.

Exercise 10.5. Using what you learned in Exercise 10.4, design and implement a *DaryHeap*, the d-ary generalization of a BinaryHeap. Analyze the running times of operations on a DaryHeap and test the performance of your DaryHeap implementation against that of the BinaryHeap implementation given here.

Exercise 10.6. Illustrate the addition of the values 17 and then 82 in the MeldableHeap h1 shown in Figure 10.4. Use a coin to simulate a random bit when needed.

Exercise 10.7. Illustrate the removal of the next two values (4 and 8) in the MeldableHeap h1 shown in Figure 10.4. Use a coin to simulate a random bit when needed.

Exercise 10.8. Implement the remove(u) method, that removes the node u from a MeldableHeap. This method should run in $O(\log n)$ expected time.

Exercise 10.9. Show how to find the second smallest value in a BinaryHeap or MeldableHeap in constant time.

Exercise 10.10. Show how to find the kth smallest value in a BinaryHeap or MeldableHeap in $O(k \log k)$ time. (Hint: Using another heap might help.)

Exercise 10.11. Suppose you are given k sorted lists, of total length n. Using a heap, show how to merge these into a single sorted list in $O(n \log k)$ time. (Hint: Starting with the case $k = 2$ can be instructive.)

Chapter 11

Sorting Algorithms

This chapter discusses algorithms for sorting a set of n items. This might seem like a strange topic for a book on data structures, but there are several good reasons for including it here. The most obvious reason is that two of these sorting algorithms (quicksort and heap-sort) are intimately related to two of the data structures we have already studied (random binary search trees and heaps, respectively).

The first part of this chapter discusses algorithms that sort using only comparisons and presents three algorithms that run in $O(n \log n)$ time. As it turns out, all three algorithms are asymptotically optimal; no algorithm that uses only comparisons can avoid doing roughly $n \log n$ comparisons in the worst case and even the average case.

Before continuing, we should note that any of the SSet or priority Queue implementations presented in previous chapters can also be used to obtain an $O(n \log n)$ time sorting algorithm. For example, we can sort n items by performing n add(x) operations followed by n remove() operations on a BinaryHeap or MeldableHeap. Alternatively, we can use n add(x) operations on any of the binary search tree data structures and then perform an in-order traversal (Exercise 6.8) to extract the elements in sorted order. However, in both cases we go through a lot of overhead to build a structure that is never fully used. Sorting is such an important problem that it is worthwhile developing direct methods that are as fast, simple, and space-efficient as possible.

The second part of this chapter shows that, if we allow other operations besides comparisons, then all bets are off. Indeed, by using array-indexing, it is possible to sort a set of n integers in the range $\{0,\ldots,n^c-1\}$ in $O(cn)$ time.

11.1 Comparison-Based Sorting

In this section, we present three sorting algorithms: merge-sort, quick-sort, and heap-sort. Each of these algorithms takes an input array a and sorts the elements of a into non-decreasing order in $O(n \log n)$ (expected) time. These algorithms are all *comparison-based*. Their second argument, c, is a Comparator that implements the compare(a,b) method. These algorithms don't care what type of data is being sorted; the only operation they do on the data is comparisons using the compare(a,b) method. Recall, from Section 1.2.4, that compare(a,b) returns a negative value if $a < b$, a positive value if $a > b$, and zero if $a = b$.

11.1.1 Merge-Sort

The *merge-sort* algorithm is a classic example of recursive divide and conquer: If the length of a is at most 1, then a is already sorted, so we do nothing. Otherwise, we split a into two halves, $a0 = a[0],\ldots,a[n/2-1]$ and $a1 = a[n/2],\ldots,a[n-1]$. We recursively sort a0 and a1, and then we merge (the now sorted) a0 and a1 to get our fully sorted array a:

```
Algorithms
<T> void mergeSort(T[] a, Comparator<T> c) {
  if (a.length <= 1) return;
  T[] a0 = Arrays.copyOfRange(a, 0, a.length/2);
  T[] a1 = Arrays.copyOfRange(a, a.length/2, a.length);
  mergeSort(a0, c);
  mergeSort(a1, c);
  merge(a0, a1, a, c);
}
```

An example is shown in Figure 11.1.

Compared to sorting, merging the two sorted arrays a0 and a1 is fairly easy. We add elements to a one at a time. If a0 or a1 is empty, then we add the next elements from the other (non-empty) array. Otherwise, we

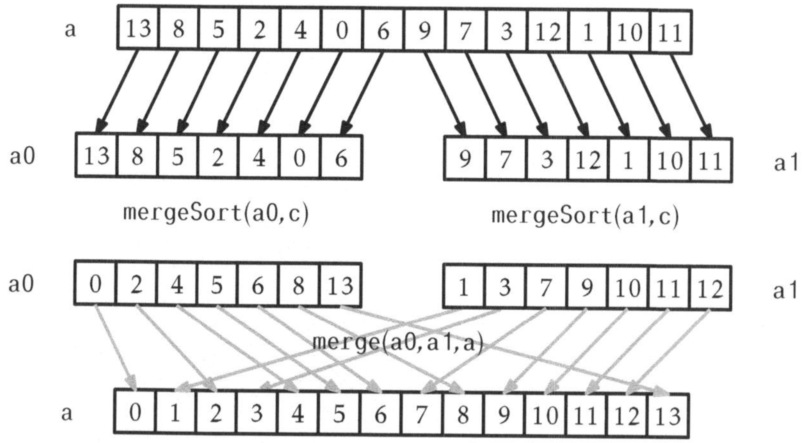

Figure 11.1: The execution of mergeSort(a,c)

take the minimum of the next element in a0 and the next element in a1 and add it to a:

```
                          Algorithms
<T> void merge(T[] a0, T[] a1, T[] a, Comparator<T> c) {
  int i0 = 0, i1 = 0;
  for (int i = 0; i < a.length; i++) {
    if (i0 == a0.length)
      a[i] = a1[i1++];
    else if (i1 == a1.length)
      a[i] = a0[i0++];
    else if (compare(a0[i0], a1[i1]) < 0)
      a[i] = a0[i0++];
    else
      a[i] = a1[i1++];
  }
}
```

Notice that the merge(a0,a1,a,c) algorithm performs at most $n-1$ comparisons before running out of elements in one of a0 or a1.

To understand the running-time of merge-sort, it is easiest to think of it in terms of its recursion tree. Suppose for now that n is a power of

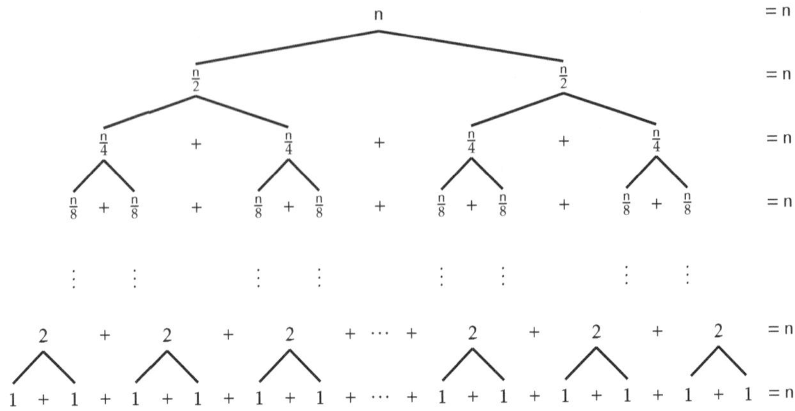

Figure 11.2: The merge-sort recursion tree.

two, so that $n = 2^{\log n}$, and $\log n$ is an integer. Refer to Figure 11.2. Merge-sort turns the problem of sorting n elements into two problems, each of sorting $n/2$ elements. These two subproblem are then turned into two problems each, for a total of four subproblems, each of size $n/4$. These four subproblems become eight subproblems, each of size $n/8$, and so on. At the bottom of this process, $n/2$ subproblems, each of size two, are converted into n problems, each of size one. For each subproblem of size $n/2^i$, the time spent merging and copying data is $O(n/2^i)$. Since there are 2^i subproblems of size $n/2^i$, the total time spent working on problems of size 2^i, not counting recursive calls, is

$$2^i \times O(n/2^i) = O(n) \ .$$

Therefore, the total amount of time taken by merge-sort is

$$\sum_{i=0}^{\log n} O(n) = O(n \log n) \ .$$

The proof of the following theorem is based on preceding analysis, but has to be a little more careful to deal with the cases where n is not a power of 2.

Theorem 11.1. *The* `mergeSort(a,c)` *algorithm runs in* $O(n \log n)$ *time and performs at most* $n \log n$ *comparisons.*

Proof. The proof is by induction on n. The base case, in which $n = 1$, is trivial; when presented with an array of length 0 or 1 the algorithm simply returns without performing any comparisons.

Merging two sorted lists of total length n requires at most $n-1$ comparisons. Let $C(n)$ denote the maximum number of comparisons performed by `mergeSort(a,c)` on an array a of length n. If n is even, then we apply the inductive hypothesis to the two subproblems and obtain

$$\begin{aligned} C(n) &\le n-1+2C(n/2) \\ &\le n-1+2((n/2)\log(n/2)) \\ &= n-1+n\log(n/2) \\ &= n-1+n\log n - n \\ &< n\log n \ . \end{aligned}$$

The case where n is odd is slightly more complicated. For this case, we use two inequalities that are easy to verify:

$$\log(x+1) \le \log(x)+1 \ , \tag{11.1}$$

for all $x \ge 1$ and

$$\log(x+1/2)+\log(x-1/2) \le 2\log(x) \ , \tag{11.2}$$

for all $x \ge 1/2$. Inequality (11.1) comes from the fact that $\log(x)+1 = \log(2x)$ while (11.2) follows from the fact that log is a concave function. With these tools in hand we have, for odd n,

$$\begin{aligned} C(n) &\le n-1+C(\lceil n/2\rceil)+C(\lfloor n/2\rfloor) \\ &\le n-1+\lceil n/2\rceil\log\lceil n/2\rceil+\lfloor n/2\rfloor\log\lfloor n/2\rfloor \\ &= n-1+(n/2+1/2)\log(n/2+1/2)+(n/2-1/2)\log(n/2-1/2) \\ &\le n-1+n\log(n/2)+(1/2)(\log(n/2+1/2)-\log(n/2-1/2)) \\ &\le n-1+n\log(n/2)+1/2 \\ &< n+n\log(n/2) \\ &= n+n(\log n-1) \\ &= n\log n \ . \end{aligned}$$

□

11.1.2 Quicksort

The *quicksort* algorithm is another classic divide and conquer algorithm. Unlike merge-sort, which does merging after solving the two subproblems, quicksort does all of its work upfront.

Quicksort is simple to describe: Pick a random *pivot* element, x, from a; partition a into the set of elements less than x, the set of elements equal to x, and the set of elements greater than x; and, finally, recursively sort the first and third sets in this partition. An example is shown in Figure 11.3.

```
Algorithms
<T> void quickSort(T[] a, Comparator<T> c) {
  quickSort(a, 0, a.length, c);
}
<T> void quickSort(T[] a, int i, int n, Comparator<T> c) {
  if (n <= 1) return;
  T x = a[i + rand.nextInt(n)];
  int p = i-1, j = i, q = i+n;
  // a[i..p]<x,  a[p+1..q-1]??x, a[q..i+n-1]>x
  while (j < q) {
    int comp = compare(a[j], x);
    if (comp < 0) {       // move to beginning of array
      swap(a, j++, ++p);
    } else if (comp > 0) {
      swap(a, j, --q);  // move to end of array
    } else {
      j++;              // keep in the middle
    }
  }
  // a[i..p]<x,  a[p+1..q-1]=x, a[q..i+n-1]>x
  quickSort(a, i, p-i+1, c);
  quickSort(a, q, n-(q-i), c);
}
```

All of this is done in place, so that instead of making copies of subarrays being sorted, the quickSort(a, i, n, c) method only sorts the subarray a[i],...,a[i + n − 1]. Initially, this method is invoked with the arguments quickSort(a, 0, a.length, c).

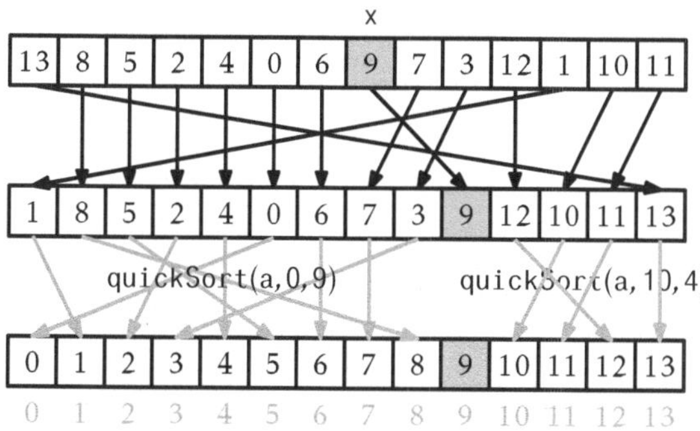

Figure 11.3: An example execution of quickSort(a,0,14,c)

At the heart of the quicksort algorithm is the in-place partitioning algorithm. This algorithm, without using any extra space, swaps elements in a and computes indices p and q so that

$$a[i]\begin{cases} < x & \text{if } 0 \leq i \leq p \\ = x & \text{if } p < i < q \\ > x & \text{if } q \leq i \leq n-1 \end{cases}$$

This partitioning, which is done by the while loop in the code, works by iteratively increasing p and decreasing q while maintaining the first and last of these conditions. At each step, the element at position j is either moved to the front, left where it is, or moved to the back. In the first two cases, j is incremented, while in the last case, j is not incremented since the new element at position j has not yet been processed.

Quicksort is very closely related to the random binary search trees studied in Section 7.1. In fact, if the input to quicksort consists of n distinct elements, then the quicksort recursion tree is a random binary search tree. To see this, recall that when constructing a random binary search tree the first thing we do is pick a random element x and make it the root of the tree. After this, every element will eventually be compared to x, with smaller elements going into the left subtree and larger elements into the right.

In quicksort, we select a random element x and immediately compare everything to x, putting the smaller elements at the beginning of the array and larger elements at the end of the array. Quicksort then recursively sorts the beginning of the array and the end of the array, while the random binary search tree recursively inserts smaller elements in the left subtree of the root and larger elements in the right subtree of the root.

The above correspondence between random binary search trees and quicksort means that we can translate Lemma 7.1 to a statement about quicksort:

Lemma 11.1. *When quicksort is called to sort an array containing the integers* $0,\ldots,n-1$*, the expected number of times element* i *is compared to a pivot element is at most* $H_{i+1} + H_{n-i}$.

A little summing up of harmonic numbers gives us the following theorem about the running time of quicksort:

Theorem 11.2. *When quicksort is called to sort an array containing* n *distinct elements, the expected number of comparisons performed is at most* $2n\ln n + O(n)$.

Proof. Let T be the number of comparisons performed by quicksort when sorting n distinct elements. Using Lemma 11.1 and linearity of expectation, we have:

$$\begin{aligned} \mathrm{E}[T] &= \sum_{i=0}^{n-1}(H_{i+1} + H_{n-i}) \\ &= 2\sum_{i=1}^{n} H_i \\ &\le 2\sum_{i=1}^{n} H_n \\ &\le 2n\ln n + 2n = 2n\ln n + O(n) \end{aligned}$$

□

Theorem 11.3 describes the case where the elements being sorted are all distinct. When the input array, a, contains duplicate elements, the expected running time of quicksort is no worse, and can be even better; any time a duplicate element x is chosen as a pivot, all occurrences of x get grouped together and do not take part in either of the two subproblems.

Theorem 11.3. *The* `quickSort(a,c)` *method runs in* $O(n\log n)$ *expected time and the expected number of comparisons it performs is at most* $2n\ln n + O(n)$.

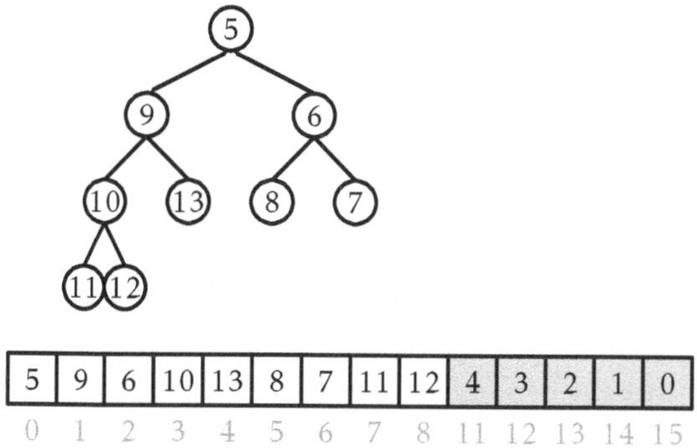

Figure 11.4: A snapshot of the execution of heapSort(a,c). The shaded part of the array is already sorted. The unshaded part is a BinaryHeap. During the next iteration, element 5 will be placed into array location 8.

11.1.3 Heap-sort

The *heap-sort* algorithm is another in-place sorting algorithm. Heap-sort uses the binary heaps discussed in Section 10.1. Recall that the BinaryHeap data structure represents a heap using a single array. The heap-sort algorithm converts the input array a into a heap and then repeatedly extracts the minimum value.

More specifically, a heap stores n elements in an array, a, at array locations a[0],...,a[n − 1] with the smallest value stored at the root, a[0]. After transforming a into a BinaryHeap, the heap-sort algorithm repeatedly swaps a[0] and a[n − 1], decrements n, and calls trickleDown(0) so that a[0],...,a[n − 2] once again are a valid heap representation. When this process ends (because n = 0) the elements of a are stored in decreasing order, so a is reversed to obtain the final sorted order.[1] Figure 11.4 shows an example of the execution of heapSort(a,c).

BinaryHeap

```
<T> void sort(T[] a, Comparator<T> c) {
  BinaryHeap<T> h = new BinaryHeap<T>(a, c);
  while (h.n > 1) {
```

[1]The algorithm could alternatively redefine the compare(x,y) function so that the heap sort algorithm stores the elements directly in ascending order.

```
    h.swap(--h.n, 0);
    h.trickleDown(0);
  }
  Collections.reverse(Arrays.asList(a));
}
```

A key subroutine in heap sort is the constructor for turning an unsorted array a into a heap. It would be easy to do this in $O(n \log n)$ time by repeatedly calling the BinaryHeap add(x) method, but we can do better by using a bottom-up algorithm. Recall that, in a binary heap, the children of a[i] are stored at positions a[2i + 1] and a[2i + 2]. This implies that the elements $a[\lfloor n/2 \rfloor],\ldots,a[n-1]$ have no children. In other words, each of $a[\lfloor n/2 \rfloor],\ldots,a[n-1]$ is a sub-heap of size 1. Now, working backwards, we can call trickleDown(i) for each $i \in \{\lfloor n/2 \rfloor - 1,\ldots,0\}$. This works, because by the time we call trickleDown(i), each of the two children of a[i] are the root of a sub-heap, so calling trickleDown(i) makes a[i] into the root of its own subheap.

```
BinaryHeap
BinaryHeap(T[] a, Comparator<T> c) {
  this.c = c;
  this.a = a;
  n = a.length;
  for (int i = n/2-1; i >= 0; i--) {
    trickleDown(i);
  }
}
```

The interesting thing about this bottom-up strategy is that it is more efficient than calling add(x) n times. To see this, notice that, for n/2 elements, we do no work at all, for n/4 elements, we call trickleDown(i) on a subheap rooted at a[i] and whose height is one, for n/8 elements, we call trickleDown(i) on a subheap whose height is two, and so on. Since the work done by trickleDown(i) is proportional to the height of the sub-heap rooted at a[i], this means that the total work done is at most

$$\sum_{i=1}^{\log n} O((i-1)n/2^i) \le \sum_{i=1}^{\infty} O(in/2^i) = O(n)\sum_{i=1}^{\infty} i/2^i = O(2n) = O(n) \ .$$

The second-last equality follows by recognizing that the sum $\sum_{i=1}^{\infty} i/2^i$ is equal, by definition of expected value, to the expected number of times we toss a coin up to and including the first time the coin comes up as heads and applying Lemma 4.2.

The following theorem describes the performance of `heapSort(a,c)`.

Theorem 11.4. *The* `heapSort(a,c)` *method runs in* $O(n \log n)$ *time and performs at most* $2n \log n + O(n)$ *comparisons.*

Proof. The algorithm runs in three steps: (1) transforming a into a heap, (2) repeatedly extracting the minimum element from a, and (3) reversing the elements in a. We have just argued that step 1 takes $O(n)$ time and performs $O(n)$ comparisons. Step 3 takes $O(n)$ time and performs no comparisons. Step 2 performs n calls to `trickleDown(0)`. The ith such call operates on a heap of size $n-i$ and performs at most $2\log(n-i)$ comparisons. Summing this over i gives

$$\sum_{i=0}^{n-i} 2\log(n-i) \le \sum_{i=0}^{n-i} 2\log n = 2n\log n$$

Adding the number of comparisons performed in each of the three steps completes the proof. □

11.1.4 A Lower-Bound for Comparison-Based Sorting

We have now seen three comparison-based sorting algorithms that each run in $O(n \log n)$ time. By now, we should be wondering if faster algorithms exist. The short answer to this question is no. If the only operations allowed on the elements of a are comparisons, then no algorithm can avoid doing roughly $n \log n$ comparisons. This is not difficult to prove, but requires a little imagination. Ultimately, it follows from the fact that

$$\log(n!) = \log n + \log(n-1) + \dots + \log(1) = n\log n - O(n) \ .$$

(Proving this fact is left as Exercise 11.11.)

We will start by focusing our attention on deterministic algorithms like merge-sort and heap-sort and on a particular fixed value of n. Imagine such an algorithm is being used to sort n distinct elements. The key

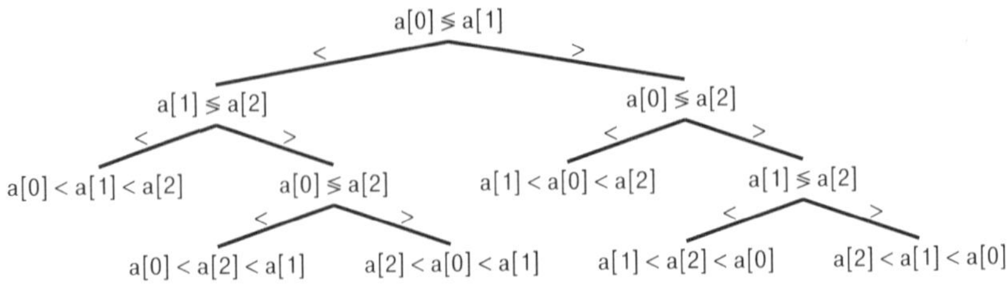

Figure 11.5: A comparison tree for sorting an array a[0], a[1], a[2] of length $n = 3$.

to proving the lower-bound is to observe that, for a deterministic algorithm with a fixed value of n, the first pair of elements that are compared is always the same. For example, in `heapSort(a,c)`, when n is even, the first call to `trickleDown(i)` is with $i = n/2 - 1$ and the first comparison is between elements $a[n/2-1]$ and $a[n-1]$.

Since all input elements are distinct, this first comparison has only two possible outcomes. The second comparison done by the algorithm may depend on the outcome of the first comparison. The third comparison may depend on the results of the first two, and so on. In this way, any deterministic comparison-based sorting algorithm can be viewed as a rooted binary *comparison tree*. Each internal node, u, of this tree is labelled with a pair of indices u.i and u.j. If $a[u.i] < a[u.j]$ the algorithm proceeds to the left subtree, otherwise it proceeds to the right subtree. Each leaf w of this tree is labelled with a permutation $w.p[0], \ldots, w.p[n-1]$ of $0, \ldots, n-1$. This permutation represents the one that is required to sort a if the comparison tree reaches this leaf. That is,

$$a[w.p[0]] < a[w.p[1]] < \cdots < a[w.p[n-1]] \ .$$

An example of a comparison tree for an array of size $n = 3$ is shown in Figure 11.5.

The comparison tree for a sorting algorithm tells us everything about the algorithm. It tells us exactly the sequence of comparisons that will be performed for any input array, a, having n distinct elements and it tells us how the algorithm will reorder a in order to sort it. Consequently, the comparison tree must have at least $n!$ leaves; if not, then there are two distinct permutations that lead to the same leaf; therefore, the algorithm

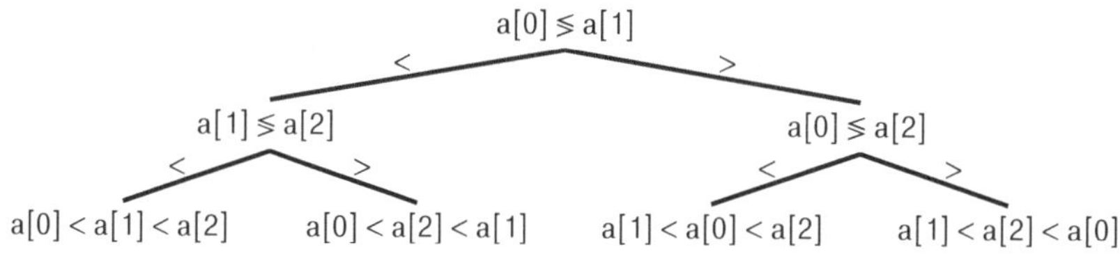

Figure 11.6: A comparison tree that does not correctly sort every input permutation.

does not correctly sort at least one of these permutations.

For example, the comparison tree in Figure 11.6 has only $4 < 3! = 6$ leaves. Inspecting this tree, we see that the two input arrays 3,1,2 and 3,2,1 both lead to the rightmost leaf. On the input 3,1,2 this leaf correctly outputs $\mathtt{a}[1] = 1, \mathtt{a}[2] = 2, \mathtt{a}[0] = 3$. However, on the input 3,2,1, this node incorrectly outputs $\mathtt{a}[1] = 2, \mathtt{a}[2] = 1, \mathtt{a}[0] = 3$. This discussion leads to the primary lower-bound for comparison-based algorithms.

Theorem 11.5. *For any deterministic comparison-based sorting algorithm $\mathcal{A}$ and any integer* $\mathtt{n} \geq 1$, *there exists an input array* a *of length* n *such that $\mathcal{A}$ performs at least* $\log(\mathtt{n}!) = \mathtt{n}\log\mathtt{n} - O(\mathtt{n})$ *comparisons when sorting* a.

Proof. By the preceding discussion, the comparison tree defined by $\mathcal{A}$ must have at least n! leaves. An easy inductive proof shows that any binary tree with k leaves has a height of at least $\log k$. Therefore, the comparison tree for $\mathcal{A}$ has a leaf, w, with a depth of at least $\log(\mathtt{n}!)$ and there is an input array a that leads to this leaf. The input array a is an input for which $\mathcal{A}$ does at least $\log(\mathtt{n}!)$ comparisons. □

Theorem 11.5 deals with deterministic algorithms like merge-sort and heap-sort, but doesn't tell us anything about randomized algorithms like quicksort. Could a randomized algorithm beat the $\log(\mathtt{n}!)$ lower bound on the number of comparisons? The answer, again, is no. Again, the way to prove it is to think differently about what a randomized algorithm is.

In the following discussion, we will assume that our decision trees have been "cleaned up" in the following way: Any node that can not be reached by some input array a is removed. This cleaning up implies that the tree has exactly n! leaves. It has at least n! leaves because, otherwise, it could not sort correctly. It has at most n! leaves since each of the possible n! permutation of n distinct elements follows exactly one root to leaf path in the decision tree.

We can think of a randomized sorting algorithm, $\mathcal{R}$, as a deterministic algorithm that takes two inputs: The input array a that should be sorted and a long sequence $b = b_1, b_2, b_3, \ldots, b_m$ of random real numbers in the range $[0,1]$. The random numbers provide the randomization for the algorithm. When the algorithm wants to toss a coin or make a random choice, it does so by using some element from b. For example, to compute the index of the first pivot in quicksort, the algorithm could use the formula $\lfloor nb_1 \rfloor$.

Now, notice that if we fix b to some particular sequence $\hat{b}$ then $\mathcal{R}$ becomes a deterministic sorting algorithm, $\mathcal{R}(\hat{b})$, that has an associated comparison tree, $\mathcal{T}(\hat{b})$. Next, notice that if we select a to be a random permutation of $\{1,\ldots,\mathrm{n}\}$, then this is equivalent to selecting a random leaf, w, from the n! leaves of $\mathcal{T}(\hat{b})$.

Exercise 11.13 asks you to prove that, if we select a random leaf from any binary tree with k leaves, then the expected depth of that leaf is at least $\log k$. Therefore, the expected number of comparisons performed by the (deterministic) algorithm $\mathcal{R}(\hat{b})$ when given an input array containing a random permutation of $\{1,\ldots,n\}$ is at least $\log(\mathrm{n}!)$. Finally, notice that this is true for every choice of $\hat{b}$, therefore it holds even for $\mathcal{R}$. This completes the proof of the lower-bound for randomized algorithms.

Theorem 11.6. *For any integer $n \geq 1$ and any (deterministic or randomized) comparison-based sorting algorithm $\mathcal{A}$, the expected number of comparisons done by $\mathcal{A}$ when sorting a random permutation of $\{1,\ldots,n\}$ is at least* $\log(\mathrm{n}!) = \mathrm{n}\log\mathrm{n} - O(\mathrm{n})$.

11.2 Counting Sort and Radix Sort

In this section we study two sorting algorithms that are not comparison-based. Specialized for sorting small integers, these algorithms elude the lower-bounds of Theorem 11.5 by using (parts of) the elements in a as indices into an array. Consider a statement of the form

$$\mathtt{c[a[i]]} = 1 \ .$$

This statement executes in constant time, but has `c.length` possible different outcomes, depending on the value of `a[i]`. This means that the execution of an algorithm that makes such a statement cannot be modelled as a binary tree. Ultimately, this is the reason that the algorithms in this section are able to sort faster than comparison-based algorithms.

11.2.1 Counting Sort

Suppose we have an input array a consisting of n integers, each in the range $0,\dots,k-1$. The *counting-sort* algorithm sorts a using an auxiliary array c of counters. It outputs a sorted version of a as an auxiliary array b.

The idea behind counting-sort is simple: For each $i \in \{0,\dots,k-1\}$, count the number of occurrences of i in a and store this in c[i]. Now, after sorting, the output will look like c[0] occurrences of 0, followed by c[1] occurrences of 1, followed by c[2] occurrences of 2,..., followed by c[k − 1] occurrences of k − 1. The code that does this is very slick, and its execution is illustrated in Figure 11.7:

Algorithms
```
int[] countingSort(int[] a, int k) {
  int c[] = new int[k];
  for (int i = 0; i < a.length; i++)
    c[a[i]]++;
  for (int i = 1; i < k; i++)
    c[i] += c[i-1];
  int b[] = new int[a.length];
  for (int i = a.length-1; i >= 0; i--)
    b[--c[a[i]]] = a[i];
  return b;
}
```

The first `for` loop in this code sets each counter c[i] so that it counts the number of occurrences of i in a. By using the values of a as indices,

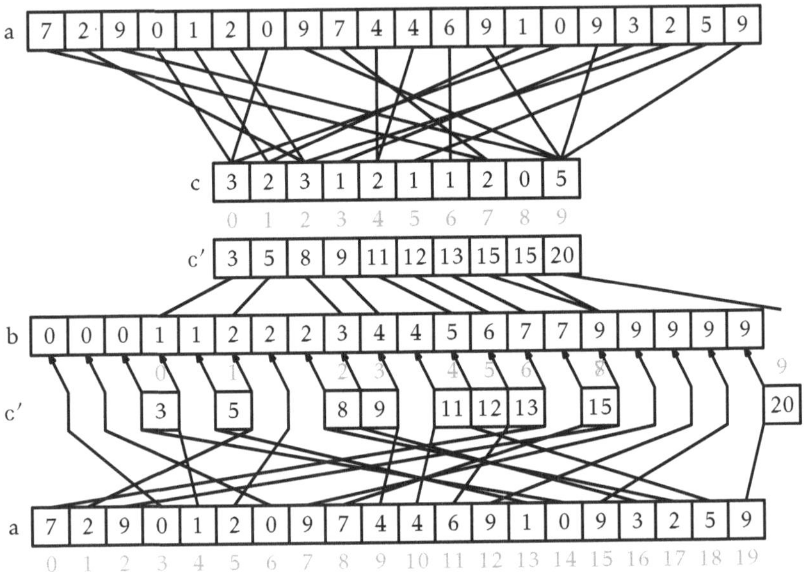

Figure 11.7: The operation of counting sort on an array of length $n = 20$ that stores integers $0,\ldots,k-1 = 9$.

these counters can all be computed in $O(n)$ time with a single for loop. At this point, we could use c to fill in the output array b directly. However, this would not work if the elements of a have associated data. Therefore we spend a little extra effort to copy the elements of a into b.

The next `for` loop, which takes $O(k)$ time, computes a running-sum of the counters so that c[i] becomes the number of elements in a that are less than or equal to i. In particular, for every $i \in \{0,\dots,k-1\}$, the output array, b, will have

$$b[c[i-1]] = b[c[i-1]+1] = \cdots = b[c[i]-1] = i \ .$$

Finally, the algorithm scans a backwards to place its elements, in order, into an output array b. When scanning, the element a[i] = j is placed at location b[c[j] − 1] and the value c[j] is decremented.

Theorem 11.7. *The* countingSort(a, k) *method can sort an array* a *containing* n *integers in the set* $\{0,\dots,k-1\}$ *in* $O(n+k)$ *time.*

The counting-sort algorithm has the nice property of being *stable*; it preserves the relative order of equal elements. If two elements a[i] and a[j] have the same value, and i < j then a[i] will appear before a[j] in b. This will be useful in the next section.

11.2.2 Radix-Sort

Counting-sort is very efficient for sorting an array of integers when the length, n, of the array is not much smaller than the maximum value, $k-1$, that appears in the array. The *radix-sort* algorithm, which we now describe, uses several passes of counting-sort to allow for a much greater range of maximum values.

Radix-sort sorts w-bit integers by using w/d passes of counting-sort to sort these integers d bits at a time.[2] More precisely, radix sort first sorts the integers by their least significant d bits, then their next significant d bits, and so on until, in the last pass, the integers are sorted by their most significant d bits.

[2]We assume that d divides w, otherwise we can always increase w to $d\lceil w/d\rceil$.

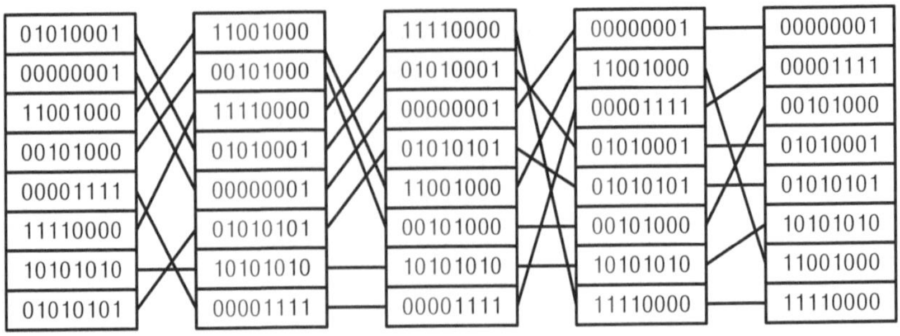

Figure 11.8: Using radixsort to sort w = 8-bit integers by using 4 passes of counting sort on d = 2-bit integers.

Algorithms
```
int[] radixSort(int[] a) {
  int[] b = null;
  for (int p = 0; p < w/d; p++) {
    int c[] = new int[1<<d];
    // the next three for loops implement counting-sort
    b = new int[a.length];
    for (int i = 0; i < a.length; i++)
      c[(a[i] >> d*p)&((1<<d)-1)]++;
    for (int i = 1; i < 1<<d; i++)
      c[i] += c[i-1];
    for (int i = a.length-1; i >= 0; i--)
      b[--c[(a[i] >> d*p)&((1<<d)-1)]] = a[i];
    a = b;
  }
  return b;
}
```

(In this code, the expression $(\mathtt{a[i]}>>\mathtt{d}*\mathtt{p})\&((1<<\mathtt{d})-1)$ extracts the integer whose binary representation is given by bits $(\mathtt{p}+1)\mathtt{d}-1,\dots,\mathtt{pd}$ of a[i].) An example of the steps of this algorithm is shown in Figure 11.8.

This remarkable algorithm sorts correctly because counting-sort is a stable sorting algorithm. If x < y are two elements of a, and the most significant bit at which x differs from y has index r, then x will be placed before y during pass $\lfloor r/\mathtt{d}\rfloor$ and subsequent passes will not change the relative order of x and y.

Radix-sort performs w/d passes of counting-sort. Each pass requires $O(n + 2^d)$ time. Therefore, the performance of radix-sort is given by the following theorem.

Theorem 11.8. *For any integer* $d > 0$, *the* radixSort(a,k) *method can sort an array* a *containing* n w*-bit integers in* $O((w/d)(n + 2^d))$ *time.*

If we think, instead, of the elements of the array being in the range $\{0,\ldots,n^c - 1\}$, and take $d = \lceil \log n \rceil$ we obtain the following version of Theorem 11.8.

Corollary 11.1. *The* radixSort(a,k) *method can sort an array* a *containing* n *integer values in the range* $\{0,\ldots,n^c - 1\}$ *in* $O(cn)$ *time.*

11.3 Discussion and Exercises

Sorting is *the* fundamental algorithmic problem in computer science, and it has a long history. Knuth [48] attributes the merge-sort algorithm to von Neumann (1945). Quicksort is due to Hoare [39]. The original heap-sort algorithm is due to Williams [78], but the version presented here (in which the heap is constructed bottom-up in $O(n)$ time) is due to Floyd [28]. Lower-bounds for comparison-based sorting appear to be folklore. The following table summarizes the performance of these comparison-based algorithms:

	comparisons		in-place
Merge-sort	$n \log n$	worst-case	No
Quicksort	$1.38 n \log n + O(n)$	expected	Yes
Heap-sort	$2n \log n + O(n)$	worst-case	Yes

Each of these comparison-based algorithms has its advantages and disadvantages. Merge-sort does the fewest comparisons and does not rely on randomization. Unfortunately, it uses an auxilliary array during its merge phase. Allocating this array can be expensive and is a potential point of failure if memory is limited. Quicksort is an *in-place* algorithm and is a close second in terms of the number of comparisons, but is randomized, so this running time is not always guaranteed. Heap-sort does the most comparisons, but it is in-place and deterministic.

There is one setting in which merge-sort is a clear-winner; this occurs when sorting a linked-list. In this case, the auxiliary array is not needed; two sorted linked lists are very easily merged into a single sorted linked-list by pointer manipulations (see Exercise 11.2).

The counting-sort and radix-sort algorithms described here are due to Seward [68, Section 2.4.6]. However, variants of radix-sort have been used since the 1920s to sort punch cards using punched card sorting machines. These machines can sort a stack of cards into two piles based on the existence (or not) of a hole in a specific location on the card. Repeating this process for different hole locations gives an implementation of radix-sort.

Finally, we note that counting sort and radix-sort can be used to sort other types of numbers besides non-negative integers. Straightforward modifications of counting sort can sort integers, in any interval $\{a,\ldots,b\}$, in $O(\mathtt{n}+b-a)$ time. Similarly, radix sort can sort integers in the same interval in $O(\mathtt{n}(\log_{\mathtt{n}}(b-a))$ time. Finally, both of these algorithms can also be used to sort floating point numbers in the IEEE 754 floating point format. This is because the IEEE format is designed to allow the comparison of two floating point numbers by comparing their values as if they were integers in a signed-magnitude binary representation [2].

Exercise 11.1. Illustrate the execution of merge-sort and heap-sort on an input array containing 1,7,4,6,2,8,3,5. Give a sample illustration of one possible execution of quicksort on the same array.

Exercise 11.2. Implement a version of the merge-sort algorithm that sorts a `DLList` without using an auxiliary array. (See Exercise 3.13.)

Exercise 11.3. Some implementations of `quickSort(a,i,n,c)` always use `a[i]` as a pivot. Give an example of an input array of length $\mathtt{n}$ in which such an implementation would perform $\binom{\mathtt{n}}{2}$ comparisons.

Exercise 11.4. Some implementations of `quickSort(a,i,n,c)` always use `a[i+n/2]` as a pivot. Given an example of an input array of length $\mathtt{n}$ in which such an implementation would perform $\binom{\mathtt{n}}{2}$ comparisons.

Exercise 11.5. Show that, for any implementation of `quickSort(a,i,n,c)` that chooses a pivot deterministically, without first looking at any values in a[i],…,a[i + n − 1], there exists an input array of length n that causes this implementation to perform $\binom{n}{2}$ comparisons.

Exercise 11.6. Design a `Comparator`, c, that you could pass as an argument to `quickSort(a, i, n, c)` and that would cause quicksort to perform $\binom{n}{2}$ comparisons. (Hint: Your comparator does not actually need to look at the values being compared.)

Exercise 11.7. Analyze the expected number of comparisons done by Quicksort a little more carefully than the proof of Theorem 11.3. In particular, show that the expected number of comparisons is $2nH_n - n + H_n$.

Exercise 11.8. Describe an input array that causes heap sort to perform at least $2n\log n - O(n)$ comparisons. Justify your answer.

Exercise 11.9. The heap sort implementation described here sorts the elements into reverse sorted order and then reverses the array. This last step could be avoided by defining a new `Comparator` that negates the results of the input `Comparator`, c. Explain why this would not be a good optimization. (Hint: Consider how many negations would need to be done in relation to how long it takes to reverse the array.)

Exercise 11.10. Find another pair of permutations of 1, 2, 3 that are not correctly sorted by the comparison tree in Figure 11.6.

Exercise 11.11. Prove that $\log n! = n\log n - O(n)$.

Exercise 11.12. Prove that a binary tree with k leaves has height at least $\log k$.

Exercise 11.13. Prove that, if we pick a random leaf from a binary tree with k leaves, then the expected height of this leaf is at least $\log k$.

Exercise 11.14. The implementation of `radixSort(a, k)` given here works when the input array, a contains only non-negative integers. Extend this implementation so that it also works correctly when a contains both negative and non-negative integers.

Chapter 12

Graphs

In this chapter, we study two representations of graphs and basic algorithms that use these representations.

Mathematically, a *(directed) graph* is a pair $G = (V, E)$ where V is a set of *vertices* and E is a set of ordered pairs of vertices called *edges*. An edge (i, j) is *directed* from i to j; i is called the *source* of the edge and j is called the *target*. A *path* in G is a sequence of vertices $v_0, \ldots, v_k$ such that, for every $i \in \{1, \ldots, k\}$, the edge (v_{i-1}, v_i) is in E. A path $v_0, \ldots, v_k$ is a *cycle* if, additionally, the edge (v_k, v_0) is in E. A path (or cycle) is *simple* if all of its vertices are unique. If there is a path from some vertex v_i to some vertex v_j then we say that v_j is *reachable* from v_i. An example of a graph is shown in Figure 12.1.

Due to their ability to model so many phenomena, graphs have an enormous number of applications. There are many obvious examples. Computer networks can be modelled as graphs, with vertices corresponding to computers and edges corresponding to (directed) communication links between those computers. City streets can be modelled as graphs, with vertices representing intersections and edges representing streets joining consecutive intersections.

Less obvious examples occur as soon as we realize that graphs can model any pairwise relationships within a set. For example, in a university setting we might have a timetable *conflict graph* whose vertices represent courses offered in the university and in which the edge (i, j) is present if and only if there is at least one student that is taking both class i and class j. Thus, an edge indicates that the exam for class i should not

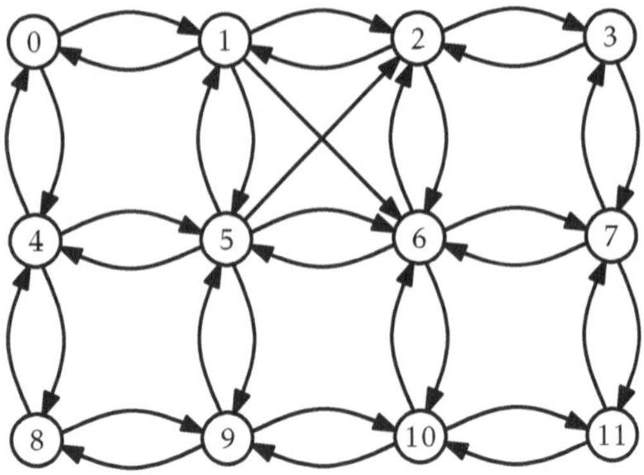

Figure 12.1: A graph with twelve vertices. Vertices are drawn as numbered circles and edges are drawn as pointed curves pointing from source to target.

be scheduled at the same time as the exam for class `j`.

Throughout this section, we will use `n` to denote the number of vertices of G and `m` to denote the number of edges of G. That is, $\mathtt{n} = |V|$ and $\mathtt{m} = |E|$. Furthermore, we will assume that $V = \{0,\ldots,\mathtt{n}-1\}$. Any other data that we would like to associate with the elements of V can be stored in an array of length `n`.

Some typical operations performed on graphs are:

- `addEdge(i, j)`: Add the edge `(i, j)` to E.
- `removeEdge(i, j)`: Remove the edge `(i, j)` from E.
- `hasEdge(i, j)`: Check if the edge $(\mathtt{i},\mathtt{j}) \in E$
- `outEdges(i)`: Return a `List` of all integers `j` such that $(\mathtt{i},\mathtt{j}) \in E$
- `inEdges(i)`: Return a `List` of all integers `j` such that $(\mathtt{j},\mathtt{i}) \in E$

Note that these operations are not terribly difficult to implement efficiently. For example, the first three operations can be implemented directly by using a `USet`, so they can be implemented in constant expected time using the hash tables discussed in Chapter 5. The last two operations can be implemented in constant time by storing, for each vertex, a list of its adjacent vertices.

However, different applications of graphs have different performance requirements for these operations and, ideally, we can use the simplest implementation that satisfies all the application's requirements. For this reason, we discuss two broad categories of graph representations.

12.1 AdjacencyMatrix: Representing a Graph by a Matrix

An *adjacency matrix* is a way of representing an n vertex graph $G = (V, E)$ by an $n \times n$ matrix, a, whose entries are boolean values.

```
AdjacencyMatrix
int n;
boolean[][] a;
AdjacencyMatrix(int n0) {
  n = n0;
  a = new boolean[n][n];
}
```

The matrix entry a[i][j] is defined as

$$\mathtt{a[i][j]} = \begin{cases} \mathtt{true} & \text{if } (\mathtt{i},\mathtt{j}) \in E \\ \mathtt{false} & \text{otherwise} \end{cases}$$

The adjacency matrix for the graph in Figure 12.1 is shown in Figure 12.2.

In this representation, the operations addEdge(i, j), removeEdge(i, j), and hasEdge(i, j) just involve setting or reading the matrix entry a[i][j]:

```
AdjacencyMatrix
void addEdge(int i, int j) {
  a[i][j] = true;
}
void removeEdge(int i, int j) {
  a[i][j] = false;
}
boolean hasEdge(int i, int j) {
  return a[i][j];
}
```

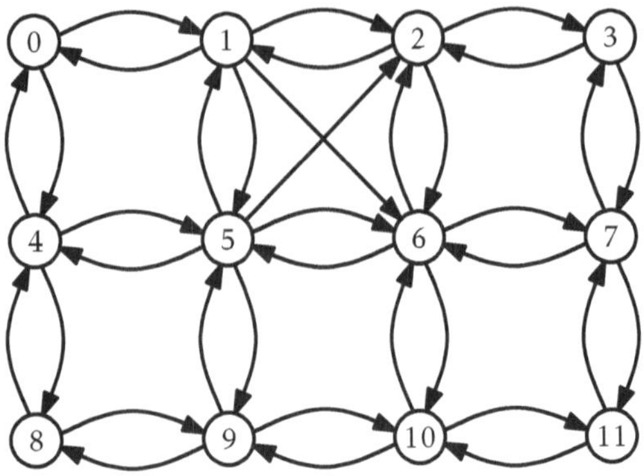

	0	1	2	3	4	5	6	7	8	9	10	11
0	0	1	0	0	1	0	0	0	0	0	0	0
1	1	0	1	0	0	1	1	0	0	0	0	0
2	1	0	0	1	0	0	1	0	0	0	0	0
3	0	0	1	0	0	0	0	1	0	0	0	0
4	1	0	0	0	0	1	0	0	1	0	0	0
5	0	1	1	0	1	0	1	0	0	1	0	0
6	0	0	1	0	0	1	0	1	0	0	1	0
7	0	0	0	1	0	0	1	0	0	0	0	1
8	0	0	0	0	1	0	0	0	0	1	0	0
9	0	0	0	0	0	1	0	0	1	0	1	0
10	0	0	0	0	0	0	1	0	0	1	0	1
11	0	0	0	0	0	0	0	1	0	0	1	0

Figure 12.2: A graph and its adjacency matrix.

These operations clearly take constant time per operation.

Where the adjacency matrix performs poorly is with the outEdges(i) and inEdges(i) operations. To implement these, we must scan all n entries in the corresponding row or column of a and gather up all the indices, j, where a[i][j], respectively a[j][i], is true.

```
AdjacencyMatrix
List<Integer> outEdges(int i) {
  List<Integer> edges = new ArrayList<Integer>();
  for (int j = 0; j < n; j++)
    if (a[i][j]) edges.add(j);
  return edges;
}
List<Integer> inEdges(int i) {
  List<Integer> edges = new ArrayList<Integer>();
  for (int j = 0; j < n; j++)
    if (a[j][i]) edges.add(j);
  return edges;
}
```

These operations clearly take $O(n)$ time per operation.

Another drawback of the adjacency matrix representation is that it is large. It stores an $n \times n$ boolean matrix, so it requires at least n^2 bits of memory. The implementation here uses a matrix of boolean values so it actually uses on the order of n^2 bytes of memory. A more careful implementation, which packs w boolean values into each word of memory, could reduce this space usage to $O(n^2/w)$ words of memory.

Theorem 12.1. *The* AdjacencyMatrix *data structure implements the* Graph *interface. An* AdjacencyMatrix *supports the operations*

- addEdge(i, j), removeEdge(i, j), *and* hasEdge(i, j) *in constant time per operation; and*
- inEdges(i), *and* outEdges(i) *in* $O(n)$ *time per operation.*

The space used by an AdjacencyMatrix *is* $O(n^2)$.

Despite its high memory requirements and poor performance of the inEdges(i) and outEdges(i) operations, an AdjacencyMatrix can still be useful for some applications. In particular, when the graph G is *dense*, i.e., it has close to n^2 edges, then a memory usage of n^2 may be acceptable.

The `AdjacencyMatrix` data structure is also commonly used because algebraic operations on the matrix a can be used to efficiently compute properties of the graph G. This is a topic for a course on algorithms, but we point out one such property here: If we treat the entries of a as integers (1 for `true` and 0 for `false`) and multiply a by itself using matrix multiplication then we get the matrix a^2. Recall, from the definition of matrix multiplication, that

$$a^2[i][j] = \sum_{k=0}^{n-1} a[i][k] \cdot a[k][j] \ .$$

Interpreting this sum in terms of the graph G, this formula counts the number of vertices, k, such that G contains both edges (i,k) and (k,j). That is, it counts the number of paths from i to j (through intermediate vertices, k) whose length is exactly two. This observation is the foundation of an algorithm that computes the shortest paths between all pairs of vertices in G using only $O(\log n)$ matrix multiplications.

12.2 AdjacencyLists: A Graph as a Collection of Lists

Adjacency list representations of graphs take a more vertex-centric approach. There are many possible implementations of adjacency lists. In this section, we present a simple one. At the end of the section, we discuss different possibilities. In an adjacency list representation, the graph $G = (V,E)$ is represented as an array, `adj`, of lists. The list `adj[i]` contains a list of all the vertices adjacent to vertex i. That is, it contains every index j such that $(i, j) \in E$.

AdjacencyLists

```
int n;
List<Integer>[] adj;
AdjacencyLists(int n0) {
  n = n0;
  adj = (List<Integer>[])new List[n];
  for (int i = 0; i < n; i++)
```

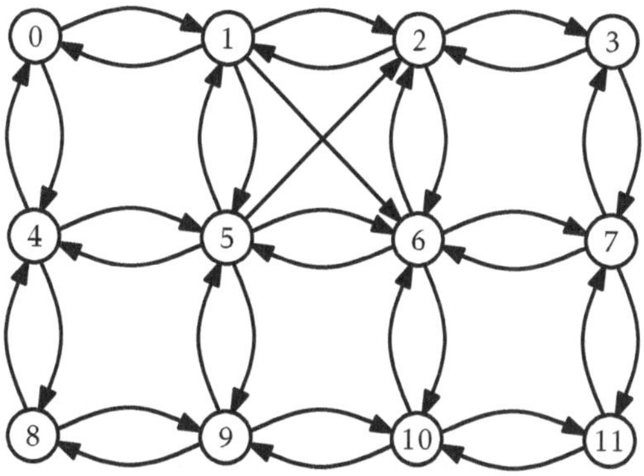

0	1	2	3	4	5	6	7	8	9	10	11
1	0	1	2	0	1	5	6	4	8	9	10
4	2	3	7	5	2	2	3	9	5	6	7
	6	6		8	6	7	11		10	11	
	5				9	10					
					4						

Figure 12.3: A graph and its adjacency lists

```
    adj[i] = new ArrayStack<Integer>();
}
```

(An example is shown in Figure 12.3.) In this particular implementation, we represent each list in adj as an ArrayStack, because we would like constant time access by position. Other options are also possible. Specifically, we could have implemented adj as a DLList.

The addEdge(i, j) operation just appends the value j to the list adj[i]:

```
AdjacencyLists
void addEdge(int i, int j) {
  adj[i].add(j);
}
```

This takes constant time.

The removeEdge(i, j) operation searches through the list adj[i] until it finds j and then removes it:

AdjacencyLists
```
void removeEdge(int i, int j) {
  Iterator<Integer> it = adj[i].iterator();
  while (it.hasNext()) {
    if (it.next() == j) {
      it.remove();
      return;
    }
  }
}
```

This takes $O(\deg(\mathtt{i}))$ time, where $\deg(\mathtt{i})$ (the *degree* of i) counts the number of edges in E that have i as their source.

The hasEdge(i, j) operation is similar; it searches through the list adj[i] until it finds j (and returns true), or reaches the end of the list (and returns false):

AdjacencyLists
```
boolean hasEdge(int i, int j) {
  return adj[i].contains(j);
}
```

This also takes $O(\deg(\mathtt{i}))$ time.

The outEdges(i) operation is very simple; it returns the list adj[i]:

AdjacencyLists
```
List<Integer> outEdges(int i) {
  return adj[i];
}
```

This clearly takes constant time.

The inEdges(i) operation is much more work. It scans over every vertex j checking if the edge (i, j) exists and, if so, adding j to the output list:

AdjacencyLists
```
List<Integer> inEdges(int i) {
  List<Integer> edges = new ArrayStack<Integer>();
```

```
  for (int j = 0; j < n; j++)
    if (adj[j].contains(i))  edges.add(j);
  return edges;
}
```

This operation is very slow. It scans the adjacency list of every vertex, so it takes $O(n+m)$ time.

The following theorem summarizes the performance of the above data structure:

Theorem 12.2. *The* AdjacencyLists *data structure implements the* Graph *interface. An* AdjacencyLists *supports the operations*

- addEdge(i, j) *in constant time per operation;*
- removeEdge(i, j) *and* hasEdge(i, j) *in $O(\deg(i))$ time per operation;*
- outEdges(i) *in constant time per operation; and*
- inEdges(i) *in $O(n+m)$ time per operation.*

The space used by a AdjacencyLists *is $O(n+m)$.*

As alluded to earlier, there are many different choices to be made when implementing a graph as an adjacency list. Some questions that come up include:

- What type of collection should be used to store each element of adj? One could use an array-based list, a linked-list, or even a hashtable.
- Should there be a second adjacency list, inadj, that stores, for each i, the list of vertices, j, such that $(j, i) \in E$? This can greatly reduce the running-time of the inEdges(i) operation, but requires slightly more work when adding or removing edges.
- Should the entry for the edge (i, j) in adj[i] be linked by a reference to the corresponding entry in inadj[j]?
- Should edges be first-class objects with their own associated data? In this way, adj would contain lists of edges rather than lists of vertices (integers).

Most of these questions come down to a tradeoff between complexity (and space) of implementation and performance features of the implementation.

12.3 Graph Traversal

In this section we present two algorithms for exploring a graph, starting at one of its vertices, i, and finding all vertices that are reachable from i. Both of these algorithms are best suited to graphs represented using an adjacency list representation. Therefore, when analyzing these algorithms we will assume that the underlying representation is an AdjacencyLists.

12.3.1 Breadth-First Search

The *bread-first-search* algorithm starts at a vertex i and visits, first the neighbours of i, then the neighbours of the neighbours of i, then the neighbours of the neighbours of the neighbours of i, and so on.

This algorithm is a generalization of the breadth-first traversal algorithm for binary trees (Section 6.1.2), and is very similar; it uses a queue, q, that initially contains only i. It then repeatedly extracts an element from q and adds its neighbours to q, provided that these neighbours have never been in q before. The only major difference between the breadth-first-search algorithm for graphs and the one for trees is that the algorithm for graphs has to ensure that it does not add the same vertex to q more than once. It does this by using an auxiliary boolean array, seen, that tracks which vertices have already been discovered.

Algorithms
```
void bfs(Graph g, int r) {
  boolean[] seen = new boolean[g.nVertices()];
  Queue<Integer> q = new SLList<Integer>();
  q.add(r);
  seen[r] = true;
  while (!q.isEmpty()) {
    int i = q.remove();
    for (Integer j : g.outEdges(i)) {
```

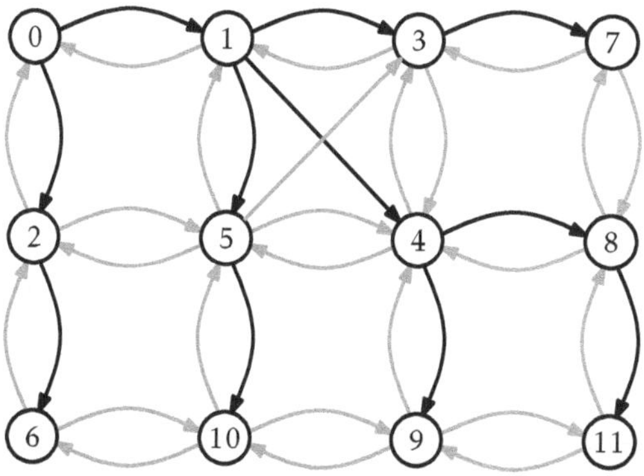

Figure 12.4: An example of bread-first-search starting at node 0. Nodes are labelled with the order in which they are added to q. Edges that result in nodes being added to q are drawn in black, other edges are drawn in grey.

```
        if (!seen[j]) {
          q.add(j);
          seen[j] = true;
        }
      }
    }
  }
```

An example of running bfs(g,0) on the graph from Figure 12.1 is shown in Figure 12.4. Different executions are possible, depending on the ordering of the adjacency lists; Figure 12.4 uses the adjacency lists in Figure 12.3.

Analyzing the running-time of the bfs(g,i) routine is fairly straightforward. The use of the seen array ensures that no vertex is added to q more than once. Adding (and later removing) each vertex from q takes constant time per vertex for a total of $O(\mathtt{n})$ time. Since each vertex is processed by the inner loop at most once, each adjacency list is processed at most once, so each edge of G is processed at most once. This processing, which is done in the inner loop takes constant time per iteration, for a total of $O(\mathtt{m})$ time. Therefore, the entire algorithm runs in $O(\mathtt{n}+\mathtt{m})$ time.

The following theorem summarizes the performance of the bfs(g,r) algorithm.

Theorem 12.3. *When given as input a* `Graph`*,* `g`*, that is implemented using the* `AdjacencyLists` *data structure, the* `bfs(g,r)` *algorithm runs in* $O(n+m)$ *time.*

A breadth-first traversal has some very special properties. Calling `bfs(g,r)` will eventually enqueue (and eventually dequeue) every vertex `j` such that there is a directed path from `r` to `j`. Moreover, the vertices at distance 0 from `r` (`r` itself) will enter `q` before the vertices at distance 1, which will enter `q` before the vertices at distance 2, and so on. Thus, the `bfs(g,r)` method visits vertices in increasing order of distance from `r` and vertices that cannot be reached from `r` are never visited at all.

A particularly useful application of the breadth-first-search algorithm is, therefore, in computing shortest paths. To compute the shortest path from `r` to every other vertex, we use a variant of `bfs(g,r)` that uses an auxilliary array, `p`, of length `n`. When a new vertex `j` is added to `q`, we set `p[j] = i`. In this way, `p[j]` becomes the second last node on a shortest path from `r` to `j`. Repeating this, by taking `p[p[j]]`, `p[p[p[j]]]`, and so on we can reconstruct the (reversal of) a shortest path from `r` to `j`.

12.3.2 Depth-First Search

The *depth-first-search* algorithm is similar to the standard algorithm for traversing binary trees; it first fully explores one subtree before returning to the current node and then exploring the other subtree. Another way to think of depth-first-search is by saying that it is similar to breadth-first search except that it uses a stack instead of a queue.

During the execution of the depth-first-search algorithm, each vertex, `i`, is assigned a colour, `c[i]`: `white` if we have never seen the vertex before, `grey` if we are currently visiting that vertex, and `black` if we are done visiting that vertex. The easiest way to think of depth-first-search is as a recursive algorithm. It starts by visiting `r`. When visiting a vertex `i`, we first mark `i` as `grey`. Next, we scan `i`'s adjacency list and recursively visit any white vertex we find in this list. Finally, we are done processing `i`, so we colour `i` black and return.

Algorithms
```
void dfs(Graph g, int r) {
```

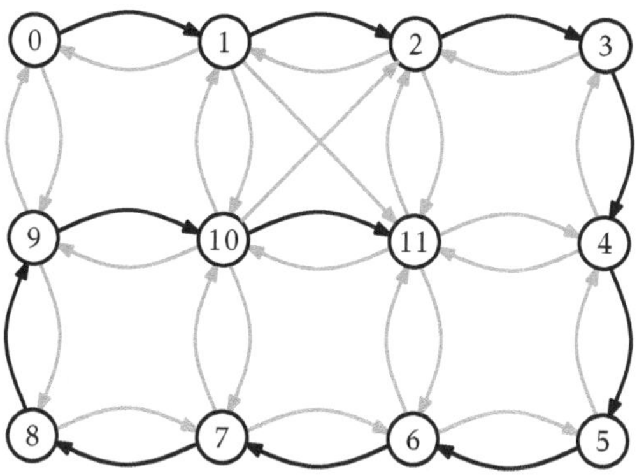

Figure 12.5: An example of depth-first-search starting at node 0. Nodes are labelled with the order in which they are processed. Edges that result in a recursive call are drawn in black, other edges are drawn in grey.

```
  byte[] c = new byte[g.nVertices()];
  dfs(g, r, c);
}
void dfs(Graph g, int i, byte[] c) {
  c[i] = grey;  // currently visiting i
  for (Integer j : g.outEdges(i)) {
    if (c[j] == white) {
      c[j] = grey;
      dfs(g, j, c);
    }
  }
  c[i] = black; // done visiting i
}
```

An example of the execution of this algorithm is shown in Figure 12.5.

Although depth-first-search may best be thought of as a recursive algorithm, recursion is not the best way to implement it. Indeed, the code given above will fail for many large graphs by causing a stack overflow. An alternative implementation is to replace the recursion stack with an explicit stack, s. The following implementation does just that:

Algorithms

```
void dfs2(Graph g, int r) {
```

```
  byte[] c = new byte[g.nVertices()];
  Stack<Integer> s = new Stack<Integer>();
  s.push(r);
  while (!s.isEmpty()) {
    int i = s.pop();
    if (c[i] == white) {
      c[i] = grey;
      for (int j : g.outEdges(i))
        s.push(j);
    }
  }
}
```

In the preceding code, when the next vertex, `i`, is processed, `i` is coloured `grey` and then replaced, on the stack, with its adjacent vertices. During the next iteration, one of these vertices will be visited.

Not surprisingly, the running times of `dfs(g,r)` and `dfs2(g,r)` are the same as that of `bfs(g,r)`:

Theorem 12.4. *When given as input a Graph, g, that is implemented using the AdjacencyLists data structure, the* `dfs(g,r)` *and* `dfs2(g,r)` *algorithms each run in* $O(n+m)$ *time.*

As with the breadth-first-search algorithm, there is an underlying tree associated with each execution of depth-first-search. When a node $i \neq r$ goes from `white` to `grey`, this is because `dfs(g,i,c)` was called recursively while processing some node i'. (In the case of `dfs2(g,r)` algorithm, `i` is one of the nodes that replaced i' on the stack.) If we think of i' as the parent of `i`, then we obtain a tree rooted at `r`. In Figure 12.5, this tree is a path from vertex 0 to vertex 11.

An important property of the depth-first-search algorithm is the following: Suppose that when node `i` is coloured `grey`, there exists a path from `i` to some other node `j` that uses only white vertices. Then `j` will be coloured first `grey` then `black` before `i` is coloured `black`. (This can be proven by contradiction, by considering any path P from `i` to `j`.)

One application of this property is the detection of cycles. Refer to Figure 12.6. Consider some cycle, C, that can be reached from `r`. Let `i` be the first node of C that is coloured `grey`, and let `j` be the node that

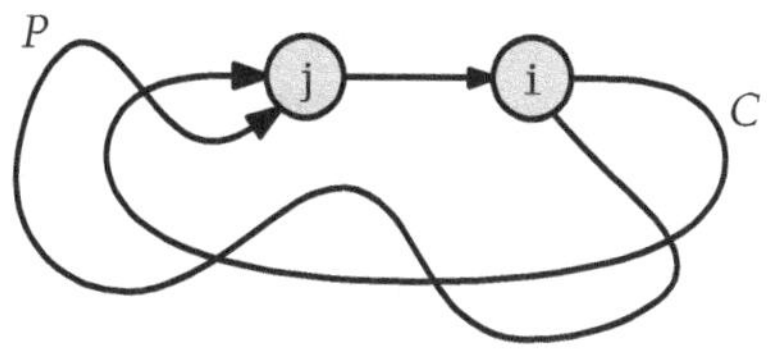

Figure 12.6: The depth-first-search algorithm can be used to detect cycles in G. The node j is coloured grey while i is still grey. This implies that there is a path, P, from i to j in the depth-first-search tree, and the edge (j, i) implies that P is also a cycle.

precedes i on the cycle C. Then, by the above property, j will be coloured grey and the edge (j, i) will be considered by the algorithm while i is still grey. Thus, the algorithm can conclude that there is a path, P, from i to j in the depth-first-search tree and the edge (j, i) exists. Therefore, P is also a cycle.

12.4 Discussion and Exercises

The running times of the depth-first-search and breadth-first-search algorithms are somewhat overstated by the Theorems 12.3 and 12.4. Define n_r as the number of vertices, i, of G, for which there exists a path from r to i. Define m_r as the number of edges that have these vertices as their sources. Then the following theorem is a more precise statement of the running times of the breadth-first-search and depth-first-search algorithms. (This more refined statement of the running time is useful in some of the applications of these algorithms outlined in the exercises.)

Theorem 12.5. *When given as input a Graph, g, that is implemented using the AdjacencyLists data structure, the* bfs(g, r), dfs(g, r) *and* dfs2(g, r) *algorithms each run in* $O(n_r + m_r)$ *time.*

Breadth-first search seems to have been discovered independently by Moore [52] and Lee [49] in the contexts of maze exploration and circuit routing, respectively.

Adjacency-list representations of graphs were presented by Hopcroft and Tarjan [40] as an alternative to the (then more common) adjacency-

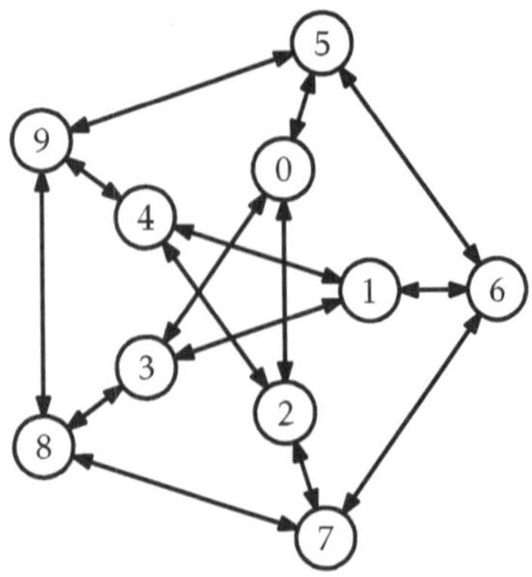

Figure 12.7: An example graph.

matrix representation. This representation, as well as depth-first-search, played a major part in the celebrated Hopcroft-Tarjan planarity testing algorithm that can determine, in $O(\mathtt{n})$ time, if a graph can be drawn, in the plane, and in such a way that no pair of edges cross each other [41].

In the following exercises, an undirected graph is one in which, for every i and j, the edge (i, j) is present if and only if the edge (j, i) is present.

Exercise 12.1. Draw an adjacency list representation and an adjacency matrix representation of the graph in Figure 12.7.

Exercise 12.2. The *incidence matrix* representation of a graph, G, is an $\mathtt{n} \times \mathtt{m}$ matrix, A, where

$$A_{i,j} = \begin{cases} -1 & \text{if vertex } i \text{ the source of edge } j \\ +1 & \text{if vertex } i \text{ the target of edge } j \\ 0 & \text{otherwise.} \end{cases}$$

1. Draw the incident matrix representation of the graph in Figure 12.7.

2. Design, analyze and implement an incidence matrix representation of a graph. Be sure to analyze the space, the cost of addEdge(i, j), removeEdge(i, j), hasEdge(i, j), inEdges(i), and outEdges(i).

Exercise 12.3. Illustrate an execution of the bfs(G, 0) and dfs(G, 0) on the graph, G, in Figure 12.7.

Exercise 12.4. Let G be an undirected graph. We say G is *connected* if, for every pair of vertices i and j in G, there is a path from i to j (since G is undirected, there is also a path from j to i). Show how to test if G is connected in $O(n + m)$ time.

Exercise 12.5. Let G be an undirected graph. A *connected-component labelling* of G partitions the vertices of G into maximal sets, each of which forms a connected subgraph. Show how to compute a connected component labelling of G in $O(n + m)$ time.

Exercise 12.6. Let G be an undirected graph. A *spanning forest* of G is a collection of trees, one per component, whose edges are edges of G and whose vertices contain all vertices of G. Show how to compute a spanning forest of of G in $O(n + m)$ time.

Exercise 12.7. We say that a graph G is *strongly-connected* if, for every pair of vertices i and j in G, there is a path from i to j. Show how to test if G is strongly-connected in $O(n + m)$ time.

Exercise 12.8. Given a graph $G = (V, E)$ and some special vertex $r \in V$, show how to compute the length of the shortest path from r to i for every vertex $i \in V$.

Exercise 12.9. Give a (simple) example where the dfs(g, r) code visits the nodes of a graph in an order that is different from that of the dfs2(g, r) code. Write a version of dfs2(g, r) that always visits nodes in exactly the same order as dfs(g, r). (Hint: Just start tracing the execution of each algorithm on some graph where r is the source of more than 1 edge.)

Exercise 12.10. A *universal sink* in a graph G is a vertex that is the target of $n - 1$ edges and the source of no edges.[1] Design and implement an algorithm that tests if a graph G, represented as an AdjacencyMatrix, has a universal sink. Your algorithm should run in $O(n)$ time.

[1] A universal sink, v, is also sometimes called a *celebrity*: Everyone in the room recognizes v, but v doesn't recognize anyone else in the room.

Chapter 13

Data Structures for Integers

In this chapter, we return to the problem of implementing an SSet. The difference now is that we assume the elements stored in the SSet are w-bit integers. That is, we want to implement add(x), remove(x), and find(x) where $x \in \{0,\ldots,2^w-1\}$. It is not too hard to think of plenty of applications where the data—or at least the key that we use for sorting the data—is an integer.

We will discuss three data structures, each building on the ideas of the previous. The first structure, the BinaryTrie performs all three SSet operations in $O(w)$ time. This is not very impressive, since any subset of $\{0,\ldots,2^w-1\}$ has size $n \le 2^w$, so that $\log n \le w$. All the other SSet implementations discussed in this book perform all operations in $O(\log n)$ time so they are all at least as fast as a BinaryTrie.

The second structure, the XFastTrie, speeds up the search in a BinaryTrie by using hashing. With this speedup, the find(x) operation runs in $O(\log w)$ time. However, add(x) and remove(x) operations in an XFastTrie still take $O(w)$ time and the space used by an XFastTrie is $O(n \cdot w)$.

The third data structure, the YFastTrie, uses an XFastTrie to store only a sample of roughly one out of every w elements and stores the remaining elements in a standard SSet structure. This trick reduces the running time of add(x) and remove(x) to $O(\log w)$ and decreases the space to $O(n)$.

The implementations used as examples in this chapter can store any type of data, as long as an integer can be associated with it. In the code samples, the variable ix is always the integer value associated with x, and

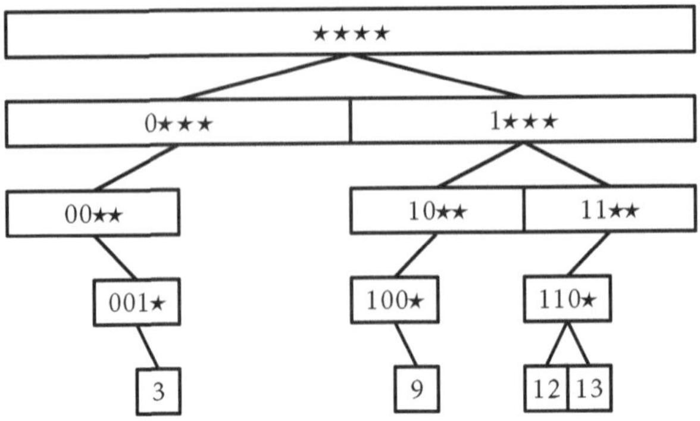

Figure 13.1: The integers stored in a binary trie are encoded as root-to-leaf paths.

the method in.intValue(x) converts x to its associated integer. In the text, however, we will simply treat x as if it is an integer.

13.1 BinaryTrie: A digital search tree

A BinaryTrie encodes a set of w bit integers in a binary tree. All leaves in the tree have depth w and each integer is encoded as a root-to-leaf path. The path for the integer x turns left at level i if the ith most significant bit of x is a 0 and turns right if it is a 1. Figure 13.1 shows an example for the case w = 4, in which the trie stores the integers 3(0011), 9(1001), 12(1100), and 13(1101).

Because the search path for a value x depends on the bits of x, it will be helpful to name the children of a node, u, u.child[0] (left) and u.child[1] (right). These child pointers will actually serve double-duty. Since the leaves in a binary trie have no children, the pointers are used to string the leaves together into a doubly-linked list. For a leaf in the binary trie u.child[0] (prev) is the node that comes before u in the list and u.child[1] (next) is the node that follows u in the list. A special node, dummy, is used both before the first node and after the last node in the list (see Section 3.2).

Each node, u, also contains an additional pointer u.jump. If u's left

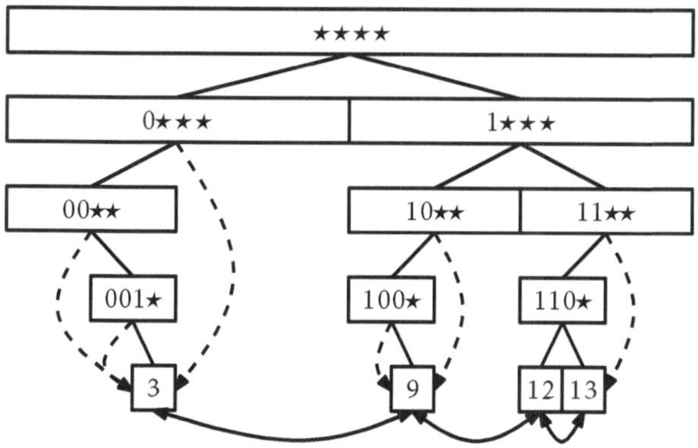

Figure 13.2: A BinaryTrie with jump pointers shown as curved dashed edges.

child is missing, then u.jump points to the smallest leaf in u's subtree. If u's right child is missing, then u.jump points to the largest leaf in u's subtree. An example of a BinaryTrie, showing jump pointers and the doubly-linked list at the leaves, is shown in Figure 13.2.

The find(x) operation in a BinaryTrie is fairly straightforward. We try to follow the search path for x in the trie. If we reach a leaf, then we have found x. If we reach a node u where we cannot proceed (because u is missing a child), then we follow u.jump, which takes us either to the smallest leaf larger than x or the largest leaf smaller than x. Which of these two cases occurs depends on whether u is missing its left or right child, respectively. In the former case (u is missing its left child), we have found the node we want. In the latter case (u is missing its right child), we can use the linked list to reach the node we want. Each of these cases is illustrated in Figure 13.3.

```
BinaryTrie
T find(T x) {
  int i, c = 0, ix = it.intValue(x);
  Node u = r;
  for (i = 0; i < w; i++) {
    c = (ix >>> w-i-1) & 1;
    if (u.child[c] == null) break;
    u = u.child[c];
  }
```

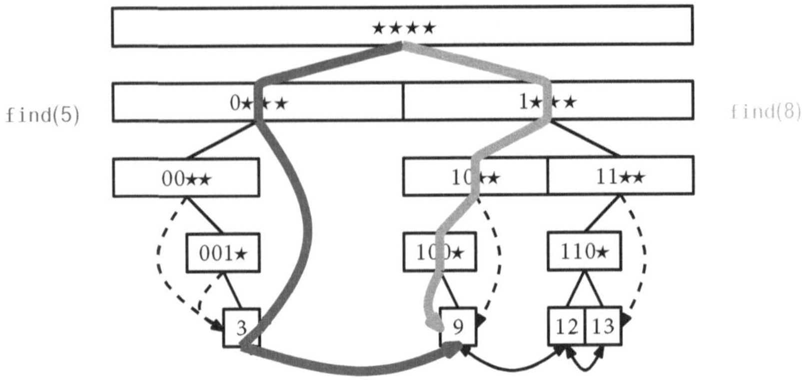

Figure 13.3: The paths followed by find(5) and find(8).

```
    if (i == w) return u.x;   // found it
    u = (c == 0) ? u.jump : u.jump.child[next];
    return u == dummy ? null : u.x;
}
```

The running-time of the find(x) method is dominated by the time it takes to follow a root-to-leaf path, so it runs in $O(\mathrm{w})$ time.

The add(x) operation in a BinaryTrie is also fairly straightforward, but has a lot of work to do:

1. It follows the search path for x until reaching a node u where it can no longer proceed.
2. It creates the remainder of the search path from u to a leaf that contains x.
3. It adds the node, u′, containing x to the linked list of leaves (it has access to the predecessor, pred, of u′ in the linked list from the jump pointer of the last node, u, encountered during step 1.)
4. It walks back up the search path for x adjusting jump pointers at the nodes whose jump pointer should now point to x.

An addition is illustrated in Figure 13.4.

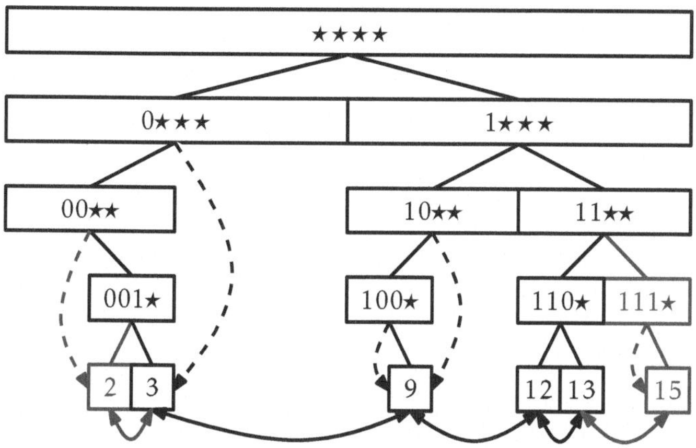

Figure 13.4: Adding the values 2 and 15 to the BinaryTrie in Figure 13.2.

```
                              BinaryTrie
boolean add(T x) {
  int i, c = 0, ix = it.intValue(x);
  Node u = r;
  // 1 - search for ix until falling out of the trie
  for (i = 0; i < w; i++) {
    c = (ix >>> w-i-1) & 1;
    if (u.child[c] == null) break;
    u = u.child[c];
  }
  if (i == w) return false; // already contains x - abort
  Node pred = (c == right) ? u.jump : u.jump.child[0];
  u.jump = null;  // u will have two children shortly
  // 2 - add path to ix
  for (; i < w; i++) {
    c = (ix >>> w-i-1) & 1;
    u.child[c] = newNode();
    u.child[c].parent = u;
    u = u.child[c];
  }
  u.x = x;
  // 3 - add u to linked list
  u.child[prev] = pred;
  u.child[next] = pred.child[next];
```

```
  u.child[prev].child[next] = u;
  u.child[next].child[prev] = u;
  // 4 - walk back up, updating jump pointers
  Node v = u.parent;
  while (v != null) {
    if ((v.child[left] == null
        && (v.jump == null || it.intValue(v.jump.x) > ix))
    || (v.child[right] == null
        && (v.jump == null || it.intValue(v.jump.x) < ix)))
      v.jump = u;
    v = v.parent;
  }
  n++;
  return true;
}
```

This method performs one walk down the search path for x and one walk back up. Each step of these walks takes constant time, so the add(x) method runs in $O(w)$ time.

The remove(x) operation undoes the work of add(x). Like add(x), it has a lot of work to do:

1. It follows the search path for x until reaching the leaf, u, containing x.
2. It removes u from the doubly-linked list.
3. It deletes u and then walks back up the search path for x deleting nodes until reaching a node v that has a child that is not on the search path for x.
4. It walks upwards from v to the root updating any jump pointers that point to u.

A removal is illustrated in Figure 13.5.

BinaryTrie

```
boolean remove(T x) {
  // 1 - find leaf, u, containing x
  int i = 0, c, ix = it.intValue(x);
  Node u = r;
```

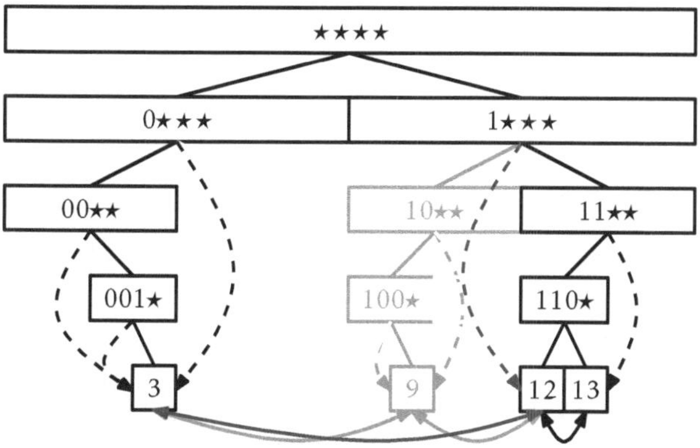

Figure 13.5: Removing the value 9 from the BinaryTrie in Figure 13.2.

```
for (i = 0; i < w; i++) {
  c = (ix >>> w-i-1) & 1;
  if (u.child[c] == null) return false;
  u = u.child[c];
}
// 2 - remove u from linked list
u.child[prev].child[next] = u.child[next];
u.child[next].child[prev] = u.child[prev];
Node v = u;
// 3 - delete nodes on path to u
for (i = w-1; i >= 0; i--) {
  c = (ix >>> w-i-1) & 1;
  v = v.parent;
  v.child[c] = null;
  if (v.child[1-c] != null) break;
}
// 4 - update jump pointers
v.jump = u;
for (; i >= 0; i--) {
  c = (ix >>> w-i-1) & 1;
  if (v.jump == u)
    v.jump = u.child[1-c];
  v = v.parent;
}
n--;
```

```
    return true;
}
```

Theorem 13.1. *A* BinaryTrie *implements the* SSet *interface for* w*-bit integers. A* BinaryTrie *supports the operations* add(x), remove(x), *and* find(x) *in* $O(\mathsf{w})$ *time per operation. The space used by a* BinaryTrie *that stores* n *values is* $O(\mathsf{n}\cdot\mathsf{w})$.

13.2 XFastTrie: Searching in Doubly-Logarithmic Time

The performance of the BinaryTrie structure is not very impressive. The number of elements, n, stored in the structure is at most 2^{w}, so $\log \mathsf{n} \le \mathsf{w}$. In other words, any of the comparison-based SSet structures described in other parts of this book are at least as efficient as a BinaryTrie, and are not restricted to only storing integers.

Next we describe the XFastTrie, which is just a BinaryTrie with $\mathsf{w}+1$ hash tables—one for each level of the trie. These hash tables are used to speed up the find(x) operation to $O(\log \mathsf{w})$ time. Recall that the find(x) operation in a BinaryTrie is almost complete once we reach a node, u, where the search path for x would like to proceed to u.right (or u.left) but u has no right (respectively, left) child. At this point, the search uses u.jump to jump to a leaf, v, of the BinaryTrie and either return v or its successor in the linked list of leaves. An XFastTrie speeds up the search process by using binary search on the levels of the trie to locate the node u.

To use binary search, we need a way to determine if the node u we are looking for is above a particular level, i, of if u is at or below level i. This information is given by the highest-order i bits in the binary representation of x; these bits determine the search path that x takes from the root to level i. For an example, refer to Figure 13.6; in this figure the last node, u, on search path for 14 (whose binary representation is 1110) is the node labelled 11★★ at level 2 because there is no node labelled 111★ at level 3. Thus, we can label each node at level i with an i-bit integer. Then, the node u we are searching for would be at or below level i if and only if there is a node at level i whose label matches the highest-order i

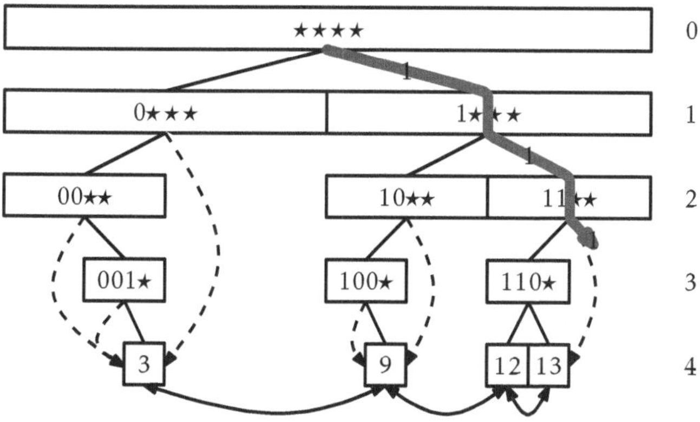

Figure 13.6: Since there is no node labelled 111★, the search path for 14 (1110) ends at the node labelled 11★★ .

bits of x.

In an XFastTrie, we store, for each $i \in \{0,\ldots,w\}$, all the nodes at level i in a USet, t[i], that is implemented as a hash table (Chapter 5). Using this USet allows us to check in constant expected time if there is a node at level i whose label matches the highest-order i bits of x. In fact, we can even find this node using t[i].find(x>>>(w − i))

The hash tables t[0],...,t[w] allow us to use binary search to find u. Initially, we know that u is at some level i with $0 \le i < w+1$. We therefore initialize l = 0 and h = w + 1 and repeatedly look at the hash table t[i], where $i = \lfloor (l+h)/2 \rfloor$. If t[i] contains a node whose label matches x's highest-order i bits then we set l = i (u is at or below level i); otherwise we set h = i (u is above level i). This process terminates when $h - l \le 1$, in which case we determine that u is at level l. We then complete the find(x) operation using u.jump and the doubly-linked list of leaves.

```
XFastTrie
T find(T x) {
  int l = 0, h = w+1, ix = it.intValue(x);
  Node v, u = r, q = newNode();
  while (h-l > 1) {
    int i = (l+h)/2;
    q.prefix = ix >>> w-i;
```

```
    if ((v = t[i].find(q)) == null) {
      h = i;
    } else {
      u = v;
      l = i;
    }
  }
  if (l == w) return u.x;
  Node pred = (((ix >>> w-l-1) & 1) == 1)
         ? u.jump : u.jump.child[0];
  return (pred.child[next] == dummy)
               ? null : pred.child[next].x;
}
```

Each iteration of the while loop in the above method decreases h − l by roughly a factor of two, so this loop finds u after $O(\log w)$ iterations. Each iteration performs a constant amount of work and one find(x) operation in a USet, which takes a constant expected amount of time. The remaining work takes only constant time, so the find(x) method in an XFastTrie takes only $O(\log w)$ expected time.

The add(x) and remove(x) methods for an XFastTrie are almost identical to the same methods in a BinaryTrie. The only modifications are for managing the hash tables t[0],...,t[w]. During the add(x) operation, when a new node is created at level i, this node is added to t[i]. During a remove(x) operation, when a node is removed form level i, this node is removed from t[i]. Since adding and removing from a hash table take constant expected time, this does not increase the running times of add(x) and remove(x) by more than a constant factor. We omit a code listing for add(x) and remove(x) since the code is almost identical to the (long) code listing already provided for the same methods in a BinaryTrie.

The following theorem summarizes the performance of an XFastTrie:

Theorem 13.2. *An XFastTrie implements the SSet interface for w-bit integers. An XFastTrie supports the operations*

- add(x) *and* remove(x) *in $O(w)$ expected time per operation and
- find(x) *in $O(\log w)$ expected time per operation.*

The space used by an XFastTrie that stores n values is $O(n \cdot w)$.

13.3 YFastTrie: A Doubly-Logarithmic Time SSet

The XFastTrie is a vast—even exponential—improvement over the BinaryTrie in terms of query time, but the add(x) and remove(x) operations are still not terribly fast. Furthermore, the space usage, $O(n \cdot w)$, is higher than the other SSet implementations described in this book, which all use $O(n)$ space. These two problems are related; if n add(x) operations build a structure of size $n \cdot w$, then the add(x) operation requires at least on the order of w time (and space) per operation.

The YFastTrie, discussed next, simultaneously improves the space and speed of XFastTries. A YFastTrie uses an XFastTrie, xft, but only stores $O(n/w)$ values in xft. In this way, the total space used by xft is only $O(n)$. Furthermore, only one out of every w add(x) or remove(x) operations in the YFastTrie results in an add(x) or remove(x) operation in xft. By doing this, the average cost incurred by calls to xft's add(x) and remove(x) operations is only constant.

The obvious question becomes: If xft only stores n/w elements, where do the remaining $n(1-1/w)$ elements go? These elements move into *secondary structures*, in this case an extended version of treaps (Section 7.2). There are roughly n/w of these secondary structures so, on average, each of them stores $O(w)$ items. Treaps support logarithmic time SSet operations, so the operations on these treaps will run in $O(\log w)$ time, as required.

More concretely, a YFastTrie contains an XFastTrie, xft, that contains a random sample of the data, where each element appears in the sample independently with probability 1/w. For convenience, the value $2^w - 1$, is always contained in xft. Let $x_0 < x_1 < \cdots < x_{k-1}$ denote the elements stored in xft. Associated with each element, x_i, is a treap, t_i, that stores all values in the range $x_{i-1}+1,\ldots,x_i$. This is illustrated in Figure 13.7.

The find(x) operation in a YFastTrie is fairly easy. We search for x in xft and find some value x_i associated with the treap t_i. We then use the treap find(x) method on t_i to answer the query. The entire method is a one-liner:

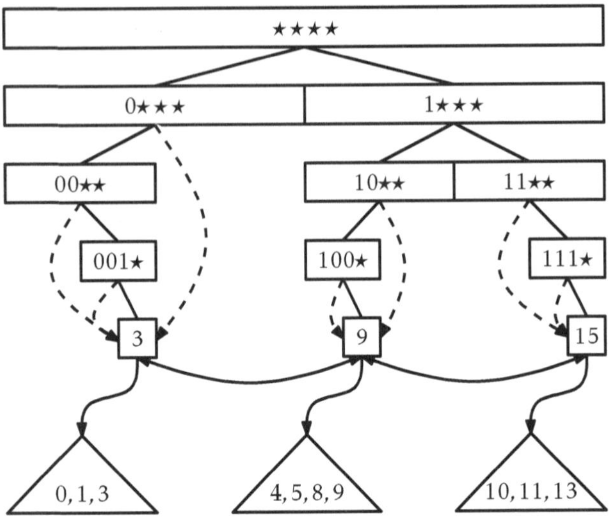

Figure 13.7: A YFastTrie containing the values 0, 1, 3, 4, 6, 8, 9, 10, 11, and 13.

```
YFastTrie
T find(T x) {
  return xft.find(new Pair<T>(it.intValue(x))).t.find(x);
}
```

The first find(x) operation (on xft) takes $O(\log w)$ time. The second find(x) operation (on a treap) takes $O(\log r)$ time, where r is the size of the treap. Later in this section, we will show that the expected size of the treap is $O(w)$ so that this operation takes $O(\log w)$ time.[1]

Adding an element to a YFastTrie is also fairly simple—most of the time. The add(x) method calls xft.find(x) to locate the treap, t, into which x should be inserted. It then calls t.add(x) to add x to t. At this point, it tosses a biased coin that comes up as heads with probability $1/w$ and as tails with probability $1 - 1/w$. If this coin comes up heads, then x will be added to xft.

This is where things get a little more complicated. When x is added to xft, the treap t needs to be split into two treaps, t1 and t′. The treap t1 contains all the values less than or equal to x; t′ is the original treap,

[1]This is an application of *Jensen's Inequality*: If $E[r] = w$, then $E[\log r] \le \log w$.

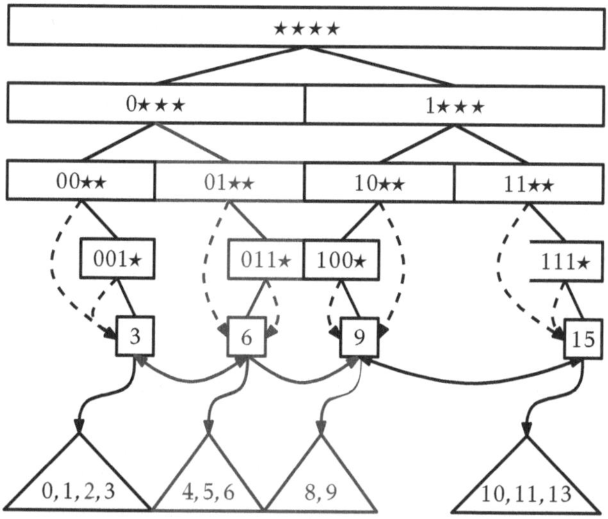

Figure 13.8: Adding the values 2 and 6 to a YFastTrie. The coin toss for 6 came up heads, so 6 was added to xft and the treap containing 4,5,6,8,9 was split.

t, with the elements of t1 removed. Once this is done, we add the pair (x, t1) to xft. Figure 13.8 shows an example.

```
                         YFastTrie
boolean add(T x) {
  int ix = it.intValue(x);
  STreap<T> t = xft.find(new Pair<T>(ix)).t;
  if (t.add(x)) {
    n++;
    if (rand.nextInt(w) == 0) {
      STreap<T> t1 = t.split(x);
      xft.add(new Pair<T>(ix, t1));
    }
    return true;
  }
  return false;
}
```

Adding x to t takes $O(\log w)$ time. Exercise 7.12 shows that splitting t into t1 and t′ can also be done in $O(\log w)$ expected time. Adding the pair (x,t1) to xft takes $O(w)$ time, but only happens with probability $1/w$. Therefore, the expected running time of the add(x) operation is

$$O(\log w) + \frac{1}{w}O(w) = O(\log w) \ .$$

The remove(x) method undoes the work performed by add(x). We use xft to find the leaf, u, in xft that contains the answer to xft.find(x). From u, we get the treap, t, containing x and remove x from t. If x was also stored in xft (and x is not equal to $2^w - 1$) then we remove x from xft and add the elements from x's treap to the treap, t2, that is stored by u's successor in the linked list. This is illustrated in Figure 13.9.

```
                                YFastTrie
boolean remove(T x) {
  int ix = it.intValue(x);
  Node<T> u = xft.findNode(ix);
  boolean ret = u.x.t.remove(x);
  if (ret) n--;
  if (u.x.x == ix && ix != 0xffffffff) {
    STreap<T> t2 = u.child[1].x.t;
    t2.absorb(u.x.t);
    xft.remove(u.x);
  }
  return ret;
}
```

Finding the node u in xft takes $O(\log w)$ expected time. Removing x from t takes $O(\log w)$ expected time. Again, Exercise 7.12 shows that merging all the elements of t into t2 can be done in $O(\log w)$ time. If necessary, removing x from xft takes $O(w)$ time, but x is only contained in xft with probability $1/w$. Therefore, the expected time to remove an element from a YFastTrie is $O(\log w)$.

Earlier in the discussion, we delayed arguing about the sizes of treaps in this structure until later. Before finishing this chapter, we prove the result we need.

Lemma 13.1. *Let* x *be an integer stored in a* YFastTrie *and let* n_x *denote the number of elements in the treap,* t, *that contains* x. *Then* $E[n_x] \le 2w - 1$.

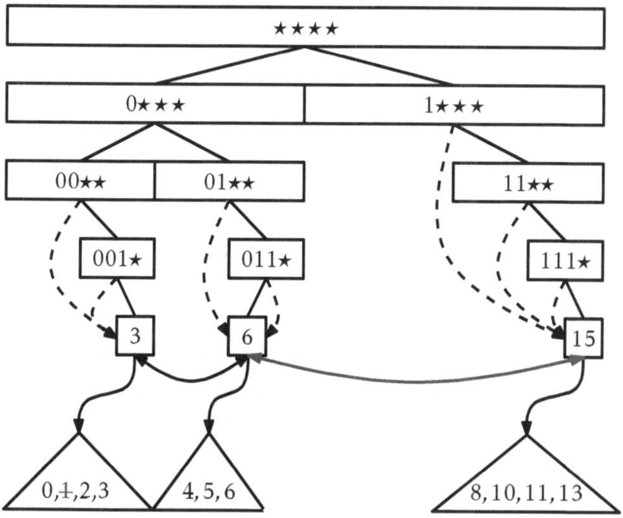

Figure 13.9: Removing the values 1 and 9 from a YFastTrie in Figure 13.8.

Proof. Refer to Figure 13.10. Let $x_1 < x_2 < \cdots < x_i = x < x_{i+1} < \cdots < x_n$ denote the elements stored in the YFastTrie. The treap t contains some elements greater than or equal to x. These are $x_i, x_{i+1}, \ldots, x_{i+j-1}$, where x_{i+j-1} is the only one of these elements in which the biased coin toss performed in the add(x) method turned up as heads. In other words, $E[j]$ is equal to the expected number of biased coin tosses required to obtain the first heads.[2] Each coin toss is independent and turns up as heads with probability 1/w, so $E[j] \leq w$. (See Lemma 4.2 for an analysis of this for the case $w = 2$.)

Similarly, the elements of t smaller than x are $x_{i-1}, \ldots, x_{i-k}$ where all these k coin tosses turn up as tails and the coin toss for x_{i-k-1} turns up as heads. Therefore, $E[k] \leq w - 1$, since this is the same coin tossing experiment considered in the preceding paragraph, but one in which the last toss is not counted. In summary, $n_x = j + k$, so

$$E[n_x] = E[j + k] = E[j] + E[k] \leq 2w - 1 \ . \qquad \square$$

[2]This analysis ignores the fact that j never exceeds $n - i + 1$. However, this only decreases $E[j]$, so the upper bound still holds.

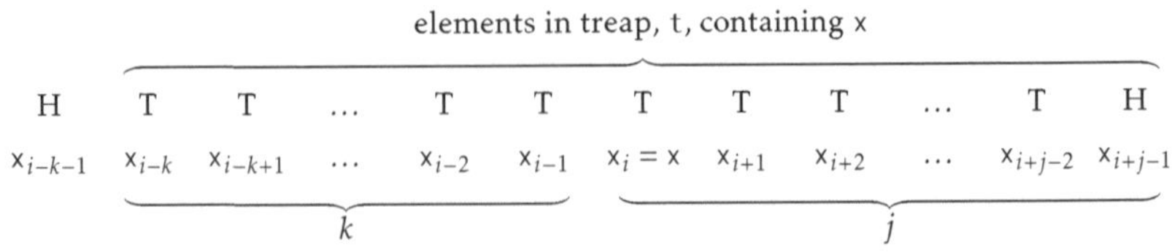

Figure 13.10: The number of elements in the treap t containing x is determined by two coin tossing experiments.

Lemma 13.1 was the last piece in the proof of the following theorem, which summarizes the performance of the YFastTrie:

Theorem 13.3. *A* YFastTrie *implements the* SSet *interface for* w*-bit integers. A* YFastTrie *supports the operations* add(x), remove(x), *and* find(x) *in* $O(\log w)$ *expected time per operation. The space used by a* YFastTrie *that stores* n *values is* $O(n+w)$.

The w term in the space requirement comes from the fact that xft always stores the value $2^w - 1$. The implementation could be modified (at the expense of adding some extra cases to the code) so that it is unnecessary to store this value. In this case, the space requirement in the theorem becomes $O(n)$.

13.4 Discussion and Exercises

The first data structure to provide $O(\log w)$ time add(x), remove(x), and find(x) operations was proposed by van Emde Boas and has since become known as the *van Emde Boas* (or *stratified*) *tree* [74]. The original van Emde Boas structure had size 2^w, making it impractical for large integers.

The XFastTrie and YFastTrie data structures were discovered by Willard [77]. The XFastTrie structure is closely related to van Emde Boas trees; for instance, the hash tables in an XFastTrie replace arrays in a van Emde Boas tree. That is, instead of storing the hash table t[i], a van Emde Boas tree stores an array of length 2^i.

Another structure for storing integers is Fredman and Willard's fusion trees [32]. This structure can store n w-bit integers in $O(n)$ space so that the find(x) operation runs in $O((\log n)/(\log w))$ time. By using a fusion tree when $\log w > \sqrt{\log n}$ and a YFastTrie when $\log w \le \sqrt{\log n}$, one obtains an $O(n)$ space data structure that can implement the find(x) operation in $O(\sqrt{\log n})$ time. Recent lower-bound results of Pătraşcu and Thorup [59] show that these results are more or less optimal, at least for structures that use only $O(n)$ space.

Exercise 13.1. Design and implement a simplified version of a BinaryTrie that does not have a linked list or jump pointers, but for which find(x)

still runs in $O(w)$ time.

Exercise 13.2. Design and implement a simplified implementation of an XFastTrie that doesn't use a binary trie at all. Instead, your implementation should store everything in a doubly-linked list and $w+1$ hash tables.

Exercise 13.3. We can think of a BinaryTrie as a structure that stores bit strings of length w in such a way that each bitstring is represented as a root to leaf path. Extend this idea into an SSet implementation that stores variable-length strings and implements add(s), remove(s), and find(s) in time proporitional to the length of s.
Hint: Each node in your data structure should store a hash table that is indexed by character values.

Exercise 13.4. For an integer $x \in \{0,\dots 2^w-1\}$, let $d(x)$ denote the difference between x and the value returned by find(x) [if find(x) returns null, then define $d(x)$ as 2^w]. For example, if find(23) returns 43, then $d(23) = 20$.

1. Design and implement a modified version of the find(x) operation in an XFastTrie that runs in $O(1 + \log d(x))$ expected time. Hint: The hash table $t[w]$ contains all the values, x, such that $d(x) = 0$, so that would be a good place to start.

2. Design and implement a modified version of the find(x) operation in an XFastTrie that runs in $O(1 + \log\log d(x))$ expected time.

Chapter 14

External Memory Searching

Throughout this book, we have been using the w-bit word-RAM model of computation defined in Section 1.4. An implicit assumption of this model is that our computer has a large enough random access memory to store all of the data in the data structure. In some situations, this assumption is not valid. There exist collections of data so large that no computer has enough memory to store them. In such cases, the application must resort to storing the data on some external storage medium such as a hard disk, a solid state disk, or even a network file server (which has its own external storage).

Accessing an item from external storage is extremely slow. The hard disk attached to the computer on which this book was written has an average access time of 19ms and the solid state drive attached to the computer has an average access time of 0.3ms. In contrast, the random access memory in the computer has an average access time of less than 0.000113ms. Accessing RAM is more than 2 500 times faster than accessing the solid state drive and more than 160 000 times faster than accessing the hard drive.

These speeds are fairly typical; accessing a random byte from RAM is thousands of times faster than accessing a random byte from a hard disk or solid-state drive. Access time, however, does not tell the whole story. When we access a byte from a hard disk or solid state disk, an entire *block* of the disk is read. Each of the drives attached to the computer has a block size of 4 096; each time we read one byte, the drive gives us a block containing 4 096 bytes. If we organize our data structure carefully, this

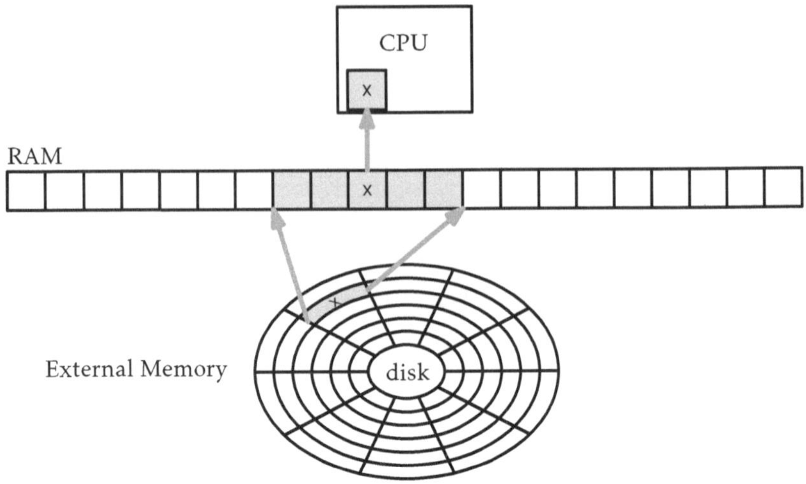

Figure 14.1: In the external memory model, accessing an individual item, x, in the external memory requires reading the entire block containing x into RAM.

means that each disk access could yield 4 096 bytes that are helpful in completing whatever operation we are doing.

This is the idea behind the *external memory model* of computation, illustrated schematically in Figure 14.1. In this model, the computer has access to a large external memory in which all of the data resides. This memory is divided into memory *blocks* each containing B words. The computer also has limited internal memory on which it can perform computations. Transferring a block between internal memory and external memory takes constant time. Computations performed within the internal memory are *free*; they take no time at all. The fact that internal memory computations are free may seem a bit strange, but it simply emphasizes the fact that external memory is so much slower than RAM.

In the full-blown external memory model, the size of the internal memory is also a parameter. However, for the data structures described in this chapter, it is sufficient to have an internal memory of size $O(B + \log_B \mathtt{n})$. That is, the memory needs to be capable of storing a constant number of blocks and a recursion stack of height $O(\log_B \mathtt{n})$. In most cases, the $O(B)$ term dominates the memory requirement. For example, even with the relatively small value $B = 32$, $B \geq \log_B \mathtt{n}$ for all $\mathtt{n} \leq 2^{160}$. In decimal, $B \geq \log_B n$ for any

$$n \leq 1\,461\,501\,637\,330\,902\,918\,203\,684\,832\,716\,283\,019\,655\,932\,542\,976\ .$$

14.1 The Block Store

The notion of external memory includes a large number of possible different devices, each of which has its own block size and is accessed with its own collection of system calls. To simplify the exposition of this chapter so that we can focus on the common ideas, we encapsulate external memory devices with an object called a `BlockStore`. A `BlockStore` stores a collection of memory blocks, each of size B. Each block is uniquely identified by its integer index. A `BlockStore` supports these operations:

1. `readBlock(i)`: Return the contents of the block whose index is `i`.
2. `writeBlock(i,b)`: Write contents of `b` to the block whose index is `i`.
3. `placeBlock(b)`: Return a new index and store the contents of `b` at this index.
4. `freeBlock(i)`: Free the block whose index is `i`. This indicates that the contents of this block are no longer used so the external memory allocated by this block may be reused.

The easiest way to imagine a `BlockStore` is to imagine it as storing a file on disk that is partitioned into blocks, each containing B bytes. In this way, `readBlock(i)` and `writeBlock(i,b)` simply read and write bytes $iB,\ldots,(i+1)B-1$ of this file. In addition, a simple `BlockStore` could keep a *free list* of blocks that are available for use. Blocks freed with `freeBlock(i)` are added to the free list. In this way, `placeBlock(b)` can use a block from the free list or, if none is available, append a new block to the end of the file.

14.2 B-Trees

In this section, we discuss a generalization of binary trees, called B-trees, which is efficient in the external memory model. Alternatively, B-trees can be viewed as the natural generalization of 2-4 trees described in Section 9.1. (A 2-4 tree is a special case of a B-tree that we get by setting $B = 2$.)

For any integer $B \geq 2$, a *B-tree* is a tree in which all of the leaves have the same depth and every non-root internal node, u, has at least B children and at most $2B$ children. The children of u are stored in an array, `u.children`. The required number of children is relaxed at the root, which can have anywhere between 2 and $2B$ children.

If the height of a B-tree is h, then it follows that the number, ℓ, of leaves in the B-tree satisfies

$$2B^{h-1} \leq \ell \leq 2(2B)^{h-1} \ .$$

Taking the logarithm of the first inequality and rearranging terms yields:

$$\begin{aligned} h &\leq \frac{\log \ell - 1}{\log B} + 1 \\ &\leq \frac{\log \ell}{\log B} + 1 \\ &= \log_B \ell + 1 \ . \end{aligned}$$

That is, the height of a B-tree is proportional to the base-B logarithm of the number of leaves.

Each node, u, in B-tree stores an array of keys $\mathtt{u.keys}[0],\ldots,\mathtt{u.keys}[2B-1]$. If u is an internal node with k children, then the number of keys stored at u is exactly $k-1$ and these are stored in $\mathtt{u.keys}[0],\ldots,\mathtt{u.keys}[k-2]$. The remaining $2B-k+1$ array entries in u.keys are set to `null`. If u is a non-root leaf node, then u contains between $B-1$ and $2B-1$ keys. The keys in a B-tree respect an order similar to the keys in a binary search tree. For any node, u, that stores $k-1$ keys,

$$\mathtt{u.keys}[0] < \mathtt{u.keys}[1] < \cdots < \mathtt{u.keys}[k-2] \ .$$

If u is an internal node, then for every $\mathtt{i} \in \{0,\ldots,k-2\}$, $\mathtt{u.keys}[\mathtt{i}]$ is larger than every key stored in the subtree rooted at $\mathtt{u.children}[\mathtt{i}]$ but smaller than every key stored in the subtree rooted at $\mathtt{u.children}[\mathtt{i}+1]$. Informally,

$$\mathtt{u.children}[\mathtt{i}] \prec \mathtt{u.keys}[\mathtt{i}] \prec \mathtt{u.children}[\mathtt{i}+1] \ .$$

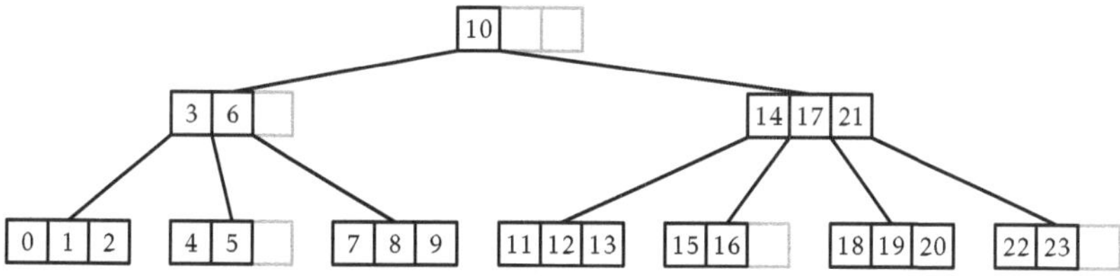

Figure 14.2: A B-tree with $B = 2$.

An example of a B-tree with $B = 2$ is shown in Figure 14.2.

Note that the data stored in a B-tree node has size $O(B)$. Therefore, in an external memory setting, the value of B in a B-tree is chosen so that a node fits into a single external memory block. In this way, the time it takes to perform a B-tree operation in the external memory model is proportional to the number of nodes that are accessed (read or written) by the operation.

For example, if the keys are 4 byte integers and the node indices are also 4 bytes, then setting $B = 256$ means that each node stores

$$(4+4) \times 2B = 8 \times 512 = 4096$$

bytes of data. This would be a perfect value of B for the hard disk or solid state drive discussed in the introduction to this chaper, which have a block size of 4096 bytes.

The `BTree` class, which implements a B-tree, stores a `BlockStore`, `bs`, that stores `BTree` nodes as well as the index, `ri`, of the root node. As usual, an integer, `n`, is used to keep track of the number of items in the data structure:

BTree
```
int n;
BlockStore<Node> bs;
int ri;
```

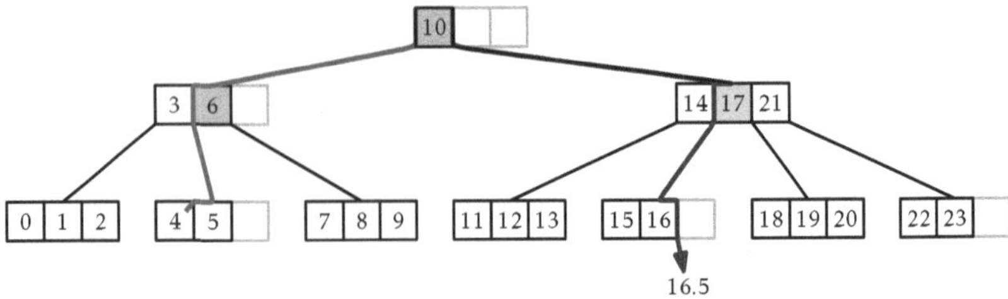

Figure 14.3: A successful search (for the value 4) and an unsuccessful search (for the value 16.5) in a *B*-tree. Shaded nodes show where the value of z is updated during the searches.

14.2.1 Searching

The implementation of the `find(x)` operation, which is illustrated in Figure 14.3, generalizes the `find(x)` operation in a binary search tree. The search for x starts at the root and uses the keys stored at a node, u, to determine in which of u's children the search should continue.

More specifically, at a node u, the search checks if x is stored in u.keys. If so, x has been found and the search is complete. Otherwise, the search finds the smallest integer, i, such that u.keys[i] > x and continues the search in the subtree rooted at u.children[i]. If no key in u.keys is greater than x, then the search continues in u's rightmost child. Just like binary search trees, the algorithm keeps track of the most recently seen key, z, that is larger than x. In case x is not found, z is returned as the smallest value that is greater or equal to x.

```
BTree
T find(T x) {
  T z = null;
  int ui = ri;
  while (ui >= 0) {
    Node u = bs.readBlock(ui);
    int i = findIt(u.keys, x);
    if (i < 0) return u.keys[-(i+1)]; // found it
    if (u.keys[i] != null)
      z = u.keys[i];
    ui = u.children[i];
  }
```

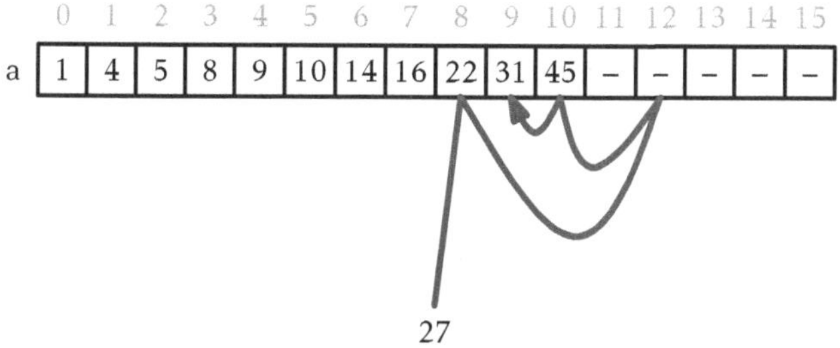

Figure 14.4: The execution of `findIt(a,27)`.

```
  return z;
}
```

Central to the `find`(x) method is the `findIt`(a, x) method that searches in a `null`-padded sorted array, a, for the value x. This method, illustrated in Figure 14.4, works for any array, a, where a[0],...,a[$k-1$] is a sequence of keys in sorted order and a[k],...,a[a.`length`-1] are all set to `null`. If x is in the array at position i, then `findIt`(a, x) returns $-$i $-$ 1. Otherwise, it returns the smallest index, i, such that a[i] > x or a[i] = `null`.

```
BTree
int findIt(T[] a, T x) {
  int lo = 0, hi = a.length;
  while (hi != lo) {
    int m = (hi+lo)/2;
    int cmp = a[m] == null ? -1 : compare(x, a[m]);
    if (cmp < 0)
      hi = m;        // look in first half
    else if (cmp > 0)
      lo = m+1;      // look in second half
    else
      return -m-1; // found it
  }
  return lo;
}
```

The `findIt`(a, x) method uses a binary search that halves the search space at each step, so it runs in $O(\log(\text{a.length}))$ time. In our setting, a.`length` = $2B$, so `findIt`(a, x) runs in $O(\log B)$ time.

We can analyze the running time of a B-tree find(x) operation both in the usual word-RAM model (where every instruction counts) and in the external memory model (where we only count the number of nodes accessed). Since each leaf in a B-tree stores at least one key and the height of a B-Tree with ℓ leaves is $O(\log_B \ell)$, the height of a B-tree that stores n keys is $O(\log_B n)$. Therefore, in the external memory model, the time taken by the find(x) operation is $O(\log_B n)$. To determine the running time in the word-RAM model, we have to account for the cost of calling findIt(a, x) for each node we access, so the running time of find(x) in the word-RAM model is

$$O(\log_B n) \times O(\log B) = O(\log n) \enspace .$$

14.2.2 Addition

One important difference between B-trees and the BinarySearchTree data structure from Section 6.2 is that the nodes of a B-tree do not store pointers to their parents. The reason for this will be explained shortly. The lack of parent pointers means that the add(x) and remove(x) operations on B-trees are most easily implemented using recursion.

Like all balanced search trees, some form of rebalancing is required during an add(x) operation. In a B-tree, this is done by *splitting* nodes. Refer to Figure 14.5 for what follows. Although splitting takes place across two levels of recursion, it is best understood as an operation that takes a node u containing $2B$ keys and having $2B+1$ children. It creates a new node, w, that adopts u.children[B],...,u.children[$2B$]. The new node w also takes u's B largest keys, u.keys[B],...,u.keys[$2B-1$]. At this point, u has B children and B keys. The extra key, u.keys[$B-1$], is passed up to the parent of u, which also adopts w.

Notice that the splitting operation modifies three nodes: u, u's parent, and the new node, w. This is why it is important that the nodes of a B-tree do not maintain parent pointers. If they did, then the $B+1$ children adopted by w would all need to have their parent pointers modified. This would increase the number of external memory accesses from 3 to $B+4$ and would make B-trees much less efficient for large values of B.

The add(x) method in a B-tree is illustrated in Figure 14.6. At a high

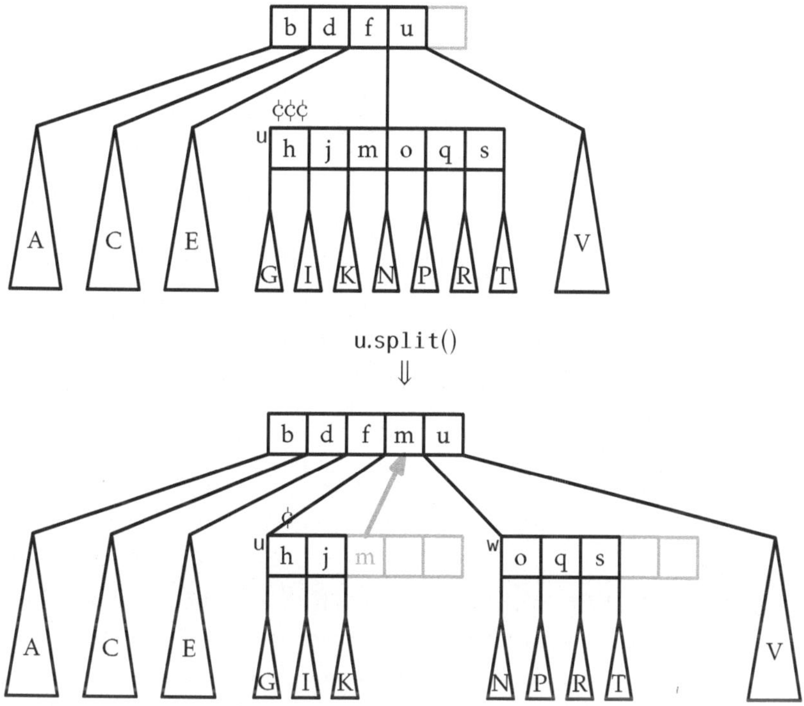

Figure 14.5: Splitting the node u in a B-tree ($B = 3$). Notice that the key u.keys[2] = m passes from u to its parent.

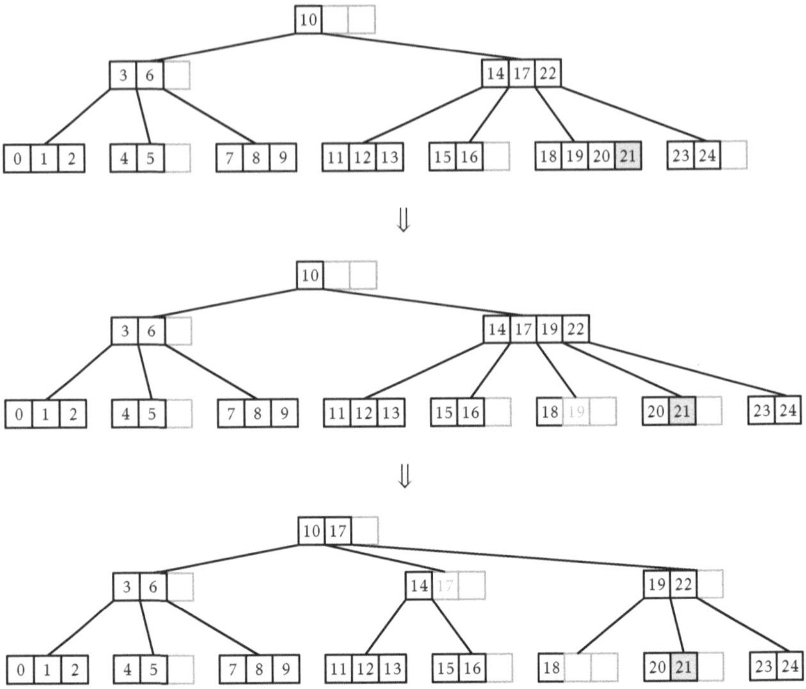

Figure 14.6: The add(x) operation in a BTree. Adding the value 21 results in two nodes being split.

level, this method finds a leaf, u, at which to add the value x. If this causes u to become overfull (because it already contained $B-1$ keys), then u is split. If this causes u's parent to become overfull, then u's parent is also split, which may cause u's grandparent to become overfull, and so on. This process continues, moving up the tree one level at a time until reaching a node that is not overfull or until the root is split. In the former case, the process stops. In the latter case, a new root is created whose two children become the nodes obtained when the original root was split.

The executive summary of the add(x) method is that it walks from the root to a leaf searching for x, adds x to this leaf, and then walks back up to the root, splitting any overfull nodes it encounters along the way. With this high level view in mind, we can now delve into the details of how this method can be implemented recursively.

The real work of add(x) is done by the addRecursive(x,ui) method, which adds the value x to the subtree whose root, u, has the identifier ui. If u is a leaf, then x is simply inserted into u.keys. Otherwise, x is added recursively into the appropriate child, u′, of u. The result of this recursive call is normally null but may also be a reference to a newly-created node, w, that was created because u′ was split. In this case, u adopts w and takes its first key, completing the splitting operation on u′.

After the value x has been added (either to u or to a descendant of u), the addRecursive(x,ui) method checks to see if u is storing too many (more than $2B-1$) keys. If so, then u needs to be *split* with a call to the u.split() method. The result of calling u.split() is a new node that is used as the return value for addRecursive(x,ui).

BTree

```
Node addRecursive(T x, int ui) {
  Node u = bs.readBlock(ui);
  int i = findIt(u.keys, x);
  if (i < 0) throw new DuplicateValueException();
  if (u.children[i] < 0) { // leaf node, just add it
    u.add(x, -1);
    bs.writeBlock(u.id, u);
  } else {
    Node w = addRecursive(x, u.children[i]);
    if (w != null) {  // child was split, w is new child
      x = w.remove(0);
      bs.writeBlock(w.id, w);
      u.add(x, w.id);
      bs.writeBlock(u.id, u);
    }
  }
  return u.isFull() ? u.split() : null;
}
```

The addRecursive(x,ui) method is a helper for the add(x) method, which calls addRecursive(x,ri) to insert x into the root of the *B*-tree. If addRecursive(x,ri) causes the root to split, then a new root is created that takes as its children both the old root and the new node created by the splitting of the old root.

BTree
```
boolean add(T x) {
  Node w;
  try {
    w = addRecursive(x, ri);
  } catch (DuplicateValueException e) {
    return false;
  }
  if (w != null) {   // root was split, make new root
    Node newroot = new Node();
    x = w.remove(0);
    bs.writeBlock(w.id, w);
    newroot.children[0] = ri;
    newroot.keys[0] = x;
    newroot.children[1] = w.id;
    ri = newroot.id;
    bs.writeBlock(ri, newroot);
  }
  n++;
  return true;
}
```

The add(x) method and its helper, addRecursive(x,ui), can be analyzed in two phases:

Downward phase: During the downward phase of the recursion, before x has been added, they access a sequence of BTree nodes and call findIt(a, x) on each node. As with the find(x) method, this takes $O(\log_B n)$ time in the external memory model and $O(\log n)$ time in the word-RAM model.

Upward phase: During the upward phase of the recursion, after x has been added, these methods perform a sequence of at most $O(\log_B n)$ splits. Each split involves only three nodes, so this phase takes $O(\log_B n)$ time in the external memory model. However, each split involves moving B keys and children from one node to another, so in the word-RAM model, this takes $O(B \log n)$ time.

Recall that the value of B can be quite large, much larger than even $\log n$. Therefore, in the word-RAM model, adding a value to a B-tree can be much slower than adding into a balanced binary search tree. Later, in Section 14.2.4, we will show that the situation is not quite so bad; the amortized number of split operations done during an add(x) operation is constant. This shows that the (amortized) running time of the add(x) operation in the word-RAM model is $O(B + \log n)$.

14.2.3 Removal

The remove(x) operation in a BTree is, again, most easily implemented as a recursive method. Although the recursive implementation of remove(x) spreads the complexity across several methods, the overall process, which is illustrated in Figure 14.7, is fairly straightforward. By shuffling keys around, removal is reduced to the problem of removing a value, x′, from some leaf, u. Removing x′ may leave u with less than $B-1$ keys; this situation is called an *underflow*.

When an underflow occurs, u either borrows keys from, or is merged with, one of its siblings. If u is merged with a sibling, then u's parent will now have one less child and one less key, which can cause u's parent to underflow; this is again corrected by borrowing or merging, but merging may cause u's grandparent to underflow. This process works its way back up to the root until there is no more underflow or until the root has its last two children merged into a single child. When the latter case occurs, the root is removed and its lone child becomes the new root.

Next we delve into the details of how each of these steps is implemented. The first job of the remove(x) method is to find the element x that should be removed. If x is found in a leaf, then x is removed from this leaf. Otherwise, if x is found at u.keys[i] for some internal node, u, then the algorithm removes the smallest value, x′, in the subtree rooted at u.children[i + 1]. The value x′ is the smallest value stored in the BTree that is greater than x. The value of x′ is then used to replace x in u.keys[i]. This process is illustrated in Figure 14.8.

The removeRecursive(x,ui) method is a recursive implementation of the preceding algorithm:

```
                              BTree
boolean removeRecursive(T x, int ui) {
```

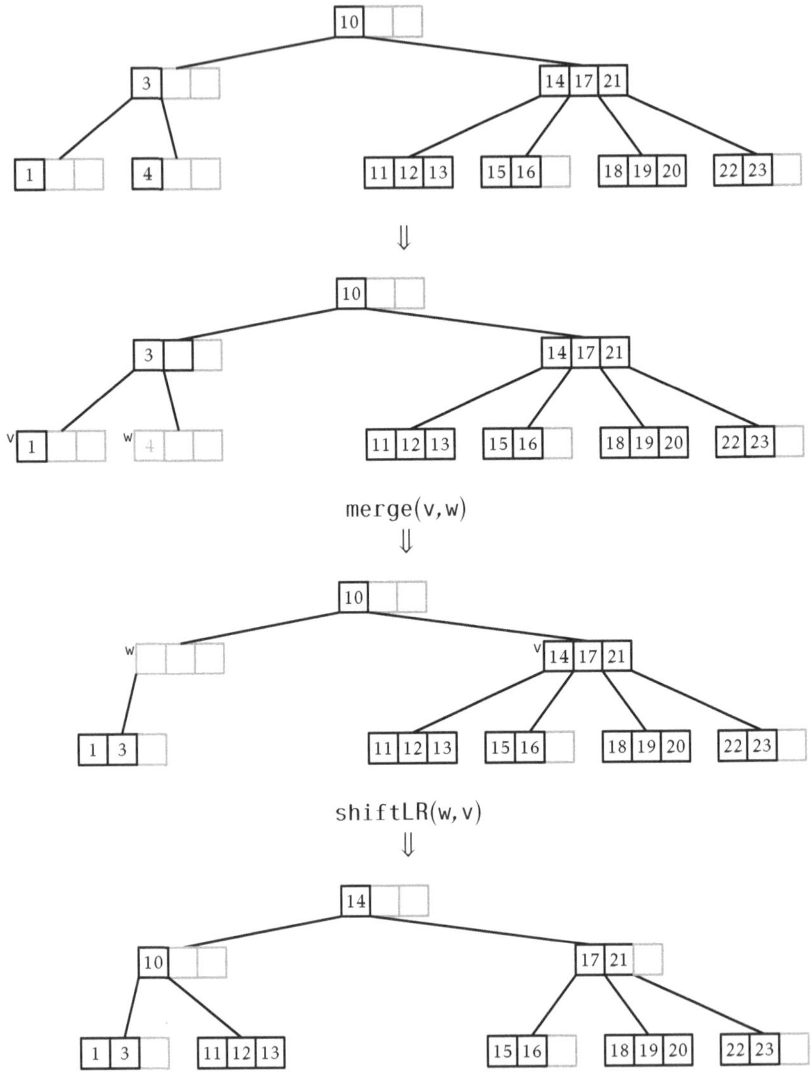

Figure 14.7: Removing the value 4 from a B-tree results in one merge and one borrowing operation.

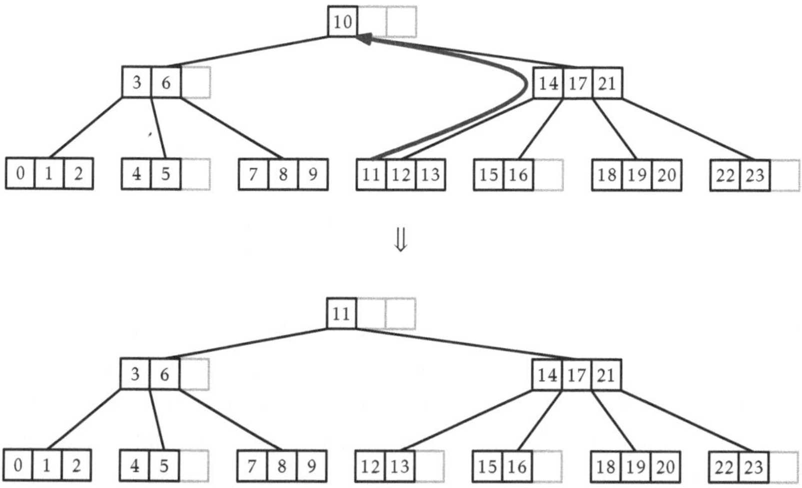

Figure 14.8: The remove(x) operation in a BTree. To remove the value x = 10 we replace it with the the value x′ = 11 and remove 11 from the leaf that contains it.

```
    if (ui < 0) return false;  // didn't find it
    Node u = bs.readBlock(ui);
    int i = findIt(u.keys, x);
    if (i < 0) { // found it
      i = -(i+1);
      if (u.isLeaf()) {
        u.remove(i);
      } else {
        u.keys[i] = removeSmallest(u.children[i+1]);
        checkUnderflow(u, i+1);
      }
      return true;
    } else if (removeRecursive(x, u.children[i])) {
      checkUnderflow(u, i);
      return true;
    }
    return false;
  }
  T removeSmallest(int ui) {
    Node u = bs.readBlock(ui);
    if (u.isLeaf())
```

```
    return u.remove(0);
  T y = removeSmallest(u.children[0]);
  checkUnderflow(u, 0);
  return y;
}
```

Note that, after recursively removing the value x from the ith child of u, removeRecursive(x,ui) needs to ensure that this child still has at least $B-1$ keys. In the preceding code, this is done using a method called checkUnderflow(x, i), which checks for and corrects an underflow in the ith child of u. Let w be the ith child of u. If w has only $B-2$ keys, then this needs to be fixed. The fix requires using a sibling of w. This can be either child $i+1$ of u or child $i-1$ of u. We will usually use child $i-1$ of u, which is the sibling, v, of w directly to its left. The only time this doesn't work is when $i = 0$, in which case we use the sibling directly to w's right.

```
BTree
void checkUnderflow(Node u, int i) {
  if (u.children[i] < 0) return;
  if (i == 0)
    checkUnderflowZero(u, i); // use u's right sibling
  else
    checkUnderflowNonZero(u,i);
}
```

In the following, we focus on the case when $i \neq 0$ so that any underflow at the ith child of u will be corrected with the help of the $(i-1)$st child of u. The case $i = 0$ is similar and the details can be found in the accompanying source code.

To fix an underflow at node w, we need to find more keys (and possibly also children), for w. There are two ways to do this:

Borrowing: If w has a sibling, v, with more than $B-1$ keys, then w can borrow some keys (and possibly also children) from v. More specifically, if v stores size(v) keys, then between them, v and w have a total of

$$B-2+\texttt{size}(w) \geq 2B-2$$

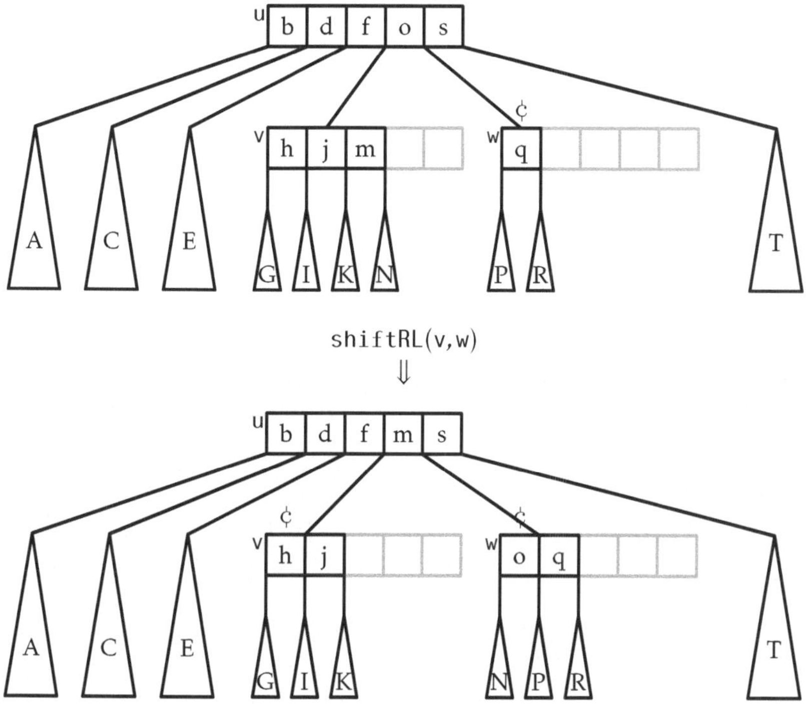

Figure 14.9: If v has more than $B-1$ keys, then w can borrow keys from v.

keys. We can therefore shift keys from v to w so that each of v and w has at least $B-1$ keys. This process is illustrated in Figure 14.9.

Merging: If v has only $B-1$ keys, we must do something more drastic, since v cannot afford to give any keys to w. Therefore, we *merge* v and w as shown in Figure 14.10. The merge operation is the opposite of the split operation. It takes two nodes that contain a total of $2B-3$ keys and merges them into a single node that contains $2B-2$ keys. (The additional key comes from the fact that, when we merge v and w, their common parent, u, now has one less child and therefore needs to give up one of its keys.)

BTree
```
void checkUnderflowNonZero(Node u, int i) {
  Node w = bs.readBlock(u.children[i]);  // w is child of u
```

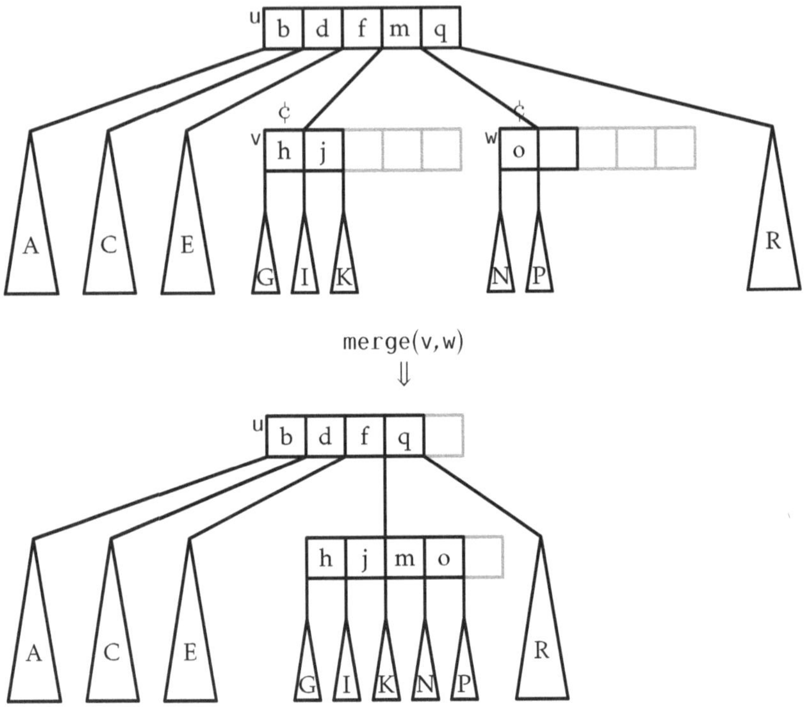

Figure 14.10: Merging two siblings v and w in a B-tree ($B = 3$).

```
    if (w.size() < B-1) {  // underflow at w
      Node v = bs.readBlock(u.children[i-1]); // v left of w
      if (v.size() > B) {  // w can borrow from v
        shiftLR(u, i-1, v, w);
      } else { // v will absorb w
        merge(u, i-1, v, w);
      }
    }
  }
  void checkUnderflowZero(Node u, int i) {
    Node w = bs.readBlock(u.children[i]); // w is child of u
    if (w.size() < B-1) {  // underflow at w
      Node v = bs.readBlock(u.children[i+1]); // v right of w
      if (v.size() > B) { // w can borrow from v
        shiftRL(u, i, v, w);
      } else { // w will absorb w
        merge(u, i, w, v);
        u.children[i] = w.id;
      }
    }
  }
```

To summarize, the remove(x) method in a B-tree follows a root to leaf path, removes a key x′ from a leaf, u, and then performs zero or more merge operations involving u and its ancestors, and performs at most one borrowing operation. Since each merge and borrow operation involves modifying only three nodes, and only $O(\log_B n)$ of these operations occur, the entire process takes $O(\log_B n)$ time in the external memory model. Again, however, each merge and borrow operation takes $O(B)$ time in the word-RAM model, so (for now) the most we can say about the running time required by remove(x) in the word-RAM model is that it is $O(B \log_B n)$.

14.2.4 Amortized Analysis of B-Trees

Thus far, we have shown that

1. In the external memory model, the running time of find(x), add(x), and remove(x) in a B-tree is $O(\log_B n)$.

2. In the word-RAM model, the running time of find(x) is $O(\log n)$ and the running time of add(x) and remove(x) is $O(B \log n)$.

The following lemma shows that, so far, we have overestimated the number of merge and split operations performed by B-trees.

Lemma 14.1. *Starting with an empty B-tree and performing any sequence of m* add(x) *and* remove(x) *operations results in at most $3m/2$ splits, merges, and borrows being performed.*

Proof. The proof of this has already been sketched in Section 9.3 for the special case in which $B = 2$. The lemma can be proven using a credit scheme, in which

1. each split, merge, or borrow operation is paid for with two credits, i.e., a credit is removed each time one of these operations occurs; and

2. at most three credits are created during any add(x) or remove(x) operation.

Since at most $3m$ credits are ever created and each split, merge, and borrow is paid for with with two credits, it follows that at most $3m/2$ splits, merges, and borrows are performed. These credits are illustrated using the ¢ symbol in Figures 14.5, 14.9, and 14.10.

To keep track of these credits the proof maintains the following *credit invariant*: Any non-root node with $B-1$ keys stores one credit and any node with $2B-1$ keys stores three credits. A node that stores at least B keys and most $2B-2$ keys need not store any credits. What remains is to show that we can maintain the credit invariant and satisfy properties 1 and 2, above, during each add(x) and remove(x) operation.

Adding: The add(x) method does not perform any merges or borrows, so we need only consider split operations that occur as a result of calls to add(x).

Each split operation occurs because a key is added to a node, u, that already contains $2B-1$ keys. When this happens, u is split into two nodes, u′ and u″ having $B-1$ and B keys, respectively. Prior to this operation, u was storing $2B-1$ keys, and hence three credits. Two of these credits can be used to pay for the split and the other credit can be given to u′ (which has $B-1$ keys) to maintain the credit invariant. Therefore, we can pay for the split and maintain the credit invariant during any split.

The only other modification to nodes that occur during an add(x) operation happens after all splits, if any, are complete. This modification involves adding a new key to some node u′. If, prior to this, u′ had $2B-2$ children, then it now has $2B-1$ children and must therefore receive three credits. These are the only credits given out by the add(x) method.

Removing: During a call to remove(x), zero or more merges occur and are possibly followed by a single borrow. Each merge occurs because two nodes, v and w, each of which had exactly $B-1$ keys prior to calling remove(x) were merged into a single node with exactly $2B-2$ keys. Each such merge therefore frees up two credits that can be used to pay for the merge.

After any merges are performed, at most one borrow operation occurs, after which no further merges or borrows occur. This borrow operation only occurs if we remove a key from a leaf, v, that has $B-1$ keys. The node v therefore has one credit, and this credit goes towards the cost of the borrow. This single credit is not enough to pay for the borrow, so we create one credit to complete the payment.

At this point, we have created one credit and we still need to show that the credit invariant can be maintained. In the worst case, v's sibling, w, has exactly B keys before the borrow so that, afterwards, both v and w have $B-1$ keys. This means that v and w each should be storing a credit when the operation is complete. Therefore, in this case, we create an additional two credits to give to v and w. Since a borrow happens at most once during a remove(x) operation, this means that we create at most three credits, as required.

If the remove(x) operation does not include a borrow operation, this is because it finishes by removing a key from some node that, prior to the operation, had B or more keys. In the worst case, this node had exactly B keys, so that it now has $B-1$ keys and must be given one credit, which we create.

In either case—whether the removal finishes with a borrow operation or not—at most three credits need to be created during a call to remove(x) to maintain the credit invariant and pay for all borrows and merges that occur. This completes the proof of the lemma. □

The purpose of Lemma 14.1 is to show that, in the word-RAM model the cost of splits, merges and joins during a sequence of m `add(x)` and `remove(x)` operations is only $O(Bm)$. That is, the amortized cost per operation is only $O(B)$, so the amortized cost of `add(x)` and `remove(x)` in the word-RAM model is $O(B + \log n)$. This is summarized by the following pair of theorems:

Theorem 14.1 (External Memory B-Trees). *A* `BTree` *implements the* `SSet` *interface. In the external memory model, a* `BTree` *supports the operations* `add(x)`, `remove(x)`, *and* `find(x)` *in* $O(\log_B n)$ *time per operation.*

Theorem 14.2 (Word-RAM B-Trees). *A* `BTree` *implements the* `SSet` *interface. In the word-RAM model, and ignoring the cost of splits, merges, and borrows, a* `BTree` *supports the operations* `add(x)`, `remove(x)`, *and* `find(x)` *in* $O(\log n)$ *time per operation. Furthermore, beginning with an empty* `BTree`, *any sequence of* m `add(x)` *and* `remove(x)` *operations results in a total of* $O(Bm)$ *time spent performing splits, merges, and borrows.*

14.3 Discussion and Exercises

The external memory model of computation was introduced by Aggarwal and Vitter [4]. It is sometimes also called the *I/O model* or the *disk access model*.

B-Trees are to external memory searching what binary search trees are to internal memory searching. B-trees were introduced by Bayer and McCreight [9] in 1970 and, less than ten years later, the title of Comer's ACM Computing Surveys article referred to them as ubiquitous [15].

Like binary search trees, there are many variants of B-Trees, including B^+-trees, B^*-trees, and counted B-trees. B-trees are indeed ubiquitous and are the primary data structure in many file systems, including Apple's HFS+, Microsoft's NTFS, and Linux's Ext4; every major database system; and key-value stores used in cloud computing. Graefe's recent survey [36] provides a 200+ page overview of the many modern applications, variants, and optimizations of B-trees.

B-trees implement the SSet interface. If only the USet interface is needed, then external memory hashing could be used as an alternative to B-trees. External memory hashing schemes do exist; see, for example, Jensen and Pagh [43]. These schemes implement the USet operations in $O(1)$ expected time in the external memory model. However, for a variety of reasons, many applications still use B-trees even though they only require USet operations.

One reason B-trees are such a popular choice is that they often perform better than their $O(\log_B n)$ running time bounds suggest. The reason for this is that, in external memory settings, the value of B is typically quite large—in the hundreds or even thousands. This means that 99% or even 99.9% of the data in a B-tree is stored in the leaves. In a database system with a large memory, it may be possible to cache all the internal nodes of a B-tree in RAM, since they only represent 1% or 0.1% of the total data set. When this happens, this means that a search in a B-tree involves a very fast search in RAM, through the internal nodes, followed by a single external memory access to retrieve a leaf.

Exercise 14.1. Show what happens when the keys 1.5 and then 7.5 are added to the B-tree in Figure 14.2.

Exercise 14.2. Show what happens when the keys 3 and then 4 are removed from the B-tree in Figure 14.2.

Exercise 14.3. What is the maximum number of internal nodes in a B-tree that stores n keys (as a function of n and B)?

Exercise 14.4. The introduction to this chapter claims that B-trees only need an internal memory of size $O(B + \log_B n)$. However, the implementation given here actually requires more memory.

1. Show that the implementation of the add(x) and remove(x) methods given in this chapter use an internal memory proportional to $B \log_B n$.

2. Describe how these methods could be modified in order to reduce their memory consumption to $O(B + \log_B n)$.

Exercise 14.5. Draw the credits used in the proof of Lemma 14.1 on the trees in Figures 14.6 and 14.7. Verify that (with three additional credits) it is possible to pay for the splits, merges, and borrows and maintain the credit invariant.

Exercise 14.6. Design a modified version of a B-tree in which nodes can have anywhere from B up to $3B$ children (and hence $B-1$ up to $3B-1$ keys). Show that this new version of B-trees performs only $O(m/B)$ splits, merges, and borrows during a sequence of m operations. (Hint: For this to work, you will have to be more agressive with merging, sometimes merging two nodes before it is strictly necessary.)

Exercise 14.7. In this exercise, you will design a modified method of splitting and merging in B-trees that asymptotically reduces the number of splits, borrows and merges by considering up to three nodes at a time.

1. Let u be an overfull node and let v be a sibling immediately to the right of u. There are two ways to fix the overflow at u:

   (a) u can give some of its keys to v; or

   (b) u can be split and the keys of u and v can be evenly distributed among u, v, and the newly created node, w.

   Show that this can always be done in such a way that, after the operation, each of the (at most 3) affected nodes has at least $B+\alpha B$ keys and at most $2B-\alpha B$ keys, for some constant $\alpha > 0$.

2. Let u be an underfull node and let v and w be siblings of u There are two ways to fix the underflow at u:

   (a) keys can be redistributed among u, v, and w; or

   (b) u, v, and w can be merged into two nodes and the keys of u, v, and w can be redistributed amongst these nodes.

   Show that this can always be done in such a way that, after the operation, each of the (at most 3) affected nodes has at least $B+\alpha B$ keys and at most $2B-\alpha B$ keys, for some constant $\alpha > 0$.

3. Show that, with these modifications, the number of merges, borrows, and splits that occur during m operations is $O(m/B)$.

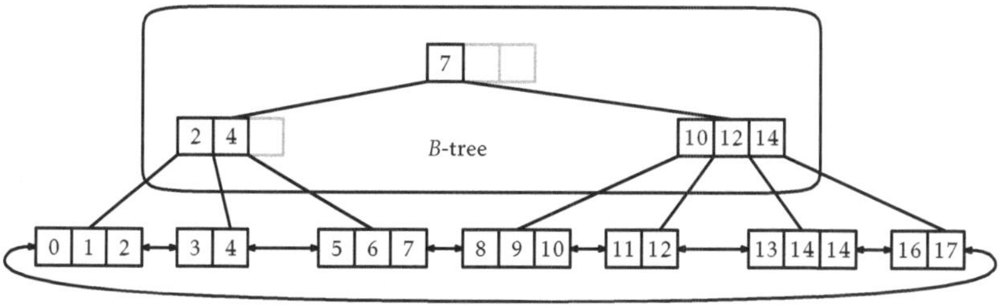

Figure 14.11: A B^+-tree is a B-tree on top of a doubly-linked list of blocks.

Exercise 14.8. A B^+-tree, illustrated in Figure 14.11 stores every key in a leaf and keeps its leaves stored as a doubly-linked list. As usual, each leaf stores between $B-1$ and $2B-1$ keys. Above this list is a standard B-tree that stores the largest value from each leaf but the last.

1. Describe fast implementations of `add(x)`, `remove(x)`, and `find(x)` in a B^+-tree.
2. Explain how to efficiently implement the `findRange(x,y)` method, that reports all values greater than `x` and less than or equal to `y`, in a B^+-tree.
3. Implement a class, `BPlusTree`, that implements `find(x)`, `add(x)`, `remove(x)`, and `findRange(x,y)`.
4. B^+-trees duplicate some of the keys because they are stored both in the B-tree and in the list. Explain why this duplication does not add up to much for large values of B.

Bibliography

[1] Free eBooks by Project Gutenberg. Available from: `http://www.gutenberg.org/` [cited 2011-10-12].

[2] IEEE Standard for Floating-Point Arithmetic. Technical report, Microprocessor Standards Committee of the IEEE Computer Society, 3 Park Avenue, New York, NY 10016-5997, USA, August 2008. `doi:10.1109/IEEESTD.2008.4610935`.

[3] G. Adelson-Velskii and E. Landis. An algorithm for the organization of information. *Soviet Mathematics Doklady*, 3(1259-1262):4, 1962.

[4] A. Aggarwal and J. S. Vitter. The input/output complexity of sorting and related problems. *Communications of the ACM*, 31(9):1116–1127, 1988.

[5] A. Andersson. Improving partial rebuilding by using simple balance criteria. In F. K. H. A. Dehne, J.-R. Sack, and N. Santoro, editors, *Algorithms and Data Structures, Workshop WADS '89, Ottawa, Canada, August 17–19, 1989, Proceedings*, volume 382 of *Lecture Notes in Computer Science*, pages 393–402. Springer, 1989.

[6] A. Andersson. Balanced search trees made simple. In F. K. H. A. Dehne, J.-R. Sack, N. Santoro, and S. Whitesides, editors, *Algorithms and Data Structures, Third Workshop, WADS '93, Montréal, Canada, August 11–13, 1993, Proceedings*, volume 709 of *Lecture Notes in Computer Science*, pages 60–71. Springer, 1993.

[7] A. Andersson. General balanced trees. *Journal of Algorithms*, 30(1):1–18, 1999.

[8] A. Bagchi, A. L. Buchsbaum, and M. T. Goodrich. Biased skip lists. In P. Bose and P. Morin, editors, *Algorithms and Computation, 13th International Symposium, ISAAC 2002 Vancouver, BC, Canada, November 21–23, 2002, Proceedings*, volume 2518 of *Lecture Notes in Computer Science*, pages 1–13. Springer, 2002.

[9] R. Bayer and E. M. McCreight. Organization and maintenance of large ordered indexes. In *SIGFIDET Workshop*, pages 107–141. ACM, 1970.

[10] Bibliography on hashing. Available from: `http://liinwww.ira.uka.de/bibliography/Theory/hash.html` [cited 2011-07-20].

[11] J. Black, S. Halevi, H. Krawczyk, T. Krovetz, and P. Rogaway. UMAC: Fast and secure message authentication. In M. J. Wiener, editor, *Advances in Cryptology - CRYPTO '99, 19th Annual International Cryptology Conference, Santa Barbara, California, USA, August 15–19, 1999, Proceedings*, volume 1666 of *Lecture Notes in Computer Science*, pages 79–79. Springer, 1999.

[12] P. Bose, K. Douïeb, and S. Langerman. Dynamic optimality for skip lists and b-trees. In S.-H. Teng, editor, *Proceedings of the Nineteenth Annual ACM-SIAM Symposium on Discrete Algorithms, SODA 2008, San Francisco, California, USA, January 20–22, 2008*, pages 1106–1114. SIAM, 2008.

[13] A. Brodnik, S. Carlsson, E. D. Demaine, J. I. Munro, and R. Sedgewick. Resizable arrays in optimal time and space. In Dehne et al. [18], pages 37–48.

[14] J. Carter and M. Wegman. Universal classes of hash functions. *Journal of computer and system sciences*, 18(2):143–154, 1979.

[15] D. Comer. The ubiquitous B-tree. *ACM Computing Surveys*, 11(2):121–137, 1979.

[16] C. Crane. Linear lists and priority queues as balanced binary trees. Technical Report STAN-CS-72-259, Computer Science Department, Stanford University, 1972.

[17] S. Crosby and D. Wallach. Denial of service via algorithmic complexity attacks. In *Proceedings of the 12th USENIX Security Symposium*, pages 29–44, 2003.

[18] F. K. H. A. Dehne, A. Gupta, J.-R. Sack, and R. Tamassia, editors. *Algorithms and Data Structures, 6th International Workshop, WADS '99, Vancouver, British Columbia, Canada, August 11–14, 1999, Proceedings*, volume 1663 of *Lecture Notes in Computer Science*. Springer, 1999.

[19] L. Devroye. Applications of the theory of records in the study of random trees. *Acta Informatica*, 26(1):123–130, 1988.

[20] P. Dietz and J. Zhang. Lower bounds for monotonic list labeling. In J. R. Gilbert and R. G. Karlsson, editors, *SWAT 90, 2nd Scandinavian Workshop on Algorithm Theory, Bergen, Norway, July 11–14, 1990, Proceedings*, volume 447 of *Lecture Notes in Computer Science*, pages 173–180. Springer, 1990.

[21] M. Dietzfelbinger. Universal hashing and *k*-wise independent random variables via integer arithmetic without primes. In C. Puech and R. Reischuk, editors, *STACS 96, 13th Annual Symposium on Theoretical Aspects of Computer Science, Grenoble, France, February 22–24, 1996, Proceedings*, volume 1046 of *Lecture Notes in Computer Science*, pages 567–580. Springer, 1996.

[22] M. Dietzfelbinger, J. Gil, Y. Matias, and N. Pippenger. Polynomial hash functions are reliable. In W. Kuich, editor, *Automata, Languages and Programming, 19th International Colloquium, ICALP92, Vienna, Austria, July 13–17, 1992, Proceedings*, volume 623 of *Lecture Notes in Computer Science*, pages 235–246. Springer, 1992.

[23] M. Dietzfelbinger, T. Hagerup, J. Katajainen, and M. Penttonen. A reliable randomized algorithm for the closest-pair problem. *Journal of Algorithms*, 25(1):19–51, 1997.

[24] M. Dietzfelbinger, A. R. Karlin, K. Mehlhorn, F. M. auf der Heide, H. Rohnert, and R. E. Tarjan. Dynamic perfect hashing: Upper and lower bounds. *SIAM J. Comput.*, 23(4):738–761, 1994.

[25] A. Elmasry. Pairing heaps with $O(\log\log n)$ decrease cost. In *Proceedings of the twentieth Annual ACM-SIAM Symposium on Discrete Algorithms*, pages 471–476. Society for Industrial and Applied Mathematics, 2009.

[26] F. Ergun, S. C. Sahinalp, J. Sharp, and R. Sinha. Biased dictionaries with fast insert/deletes. In *Proceedings of the thirty-third annual ACM symposium on Theory of computing*, pages 483–491, New York, NY, USA, 2001. ACM.

[27] M. Eytzinger. *Thesaurus principum hac aetate in Europa viventium (Cologne)*. 1590. In commentaries, 'Eytzinger' may appear in variant forms, including: Aitsingeri, Aitsingero, Aitsingerum, Eyzingern.

[28] R. W. Floyd. Algorithm 245: Treesort 3. *Communications of the ACM*, 7(12):701, 1964.

[29] M. Fredman, R. Sedgewick, D. Sleator, and R. Tarjan. The pairing heap: A new form of self-adjusting heap. *Algorithmica*, 1(1):111–129, 1986.

[30] M. Fredman and R. Tarjan. Fibonacci heaps and their uses in improved network optimization algorithms. *Journal of the ACM*, 34(3):596–615, 1987.

[31] M. L. Fredman, J. Komlós, and E. Szemerédi. Storing a sparse table with 0 (1) worst case access time. *Journal of the ACM*, 31(3):538–544, 1984.

[32] M. L. Fredman and D. E. Willard. Surpassing the information theoretic bound with fusion trees. *Journal of computer and system sciences*, 47(3):424–436, 1993.

[33] I. Galperin and R. Rivest. Scapegoat trees. In *Proceedings of the fourth annual ACM-SIAM Symposium on Discrete algorithms*, pages 165–174. Society for Industrial and Applied Mathematics, 1993.

[34] A. Gambin and A. Malinowski. Randomized meldable priority queues. In *SOFSEM98: Theory and Practice of Informatics*, pages 344–349. Springer, 1998.

[35] M. T. Goodrich and J. G. Kloss. Tiered vectors: Efficient dynamic arrays for rank-based sequences. In Dehne et al. [18], pages 205–216.

[36] G. Graefe. Modern b-tree techniques. *Foundations and Trends in Databases*, 3(4):203–402, 2010.

[37] R. L. Graham, D. E. Knuth, and O. Patashnik. *Concrete Mathematics*. Addison-Wesley, 2nd edition, 1994.

[38] L. Guibas and R. Sedgewick. A dichromatic framework for balanced trees. In *19th Annual Symposium on Foundations of Computer Science, Ann Arbor, Michigan, 16–18 October 1978, Proceedings*, pages 8–21. IEEE Computer Society, 1978.

[39] C. A. R. Hoare. Algorithm 64: Quicksort. *Communications of the ACM*, 4(7):321, 1961.

[40] J. E. Hopcroft and R. E. Tarjan. Algorithm 447: Efficient algorithms for graph manipulation. *Communications of the ACM*, 16(6):372–378, 1973.

[41] J. E. Hopcroft and R. E. Tarjan. Efficient planarity testing. *Journal of the ACM*, 21(4):549–568, 1974.

[42] HP-UX process management white paper, version 1.3, 1997. Available from: `http://h21007.www2.hp.com/portal/download/files/prot/files/STK/pdfs/proc_mgt.pdf` [cited 2011-07-20].

[43] M. S. Jensen and R. Pagh. Optimality in external memory hashing. *Algorithmica*, 52(3):403–411, 2008.

[44] P. Kirschenhofer, C. Martinez, and H. Prodinger. Analysis of an optimized search algorithm for skip lists. *Theoretical Computer Science*, 144:199–220, 1995.

[45] P. Kirschenhofer and H. Prodinger. The path length of random skip lists. *Acta Informatica*, 31:775–792, 1994.

[46] D. Knuth. *Fundamental Algorithms*, volume 1 of *The Art of Computer Programming*. Addison-Wesley, third edition, 1997.

[47] D. Knuth. *Seminumerical Algorithms*, volume 2 of *The Art of Computer Programming*. Addison-Wesley, third edition, 1997.

[48] D. Knuth. *Sorting and Searching*, volume 3 of *The Art of Computer Programming*. Addison-Wesley, second edition, 1997.

[49] C. Y. Lee. An algorithm for path connection and its applications. *IRE Transaction on Electronic Computers*, EC-10(3):346–365, 1961.

[50] E. Lehman, F. T. Leighton, and A. R. Meyer. *Mathematics for Computer Science*. 2011. Available from: `http://courses.csail.mit.edu/6.042/spring12/mcs.pdf` [cited 2012-09-06].

[51] C. Martínez and S. Roura. Randomized binary search trees. *Journal of the ACM*, 45(2):288–323, 1998.

[52] E. F. Moore. The shortest path through a maze. In *Proceedings of the International Symposium on the Theory of Switching*, pages 285–292, 1959.

[53] J. I. Munro, T. Papadakis, and R. Sedgewick. Deterministic skip lists. In *Proceedings of the third annual ACM-SIAM symposium on Discrete algorithms (SODA'92)*, pages 367–375, Philadelphia, PA, USA, 1992. Society for Industrial and Applied Mathematics.

[54] Oracle. *The Collections Framework*. Available from: `http://download.oracle.com/javase/1.5.0/docs/guide/collections/` [cited 2011-07-19].

[55] Oracle. *Java Platform Standard Ed. 6*. Available from: `http://download.oracle.com/javase/6/docs/api/` [cited 2011-07-19].

[56] Oracle. *The Java Tutorials*. Available from: `http://download.oracle.com/javase/tutorial/` [cited 2011-07-19].

[57] R. Pagh and F. Rodler. Cuckoo hashing. *Journal of Algorithms*, 51(2):122–144, 2004.

[58] T. Papadakis, J. I. Munro, and P. V. Poblete. Average search and update costs in skip lists. *BIT*, 32:316–332, 1992.

[59] M. Pătraşcu and M. Thorup. Randomization does not help searching predecessors. In N. Bansal, K. Pruhs, and C. Stein, editors, *Proceedings of the Eighteenth Annual ACM-SIAM Symposium on Discrete Algorithms, SODA 2007, New Orleans, Louisiana, USA, January 7–9, 2007*, pages 555–564. SIAM, 2007.

[60] M. Pătraşcu and M. Thorup. The power of simple tabulation hashing. *Journal of the ACM*, 59(3):14, 2012.

[61] W. Pugh. A skip list cookbook. Technical report, Institute for Advanced Computer Studies, Department of Computer Science, University of Maryland, College Park, 1989. Available from: `ftp://ftp.cs.umd.edu/pub/skipLists/cookbook.pdf` [cited 2011-07-20].

[62] W. Pugh. Skip lists: A probabilistic alternative to balanced trees. *Communications of the ACM*, 33(6):668–676, 1990.

[63] Redis. Available from: `http://redis.io/` [cited 2011-07-20].

[64] B. Reed. The height of a random binary search tree. *Journal of the ACM*, 50(3):306–332, 2003.

[65] S. M. Ross. *Probability Models for Computer Science*. Academic Press, Inc., Orlando, FL, USA, 2001.

[66] R. Sedgewick. Left-leaning red-black trees, September 2008. Available from: `http://www.cs.princeton.edu/~rs/talks/LLRB/LLRB.pdf` [cited 2011-07-21].

[67] R. Seidel and C. Aragon. Randomized search trees. *Algorithmica*, 16(4):464–497, 1996.

[68] H. H. Seward. Information sorting in the application of electronic digital computers to business operations. Master's thesis, Massachusetts Institute of Technology, Digital Computer Laboratory, 1954.

[69] Z. Shao, J. H. Reppy, and A. W. Appel. Unrolling lists. In *Proceedings of the 1994 ACM conference LISP and Functional Programming (LFP'94)*, pages 185–195, New York, 1994. ACM.

[70] P. Sinha. A memory-efficient doubly linked list. *Linux Journal*, 129, 2005. Available from: http://www.linuxjournal.com/article/6828 [cited 2013-06-05].

[71] SkipDB. Available from: http://dekorte.com/projects/opensource/SkipDB/ [cited 2011-07-20].

[72] D. Sleator and R. Tarjan. Self-adjusting binary trees. In *Proceedings of the 15th Annual ACM Symposium on Theory of Computing, 25–27 April, 1983, Boston, Massachusetts, USA*, pages 235–245. ACM, ACM, 1983.

[73] S. P. Thompson. *Calculus Made Easy*. MacMillan, Toronto, 1914. Project Gutenberg EBook 33283. Available from: http://www.gutenberg.org/ebooks/33283 [cited 2012-06-14].

[74] P. van Emde Boas. Preserving order in a forest in less than logarithmic time and linear space. *Inf. Process. Lett.*, 6(3):80–82, 1977.

[75] J. Vuillemin. A data structure for manipulating priority queues. *Communications of the ACM*, 21(4):309–315, 1978.

[76] J. Vuillemin. A unifying look at data structures. *Communications of the ACM*, 23(4):229–239, 1980.

[77] D. E. Willard. Log-logarithmic worst-case range queries are possible in space $\Theta(N)$. *Inf. Process. Lett.*, 17(2):81–84, 1983.

[78] J. Williams. Algorithm 232: Heapsort. *Communications of the ACM*, 7(6):347–348, 1964.

Index